# ADVAITA AND VIŚIṢṬĀDVAITA

# ADVAITA
# AND
# VIŚIṢṬĀDVAITA

*A study based on Vedānta Deśikā's Śatadūṣaṇī*

S.M. SRINIVASA CHARI

*Foreword by*

DR. S. RADHAKRISHNAN

MOTILAL BANARSIDASS PUBLISHING HOUSE
SINCE 1903

MOTILAL BANARSIDASS
PUBLISHING HOUSE • DELHI
*Email: naraina@mlbd.in • Website: www.mlbd.in*
*@mlbdofficial*
*+91 89 2999 9000*

*2nd Reprint : Delhi, 2020*
*Fourth Corrected Edition: Delhi, 2004*
*First Edition : Bombay, 1961*



ISBN: 978-93-5760-378-2 (Hardcover)
ISBN: 978-93-5760-388-1 (Paperback)

*Printed & Published by*
Rajendra P Jain *for*
Motilal Banarsidass Publishing House
A-44, Naraina Industrial Area, Phase I,
New Delhi–110 028 (INDIA)
*Email: naraina@mlbd.in Website: www.mlbd.in*
*Tel.: (+91-11)4751 1592*
***Showroom:***
4637/20, F-2, Hari Sadan, First Floor, Ansari Road, Daryaganj
Delhi–110 002 (Opp. Fire Station) ***Tel.*** : (+91-11)4559 7999

*To*

*The Revered Memory of*

*My Guru*

SRI GOSTIPURAM SOWMYANARAYANACHARYA SWAMI

*With Profound Respect and Gratitude*

# CONTENTS

# FOREWORD

Dr. S. M. S. Chari's book on '*Advaita and Viśiṣṭādvaita—A Study Based on the Śatadūṣaṇī*' is an important and valuable contribution to our knowledge of Vedānta in two of its major aspects. In his book *Śatadūṣaṇī*, Vedānta Deśika closely follows the arguments of *Rāmānuja's Śrībhāṣya*. Vedānta Deśika is a great dialectician and an eminent thinker and his work gives us valuable information about the way in which charges and counter-charges were handled in his time.

The *Upaniṣads* state two forms of the Supreme—Absolute Brahman and Personal God, Īśvara. The essence of religion is a mode of approach to God or to a Divine state of being. While following one path we treat the others as valid. The two are complementary to each other. There is an aspect of religion which concentrates on the worship of Personal God and requires the grace and compassion of the Supreme.

The two—*advaita* and *viśiṣṭādvaita* are not rival creeds but are recognised as fully orthodox. Even Śaṅkara who is a great protagonist of *Advaita* is said to have written poems of a devotional nature, e.g.

> " Save me from pride, O Viṣṇu, cure my restless mind
> Still my thirst for the waters of this world's mirage
> Be gracious, Lord, to this Thy humble creature,
> And rescue him from the ocean of this world."

The Marathi poet Tukārām did not feel drawn to the way of *advaita* though he knew all about it " I do not seek Divine knowledge. I shall ever desire dual consciousness. Thou shalt ever remain my Lord and I Thy worshipper."

The distinction between the Absolute Brahman and Personal God is not peculiar to Hindu Thought. A Christian classic *Theologia Germanica* says: " To God, as Godhead, appertain neither will nor knowledge, nor manifestation nor anything that we can name or say or conceive. But to God as God, it belongeth to express Himself, and know and love

Himself, and to reveal Himself to Himself".[1] Ruysbroeck says that to attain the Supreme, we must go out "beyond all things into the emptiness".[2]

No teacher of the *Advaita* holds that the world is absolutely unreal or illusory. It is real as a manifestation of being but unreal as a self-subsisting entity.

Dr. Chari's work is an excellent exposition of the *Viśiṣṭādvaita* views and will, I hope, find a large circle of readers.

12/1/61 S. Radhakrishnan

[1] XXXI Golden Treasury edition.

[2] *The Dark Light*, Book II. LXV.

# PREFACE TO THE THIRD EDITION

It is heartening that the third edition of the book is coming out. The earlier editions have presumably served to stimulate an interest in the study of Vedānta.

As the present edition is appearing after a lapse of several years, I have considered the question of revising it. The Introductory Chapter, which mainly deals with the nature and scope of the *Śatadūṣaṇī* does not need any revision. Chapters I to VIII present succinctly all the salient arguments contained in the different Vādas of the *Śatadūṣaṇī* in a systematic manner under eight broad headings. There is not much scope for revision of these chapters except by way of adding additional details but these would not be philosophically important. Chapters I to VIII are therefore retained without any change except a few verbal corrections. Regarding Chapter IX relating to the General Estimate, it is considered desirable to revise it to the extent of evaluating the soundness of the criticisms of Vedānta Désika levelled against the doctrines of Advaita Vedanta in the light of the possible answers of the Advaitins which may be found in some of the polemical Advaita works of post-Désika period and in particular the *Śatabhūṣaṇī* of Ananthakrishna Sastri written as a rejoinder to the *Śatadūṣaṇī.* This was not done earlier for reasons explained in the preface to the first and second editions. Chapter IX is now recast under the title 'General Evaluation and Conclusion'. It is hoped that this book with the revision will be found more useful for a comparative study of the two great systems of Vedānta.

Bangalore<br>May 20, 1995

S.M. SRINIVASA CHARI

## PREFACE TO THE SECOND EDITION

It is very heartening that the need for a second edition of this book has arisen. When the book was first published in 1961 I had some apprehension whether a book of this nature dealing with the most abstruse and controversial doctrines of the two systems of Vedānta would find sufficient number of readers. I am pleased to know that within a few years of the publication of the first edition, it was out of stock. The book also had a favourable reception with many complimentary references made to it. It points to the fact that the book with all its shortcomings has helped to stimulate interest in the study of Indian Philosophy in general and Vedānta in particular.

It has been suggested that in fairness to the Advaitin I should have made a critical evaluation of Vedānta Deśika's objections against Advaita in the light of the Advaita Siddhi and other later works. I had thought of this even earlier but for the reasons explained in the preface to the first edition, I have refrained from doing so. This needs an independent study and I propose to bring out a separate book on this subject.

I have not made any changes in the second edition except a few verbal corrections which are given in a note at the end of the book.

New Delhi, S. M. SRINIVASA CHARI
30th June, '76.

# PREFACE

THIS book attempts to give a comprehensive and faithful exposition of Vedānta Deśika's *Śatadūṣaṇī*. The *Śatadūṣaṇī* is an important classic of Viśiṣṭādvaita Vedānta in which, as its title suggests, one hundred philosophical issues have been chosen for systematic criticism directed against the school of Advaita. The text as available at present contains only sixty-six topics (*Vādas*). These are mainly based upon the arguments advanced by Śrī Rāmānuja in the early portion of his monumental work, *Śrī-bhāṣya*. The arguments which are stated very briefly by Śrī Rāmānuja are elaborated by Vedānta Deśika with his metaphysical profundity and mastery over the art of disputation. The topics developed in the *Śatadūṣaṇī*, each one of which is devoted to a discussion of an independent controversial doctrine of Advaita, refer to various issues bearing on epistemological, metaphysical, cosmological, religious, and ethical problems. I have attempted to bring them together and discuss in a systematic and coherent manner under eight broad headings: 1. Pramāṇas; 2. Perception; 3. Consciousness; 4. Individual Self; 5. Brahman; 6. Universe; 7. Avidyā; 8. Sādhana and Mukti.

Though Vedānta Deśika's *Śatadūṣaṇī* is essentally polemical and devoted to the criticism of the Advaita, in effect it discusses all the important doctrines of both the systems of Vedānta. In presenting the prima-facie view, Vedānta Deśika presents in great detail the Advaitin's arguments which are drawn from the great classics of the Advaita system that existed in the pre-Deśika period. In examing the same critically, he gives a good exposition of the theories of the Viśiṣṭādvaitin. The traditional dialectical method adopted by Deśika brings out clearly the differences between the two systems of Vedānta expounded by two great master-minds —Śaṃkara and Rāmānuja. In my attempt to give an exposition of the dialectics of Vedānta Deśika, I have endeavoured to develop the arguments in such a way as to present the differences between the two systems which are fundamental and emanate from the different standpoints adopted to solve the crucial problems of philosophy. In view of this, I have preferred the title '*Advaita* and *Viśiṣṭādvaita*' for this book although it is mainly devoted to the exposition of Vedānta Deśika's *Śatadūṣaṇī*. I hope that it will prove useful to students of Philosophy interested in the comparative study of Advaita and Viśiṣṭādvaita.

I wrote this book in 1948 for submission to the Madras University for the Degree of Doctor of Philosophy, after several years of research. At the time of writing this thesis, there was no work specifically written as a direct reply to the *Śatadūṣaṇī*. However, the arguments contained in the *Advaita-Siddhi* and its commentary, *Laghuchandrikā*, as well as other polemic works of post-Deśika period did provide some direct and indirect answers to the criticisms of Vedānta Deśika. But very recently Sri Anantakrishna Sastriar has brought out a book in Sanskrit entitled *Śatabhūṣaṇī* as a rejoinder to the *Śatadūṣaṇī*. With the advent of this book, the age-long controversies between these two rival schools of thought, which had remained some what dormant, have been rekindled. As a counter-reply to Sastriar's *Śatabhūṣaṇī*, Sri Uttamoor Viraraghavacharya Swami has brought out a voluminous and scholarly book entitled *Paramārthabhūṣaṇam*. Another book known as *Tattvasudhā* has been published in part by Vidwan E. S. Varadacharya. One might expect that my book coming after *Śatabhūṣaṇī* and other works should have taken up a critical examination of Vedānta Deśika's objections against Advaita in the light of the answers advanced by Sri Sastriar. I have refrained from doing so for good many reasons. First, the voluminous book brought out by Sastriar does not, in my opinion, answer satisfactorily the criticisms of Deśika. This may sound dogmatic, but a dispassionate study of the book will bear out my statement. The *Śatabhūṣaṇī*, as its very title rightly signifies, gives more an elucidation of Advaita doctrines attacked by Sri Deśika than a proper answer to the criticisms of Viśiṣṭādvaitin. Secondly, such a study is beyond the scope of the present work, whose aim is to present the arguments of Vedānta Deśika as given in the *Śatadūṣaṇī* with a view to bringing out the difference between the two systems. This needs an independent study and cannot be executed fully in this book. Thirdly, such a study would not lead one to any final conclusion as it is always possible to find a counter reply to the criticisms of one school of Vedānta against another. I have, therefore, confined myself to a general discussion of the major issues raised in the *Śatadūṣaṇī*.

The controversies between Advaita and Viśiṣṭādvaita started ever since the two systems were founded and are still alive. While this signifies the development of philosophic thought, provided it is carried on in an academic and dispassionate spirit with a genuine quest after truth, it should be borne in mind that the differences between the rival schools of thought will perforce exist as long as the approaches to the main problems of philosophy remain different. It is, therefore, no use in either condemning a system of philosophy or upholding another as a sound one. The function of criticism, in my opinion, is not to refute the opponent out of existence but only to define and distinguish one's own position from that of others with a view to establishing the soundness of one's own position. Such an attempt brings out fully the philosophical implications of the basic theories. It is from this point of view that I have attempted to give an exposition of the Advaita and Viśiṣṭādvaita based on the *Śatadūṣaṇī*. If the present work contributes even in a small measure for the understanding of the basic differences between the two systems, I feel amply rewarded.

In this book, I have covered all the *Vādas* of the *Śatadūṣaṇī* except a few which are not philosophically important. In presenting the dialectics of Vedānta Deśika, I have tried to develop all those issues which to my mind have important philosophic bearing. In stating the prima-facie views, I have mentioned only those that are generally acceptable to the Advaitins. An attempt has also been made to trace out as far as possible the prima-facie views in the original works of the pre-Deśika period. With a view to bringing out the spirit and force of the arguments as advanced by Deśika, I have presented them in a rigorous scholastic form. This has necessitated the use of Sanskrit words and quotations extensively. English renderings have, however been given side by side. Besides, these words have also been explained in the glossary.

To my knowledge this is the first attempt to give a comprehensive and systematic exposition of the *Śatadūṣaṇī*. The major portion of the work, has, however, been translated into Tamil by Mahamahopadhyaya Setlur Narasimhacharya Swami. Dr. Dasgupta has also given a very brief summary of the dialectical criticisms of Vedānta Deśika in his *History of Indian Philosophy* (Vol. III). The summary given therein covers about 39 Vādas only and is not comprehensive. In view of the importance of this classic for a comparative study of Vedānta, an attempt has been made to give a detailed and faithful exposition of the work to make it accessible to the students of Modern Philosophy. It is my hope that the present book will be a useful contribution to the study of Indian Philosophy in general and of Vedānta systems in particular.

It is with great pleasure that I record my obligations. I must first pay my respects to my revered Guru, the late Sri Sowmyanarayanacharya Swami, under whose feet I have had the good fortune of studying the original text in the traditional style. But for his initiation into the essentials of the Viśiṣṭādvaita philosophy and his blessings, it would have been well nigh impossible for me to accomplish the study of the *Śatadūṣaṇī*, which is the toughest work of Vedānta Deśika. If I have succeeded even in a small measure in interpreting the text correctly, I owe it entirely to my Acharya. I am ever indebted to him and as a token of my gratitude, I respectfully dedicate this book to him.

I should also pay my respects to His Holiness the Parakala Swami and His Holiness the Jeer of the Ahobil Mutt whose blessings and teachings have helped me considerably in understanding the Viśiṣṭādvaita Philosophy. I am deeply indebted to the late Sri Venugopalacharya, Sri Madhurantakam Viraraghavacharya and Sri Uttamoor Viraraghavacharya for helping me in interpreting some of the difficult portions of the text.

I owe a debt of gratitude to the late Sri S. S. Suryanarayana Sastri, the Head of the Department of Philosophy in the University of Madras, under whose guidance I carried on my research at the University for nearly two years (1941-43). Although he could not see the script of my book, he gave me valuable guidance in the rendering of the original text into English. My grateful thanks are due to the late Prof. M. Hiriyanna, the late Prof. P. N. Srinivasachari and Dr. R. Nagaraja Sarma for their encouragement and the valuable advice at every stage of the preparation of the book.

I am deeply indebted to my esteemed teacher, Sri M. A. Venkatarao and my esteemed friend, Dr. T. R. V. Murti who were good enough to go through the entire manuscript and offer valued criticisms and helpful suggestions. I am grateful to Dr. T. M. P. Mahadevan, Prof. R. Ramanuja Chari, Dr. P. T. Raju, Sri M. Yamunacharya, Sri S. S. Raghavachar, Sri A. Srinivasaraghavan and Sri A. S. Iyengar who read the type-script and offered useful suggestions for improvement. My thanks are specially due to my friend, Dr. R. K. Tripathy for his active help and cooperation in the preparation and revision of the book.

To Dr. S. Radhakrishnan I acknowledge my indebtedness for the very kind interest he has taken in my work and the Foreword he has written. For one who has laboured hard in writing a book of this kind amidst heavy official pre-occupations, nothing is more rewarding than the few lines of appreciation from the distinguished pen of a Philosopher-Statesman.

I should take this opportunity of acknowledging my obligations to the Madras University for not only affording me all facilities to carry on the research but also permitting me to publish the thesis accepted for the Doctorate. My thanks are due to all those who have contributed, in one way or other, to the success of this undertaking.

*Washington, D. C.* S. M. Srinivasa Chari
*14 February, 1961*

# ABBREVIATIONS

| | |
|---|---|
| Brah. | *Bṛhadāraṇyaka Upaniṣad* |
| Ch. | *Chāndogya Upaniṣad* |
| Mund. | *Muṇḍaka Upaniṣad* |
| S.B. | *Śamkara's Sūtra-bhāṣya* |
| S.D. | *Śatadūṣaṇī* |
| SLS. | *Siddhāntaleśasaṅgraha* |
| Svet. | *Śvetāśvatāra Upaniṣad* |
| Tait. | *Taittirīya Upaniṣad* |
| T.P.H. | Theosophical Publishing House |
| Up. | *Upaniṣads* |
| V.S. | *Vedānta Sūtras* |
| V.S.S. | Vizianagaram Sanskrit Series |

# INTRODUCTION

## I *Life and Works of Vedānta Deśika*

VEDĀNTA Deśika, the author of the *Śatadūṣaṇī*, was one of the most eminent thinkers of the Viśiṣṭādvaita Vedānta.[1] He was born at Himavanam, a place near Conjeevaram in 1268 A.D. in a pious Vaiṣṇavite family reputed for scholarship. Even as a boy he showed such extraordinary genius that it was predicted by Vātsya Varadācārya, a spiritual descendant of Rāmānuja, that he would establish the Viśiṣṭādvaita Vedānta and refute all rival schools of thought.[2] He studied under his maternal uncle, Ātreya Rāmānuja, who was a distinguished disciple of Vātsya Varadācārya, and acquired even by the early age of twenty, a perfect knowledge in all the different branches of traditional learning, a mastery in recognition of which the titles of *Vedāntācārya* and *Sarva Tantra Svatantra* were later bestowed on him at Śrīrangam as is evident from his own account given in the *Saṅkalpa Sūryodaya.*[3]

He led a strictly religious and saintly life and spent his time in preaching the Viśiṣṭādvaita Philosophy and writing philosophical and religious works. Though he was a man of saintly character, those who were jealous of his glory harassed him in many ways. But Deśika bore these trials and tribulations patiently. He also had to fight against the followers of the rival schools of thought. More than once he was called upon to debate with his opponents, whom he vanquished with his metaphysical profundity and unrivalled debating skill and converted to his own faith.[4] The *Paramata-bhanga* and the

[1] A detailed and authentic account of Deśika's life and works is given in *Deśika and His Works* in Tamil published by the Nigamaparimala Press, Madras. See also Mahācārya's *Vaibhava-Prakāśikā* and *Guruparamparā-Prabhāva* of Tṛtīya Brahmatantra Parakāla Swāmi.

[2] The prediction is expressed in the following verse which is believed to be the blessing bestowed on Vedānta Deśika when he met the Ācarya for the first time along with his uncle, Ātreya Rāmānuja:

pratiṣṭhāpita-vedāntaḥ pratikṣipta-bahirmataḥ
bhūyāstraividya-mānyastvam bhūri-kalyāṇa-bhājanam.

[3] *Saṅkalpa-Sūryodaya*, Act. I, pp. 12 and 14. (Nigamaparimala Press Edn.) See also the opening verse of *Adhikaraṇa-sārāvaḷī.*

[4] See *Vaibhava-Prakāśikā.*

*Śatadūṣaṇī* are held to represent the arguments advanced by Deśika in these debates. Owing to his rare mastery of poetics and dialectics and the art of disputation he won the title of *Kavitārkika-Simha*—" the lion of poets and logicians ".

His life is as inspiring as his scholarship. He was profoundly austere and humble in his way of living. He lived by receiving alms in the streets (*uñcavṛitti*). He showed utter contempt for wealth and worldly position. It is said of him that he threw away the gold coins which were mixed up in the rice offered as alms by a well-intentioned person during one of his daily rounds for alms-taking. His *vairāgya* is the most striking feature of his personality. This is borne out by his *Vairāgya-Pañcaka*, a hymn of five stanzas, written as a reply to the invitation extended by Vidyāraṇya, the Minister to the King of Vijayanagara, to come to the court to receive royal honours. He considered the deity at the temple of Hastigiri (Kānchi) as his true wealth and despised all earthly treasures. His devotion to God and respect for tradition, particularly for the teachings of Śrī Rāmānuja, were profound. The long life he led was spent entirely in devotional service to God and godly men and in the propagation of the teachings of Viśiṣṭādvaita Philosophy as expounded by Śrī Rāmānuja.[1]

The contribution of Vedānta Deśika to the Viśiṣṭādvaita Vedānta is unique and unparalleled in the history of Indian Philosophy. He has written numerous works covering various subjects. In the field of philosophy his chief works are *Tattva-muktākalāpa*, *Sarvārtha-siddhi*, *Adhikaraṇa-sārāvali*, *Nyāya-Pariśuddhi*, *Nyāya-siddhāñjana*, *Seśvara-Mīmāmsā*, *Mīmāmsā-Pādukā*, and *Śatadūṣaṇī*. In each of these works Vedānta Deśika has made some specific contribution to the Viśiṣṭādvaita Vedānta. *Tattva-muktākalāpa* which is written in the form of verse gives an exposition of the nature of *Jaḍa*, *Jīva*, *Īśvara*, *Buddhi*, and *Adravya*, according to the Viśiṣṭādvaita school of thought. *Sarvārtha-siddhi* is his own commentary on it giving a more detailed exposition of the same doctrines. *Adhikaraṇa-Sārāvalī* which is also composed in the form of verse gives a summary of the various topics or *Adhikaraṇas* contained in the *Śrī-bhāṣya*. *Nyāya-Parisuddhi* is an epistemological work of the Viśiṣṭādvaita school which discusses in detail the nature of the three pramāṇās. It reconstructs the Nyāya Vaiśeṣika system in the light of Viśiṣṭādvaita teachings by simplifying the categories and including among the pramāṇas the *Pāñcarātra* texts

[1] See the closing verse of *Rahasya-traya-sāra*.

which are regarded as divine in character. *Nyāya-siddhāñjana* sets forth in detail the metaphysics of the Viśiṣṭādvaita system which has been briefly mentioned in the *Nyāya Pariśuddhi*. *Seśvara-Mīmāmsā* and *Mīmāmsā-Pādukā* are works on Mīmāmsā. In the former work, Vedānta Deśika interprets the Mīmāmsa-Sūtras of Jaimini in such a way as to prove that the teachings of Jaimini are in consonance with the teachings of Bādarāyaṇa and that the two Mīmāmsās—Pūrva and Uttara—form an integral whole. The *Śatadūṣaṇī* is a polemical work in which the doctrines of Advaita Vedānta are criticised elaborately.

Some of the other philosophical works of Deśika are in the form of commentaries. These are *Tattvatīka* (a commentary on *Śrī-bhāṣya*), *Tātparya-candrikā* (a gloss on Rāmānujā's *Gītā-bhāṣya*), *Īśāvasyopaniṣad-bhāṣya* (a commentary on the *Īśā-vāsyopaniṣad*), *Rahasya-rakṣā* (a commentary on Yāmunā's *Stotra-ratna* and *Catuḥśloki* and Rāmānujā's *Gadya-traya*) and *Gītārtha-samgraha-rakṣā* (a commentary on Yāmunā's *Gitārtha-Samgraha*). A commentary on Rāmānuja's *Vedārtha-Samgraha* (*Vedārtha-Samgraha-vyākhyā*) and another on the works of the Alvārs (*Nigama-Parimala*) are believed to have been written but these are not available now.

In addition to the above philosophical works, all in Sanskrit, Vedānta Deśika has composed thirty-two works in the *Mani-pravāla* style, which is a mixture of Sanskrit and Tamil. In these works, he gives an exposition of the Viśiṣṭādvaita metaphysics in a popular way, easily intelligible to lay men. The *Rahasyatraya-Sāra*, which is a masterpiece of Deśika, is one of these works. Here the principles of Viśiṣṭādvaita philosophy are expounded in clear and simple language. The *Paramata-bhanga* is another important work included in this group of 32 works. In this Vedānta Deśika has advanced criticisms against seventeen schools of thought including Advaita.

The other works of Vedānta Deśika relate to Poetry, Drama and Religion. In the field of Poetry, his most important works are *Yādavābhyudaya* on the life of Lord Krishna, *Hamsa-sandeśa* written on the model of Kālidāsa's *Meghadūta*, and *Subhaṣitanivi*, a work on morals, and *Pādukā-sahasra* containing one thousand verses on the Holy Sandals of the deity of Śrīrangam. *Saṅkalpa-sūryodaya* is an allegorical drama in ten acts. In this work Vedānta Deśika presents the struggle of the Jīva in its onward march to spiritual realization. In addition to these, he has also written twenty-nine adoration-hymns known as Stotras.

Among religious works the *Pāñcarātra-rakṣā*, the *Nikṣepa-rakṣā* and *Saccaritra-rakṣā* are very important.

## II *Nature and Scope of the Śatadūṣaṇī*

The *Śatadūṣaṇī* is an important polemical work of the Viśiṣṭād-vaita Vedānta in which, as the title of the work suggests, one hundred philosophical issues have been chosen for systematic criticism. The criticism is mainly directed against the doctrines of Advaita Vedānta. The aim of the work, as is evident from the opening verse of the *Śatadūṣaṇī* as well as the statement made in the *Tattvatīka*, is to refute Śamkara and his followers.[1]

The method of criticism adopted here is purely dialectical in nature which is a characteristic feature of all such polemical works. The position of the opponent which is called the *Pūrvapakṣa* is first stated briefly. The arguments of the *Pūrvapakṣa* are then subjected to critical examination and refuted on grounds of inherent contradictions and other logical defects.

This method of criticism has a definite purpose in view. Its main object is the ascertainment of truth by eliminating all erroneous theories and partial truths. The refutation of the theories held by the opponents helps to strengthen one's own position. Thus, dialectic has a two-fold function—the destructive and the constructive—the refutation of the position held by the opponents and a constructive statement of one's own position (*paramata nirākaraṇa and svamata sthāpanā*). Such a philosophical discussion which aims at the determination of the truth is called a *Vāda* as distinguished from *Jalpa* and *Vitaṇda*. *Jalpa* is a discussion undertaken for the sake of dialectical victory and renown as a debator. *Vitaṇda* stands for a discussion the aim of which is the silencing of a clamorous opponent. It is a destructive criticism of the views of the opponent without any constructive statement of one's own

[1] See *Śatadūṣaṇī*—vol. I. p. 5 (Śāstramuktāvalī series)

vādāhaveṣu nirbhettum vedamārga vidūṣakān
prayujyatām śaraśreṇī niśitā śatadūṣaṇī.

*Tattvatīka*—Stanza 5.

śātitaḥ śatadūṣaṇyām śamkarādimudhāgrahaḥ
śārīraka śarīram-tu vyaktam-atra pradarśyate.

position.[1] *Vāda*, on the contrary, is a philosophical discussion which mainly aims at the ascertainment of truth. In polemical treatises both the *Vāda* and the *Vitaṇda* type of arguments are freely used while in others which are constructive in character the *Vāda* type of arguments is predominantly used. Sri Harṣa's *Khaṇḍana Khaṇḍa Khādya* may be mentioned as an example of the *Vitaṇda* type since the author here is more preoccupied with demolishing the Nyāya doctrines than establishing his own system. Citsukha's *Tattvapradīpikā* which is more constructive than destructive adopts mostly the *Vāda* type of arguments. Vedānta Deśika's *Śatadūṣaṇī* is both destructive and constructive and adopts only the *Vāda* type of arguments. It is, therefore, designated as a *Vāda Grantha* the aim of which is to refute the doctrines of Advaita Vedānta with a view to establishing the Viśiṣṭādvaita Vedānta on a sound logical basis. In view of this it is compared to a sword (*śastra*) used to destroy the opponents, in contrast to the purely constructive work, *Sarvārtha-siddhi*, which is compared to the shield (*kheta*) that is used to defend oneself.[2]

## III *Criticism of Advaita by Other Thinkers*

The criticism of Advaita in the *Śatadūṣaṇi* is not the first attempt of its kind. Śrī Yāmuna (916-1036 A.D.) was the first thinker of the Viśiṣṭādvaita school of thought who sought to controvert the views of the Advaitins by dialectical method. In his *Ātma-siddhi*, which is devoted to a discussion of the nature of the individual self and the Absolute from different standpoints, Śrī Yāmuna subjects to a critical examination the Advaitin's theory of the self as pure consciousness which is neither produced nor destroyed but is self-luminous—a theory which has been clearly set forth in the *Iṣṭa-siddhi* of Vimuktātman.[3] In his *Samvit-siddhi*, he criticises the other important doctrines of

[1] *Nyāya Sūtras*, I. 2. 1-3. *Nyāya Pariśuddhi*, p. 7 (Chowkamba Edn.)

See also Dr. R. N. Sarma's *Reign of Realism*, p. 48. According to Śrī Harṣa, there are only two types of argument—Vāda and Vitaṇḍa, while according to the Naiyāyikas and others there are three types of arguments. The Gauḍa Naiyāyikas recognise four types of argument—Vāda, Jalpa, Vāda-Vitaṇḍa and Jalpa-Vitaṇḍa.

[2] See *Saptatiratnamālikā*. Stanza 48.

sarvārthasiddhiḥ-śatadūṣaṇī-ca
dve kheta-śastre kathakāgragānām.

[3] The first half of the opening verse of the *Iṣṭa-siddhi* is quoted in *Ātma-siddhi*.

Advaita Vedānta such as the unity of the self, the illusoriness of the universe and the concept of *avidyā*. After, Yāmuna, Śrī Rāmānuja carried forward this task with greater fervour as the *Māyā-Vāda* had become pronounced in his time. In the portion of his *Śrī-bhāṣya* called the *Jijñāsādhikaraṇa* he states briefly the essential teachings of the Advaita Vedānta and subjects them to a critical examination. The arguments given in the *Śrī-bhāṣya* were further elaborated by Vedānta Deśika who wrote an independent work setting forth in detail and in a systematic way the criticisms against the Advaitins.

Earlier to Śrī Yāmuna, Bhāskara who is believed to have flourished in the early part of the 9th Century, had attacked vigorously the *Māyā-vāda* of Advaita Vedānta which he regarded as a version of the nihilism of Māhayānika Buddhism.[1] After Rāmānuja, Śrī Madhva figured as an uncompromising critic of Advaita Vedānta. The *Upādhikhaṇḍana*, *Māyāvāda-khaṇḍana*, *Prapañca-mithyātvānumāna-khaṇḍana* and *Tattvadyota* are independent treatises which are mainly devoted to the criticism of Advaita. Based on these works, Jayatīrtha, the greatest among the disciples of Madhva, wrote a small independent work called *Vādāvalī*, wherein he criticised the Advaitin's doctrine of the illusoriness of the universe and the theory of *māyā*. Based on the *Vādāvalī*, Vyāsarāya wrote his famous polemic work, *Nyāyāmṛtam*, which was later criticised by Madhusūdana Saraswati in his dialectical work *Advaita-siddhi*, which has become a well-known classic of Advaita Vedānta. The latter work has been criticised by Rāmācārya in his *Taranginī*, which again has been attacked in defence of *Advaita-siddhi* by Brahmānanda in his *Gauḍa-brahmānandīyam*, also known as *Laghu-candrikā*. There are many other dialectical works belonging to these three schools of Vedānta either in defence of their own systems of Vedānta or in criticism of the works of the rival schools of thought.

## IV *Conflict Between Advaita and Viśiṣṭādvaita*

Both Rāmānuja and Madhva as well as all their followers have taken a leading role as critics of the Advaita system of Vedānta. It is not difficult to find an explanation for this. The criticism of the rival schools of thought, in so far as it leads to the perfection of one's own teachings, is a common feature of all schools of thought. The second chapter of the *Vedānta-Sūtras*,

[1] See *The Philosophy of Bhedābheda*, p. 4.

known as the *Avirodhādhyāya* wherein the author of the *Sūtras* proceeds to meet the objections brought against the views set forth in the first chapter and criticises them, shows that the criticism of the rival schools of thought is essential for building one's own system of philosophy. Rāmānuja and Madhva devoted greater attention to the criticism of Advaita than to that of any other school of thought, because of the fact that the philosophy of Advaita which was opposed to their own teachings was holding an unquestioned sway in their time. A historical study of the development of the Vedāntic Monism as propounded by Śaṃkara and his followers will prove this fact. Vedāntic Monism, germs of which are discernible in the early Upaniṣads containing the idealistic thoughts, reached its culmination at the time of Gauḍapāda. Śamkara who followed Gauḍapāda gave perfection to it by his learned commentaries on the *Vedānta-Sūtras*, the ten Upaniṣads and the *Bhagavadgītā*—the three Prasthānas that constitute the foundation and supreme authority of the philosophy of Vedānta. Soon after Śamkara, other followers appeared in the field of Advaita Vedānta who wrote independent works and thereby strengthened the teachings of their master. Sureśwara's *Vārtikā* and *Naiṣkarmya-Siddhi*, Padmapāda's *Pañca-pādikā*, Prakāśātman's *Vivaraṇa*, Vimuktātman's *Iṣṭa-siddhi*, and Sarvajñātmamuni's *Samkṣepa-śārīraka*, and Vācaspati's *Bhāmatī* are some of the important Advaita classics that sprang up in the early part of the post-Śamkara period. By the 11th century, to which period Rāmānuja belongs, Advaita Vedānta had achieved full growth and prominence. Naturally a rival system of Vedānta which received great impetus at that time had to fight against the existing system in so far as the philosophical doctrines of the latter were opposed to the former. This was the position at the time of Yāmuna and Rāmanuja, as is evident from the opening verse of *Vedārtha-Samgraha*. This accounts for the elaborate criticism of Advaita Philosophy in the *Śrī-bhāṣya*.

Even in the post-Rāmānuja period, the philosophy of Advaita Vedānta was predominant despite the refutation of it by Rāmānuja. Śrī Harṣa, Ānandabodha and Citsukha are some of the leading Advaitic thinkers who flourished in the early part of the post-Rāmānuja period prior to Deśika and who strengthened the teachings of Advaita Vedānta. Thus, during the time that lapsed between Rāmānuja and Madhva as well as Deśika, there appears to have been a further development of the Advaita system, which needed elaborate criticism by others in defence of the Viśiṣṭādvaita. Deśika, whose life's mission was to establish the Viśiṣṭādvaita System as propounded by Śrī Rāmānuja by refuting the rival schools of thought, undertook this task in his masterly work entitled *Śatadūṣaṇī*.

### V *Śatadūṣaṇi and Śrī-bhāṣya*

In refuting the Advaita doctrines, Vedānta Deśika closely follows the arguments set forth by Rāmānuja in the first section of the *Śrī-bhāṣya* known as *Jijñāsādhikaraṇa*, wherein the general position of the Advaitins is stated briefly and criticised. The arguments advanced in the *Śrī-bhāṣya* are developed by Deśika into full-fledged Vādas or independent controversial topics discussing the issues in greater detail. Thus, at the close of several Vādas, Vedānta Deśika quotes from *Śrī-bhāṣya* with the following words: "Having all this in mind, the author of the Bhāṣya says".[1] In some of the Vādas he elaborates the ideas pregnant in the statement of the Bhāṣyakāra with a particular view towards the possible criticisms of the opponents.[2] From this, it would appear that the *Śatadūṣaṇī* has been written to elaborate the criticisms urged against the Advaita School of thought by Rāmānuja. But its scope is wider than that.

Though the work follows the line of arguments presented in the *Śrī-bhāṣya*, it exhibits abundant evidence of the author's originality in developing the arguments of the opponents further and exposing their hollowness.[3] The *Pūrva-pakṣa* which is stated very briefly in *Śrī-bhāṣya* is formulated in far greater detail in the *Śatadūṣaṇī* taking into consideration the development

[1] See *S.D.*, Vādas 1, 2, 10, 41.

Idam sarvam abhipretya abhāṣyata (Vāda 1).
Akhilam antar-nidhāya āha (Vāda 2).
Tadetad-āhuḥ (Vāda 10); Tadetat sarvam upakṣiptam bhāṣye (Vāda 41).

[2] See Vādas 9, 15, 18, 19, 47.

Etacca vistarāt upapādayāmaḥ (Vāda 9).
Tadidam vayam vistṛṇīmahe (Vāda 15).
Tad-vyākurmah (Vāda 18).
Tat-sarvam saṅkalayya vyākurmaḥ (Vāda 19).
Tad-vistṛṇīmahe (Vāda 47).

[3] See the discussion on Akhaṇḍārtha in Vāda 38. See also Chapter V, sec. 2.

of the Advaitic theories since the time of Rāmānuja.[1] In the critical examination of the views of the opponents, Deśika resolves them into numerous alternatives covering all the possible views on the issue.[2] The criticisms are also many-sided and are urged from different standpoints. The untenability of the arguments is shown not only from the standpoint of the *siddhānta* of the critic, but also from the point of view of the opponent himself by exposing the contradiction involved in his argument. Deśika's many-sided scholarship and his mastery over the art of dialectics enabled him to formulate even better than his predecessors had done the objections against the Advaita Philosophy taking into consideration the defence that was put forth by its exponents since the time of Rāmānuja and also what could possibly be urged at a later time. Probably it was with this idea in view that Deśika states at the outset of the work that it would be possible to win over the Advaitins by merely repeating the arguments contained in the *Śatadūṣaṇī* like a parrot (*śukavat paṭhantaḥ pracchanna bauddha vijaye parito yatadhvam*).[3] Whatever might be the correctness of this claim, there is no doubt that Vedānta Deśika strengthened the Viśiṣṭādvaita system on its critical side by his *Śatadūṣaṇī*.

## VI *Śatadūṣaṇī and Advaita Works*

The work is not directed against any particular Advaita classic. It covers in general all the important Advaita doctrines as expounded by the different Advaitins who had preceded Vedānta Deśika. In stating the *Pūrva-pakṣa* at the commencement of each Vāda, the author does not quote verbatim from any of the Advaita works except in one place where a passage from Śrī Harṣa's *Khaṇḍana-khaṇḍa khadya* has been adopted with slight alterations.[4] The other works that are directly referred to are Śamkara's *Śutra-bhāṣya*, Vācaspati's *Bhāmatī*, and Vimuktātman's *Iṣṭa-siddhi*.[5] Though there are no other direct references

[1] See Vāda 36 and Chapter IV, section 3.
The discussion on the issue whether the plurality of the Individual Self is real or illusory is very brief in *Śrī-bhāṣya*; it is only implied, as Deśika himself puts it, by way of discussing the meaning of a particular smṛti text. (*ādibharata vākya vyākhyana vyāiena bhāṣyakāraih sūcitam.*) This has been developed in great detail in the *Śatadūṣaṇī* covering the arguments put forth by the author of the *Nyāya-makaranda*, who is later than Rāmānuja. See Vāda 37.

[2] See Vāda 15 and Chapter VI. [3] See fn. p. 10 and 11. [4] See Vāda 9.

[5] See Vādas 13 and 16 where the opening sentence of *Śamkara-bhāṣya* has been quoted. See Vāda 8 . . . vācaspati kalpita prakāraiti.
Vāda 9. uktam ca iṣṭasiddhi kāraiḥ . . .

to the Advaita works, we can trace the substance of the arguments stated as *Pūrva-pakṣa* in the *Śatadūṣaṇī* in such classics as Maṇḍana's *Brahma-siddhi*, Sureśvara's *Naiṣkarmya-Siddhi* and *Vārtikā*, Padmapāda's *Pañca-pādikā*, Prakāśātman's *Vivaraṇa*, Vimuktātman's *Iṣṭa-siddhi*, Vācaspati's *Bhāmatī*, Sarvajñātmamuni's *Samkṣepa-Śarīraka*, Jñānaghanapāda's *Tattvaśuddhi*, Ānandabodhācārya's *Nyāya-makaranda* and Citaukha's *Tattva-pradīpikā*. All these are important works of Advaita Vedānta belonging to the pre-Deśika period. Our author must have had in mind the doctrines set forth in these and many other works, some of which are not available to us.

There are also many other topics discussed and criticised in the *Śatadūṣaṇī*, which are not readily traceable in the Advaita classics of the pre-Deśika period that are now extant. These might have been in vogue at the time of Deśika and having been acquainted with them in the course of the debate, he must have stated them in the *Śatadūṣaṇī*. We learn from the biographical accounts of Deśika that the *Śatadūṣaṇī* was composed after debates that Deśika had with the Advaitins and the arguments advanced in the discussions were summed up in the several Vādas of the *Śatadūṣaṇī*[1]. It is, therefore, possible that some of the arguments which are not traceable in the Advaita works now extant must have been urged in the course of the debates by the Pūrvapakṣins in defence of their own system as the possible views of their system. Or it may be that in the course of examining the position of the Pūrvapakṣin all the possible views on a particular subject, whether or not they are embodied in works by the Pūrvapakṣin, might have been stated. Such a thing is not uncommon in a polemical work. In *Khaṇḍana-Khaṇḍa Khādya*, for instance, Śrī Harṣa formulates sometimes more than fifteen alternatives against the view of the opponent and examines them critically one by one. It is not necessary that all the alternatives raised should have been textually embodied by the opponent. Vedānta Deśika who seems to have in mind Śrī Harṣa's work follows more or less the same style and manner in his refutation of Advaita doctrines.[2] Deśika himself points out in one place that

[1] See *Vaibhava-Prakāśika*. Stanza 47.
jitvā tadā vādinam āgamānta guruḥ vitene
Śatadūṣaṇīm yaḥ.

[2] See the opening verse 3 of *Khaṇḍana-Khaṇḍa Khādya*:
dhīrā yathoktam-api kīravad-etad-uktvā
lokeṣu digvijaya kautukam-ātanudhevam.

several alternatives are raised in order to clear the doubts in the minds of the laymen who are unacquainted with the philosophical truths (*mandamati sammohaśamanāya upanyasya nirastāḥ*).[1]

## VII *Sequence of Topics in the Śatadūṣaṇī*

The work, as its title suggests, should have consisted of one hundred Vādas. But the text as available at present contains only sixty-six Vādas. The remaining Vādas must have been lost as in the case of some of the other works of Vedānta Deśika such as *Tattvatīka* and *Nyāya-siddhāñjana.* There is, however, a view that the last thrity-four Vādas were directed against the Mādhva school of thought and they were not given wide publicity as the Mādhvaites are also Vaiṣṇavites and are not fundamentally opposed to the Viśiṣṭādvaitins. There is no proof in support of this view. Nor is it convincing as it directly conflicts with the main thesis of the text viz., the refutation of the Advaitins. Hence there is no room for the criticism of Dvaita doctrines in the *Śatadūṣaṇī.*

There is also a view which maintains that the text is complete with the sixty-six Vādas only. On that view the term *śata* is to be understood in the sense of 'many'.[2] The argument that may be adduced in favour of this view is that the work has a completeness in itself as far as the criticism of Advaita doctrines is concerned. Nevertheless, it is not plausible as there is no concluding verse (*upasamhāra-śloka*) which is a characteristic feature of all ancient classics in general and in particular of the works of Vedānta Deśika. Secondly, wherever Deśika employs such numerical terms as *śata*, *sahasra* or *pañcāśat* along with the titles of the works, he means them in the literal sense and in no other case has the total number required fallen short of the number indicated by the title. The original text of the *Śatadūṣaṇī* should, therefore, have consisted of one hundred Vādas and the remaining thirty-four Vādas must have been lost. It is difficult to say anything definite about the contents of these thirty-four Vādas.

cf. the opening Verse 3 of the *Śatadūṣaṇī* :
prājñā yathoditam-idam śukavat paṭhntaḥ
pracchanna baudha vijaye parito yatadhvam.
It is apparent that Deśika had in view Śrī Harṣa's *Khaṇḍana-Khaṇḍa Khādya*.

[1] See *S.D.*, Vāda 14.

[2] See Dr. Dasgupta's *History of Indian Philosophy*, Vol. III, p. 305.

The sixty-six Vādas raise numerous issues—epistemological, metaphysical, cosmological, religious and ethical. Each Vāda is devoted to a discussion of an independent controversial topic of Advaita.[1] The Vādas as such, do not appear in a logical order. The only order in which the Vādas are presented is that found in the *Laghu-siddhānta* and *Mahā-siddhānta* of the *Śrī-bhāṣya*. But even that order is not strictly adhered to by Vedānta Deśika. Thus, the first eight Vādas which deal with the discussion of the issues arising out of the interpretation of the first aphorism of the *Vedānta-Sūtras*—the import of the term, 'Brahman', the enquiry into the nature of Brahman, the preliminaries required for the purpose, the place of karma in the philosophic discipline and its relation to jñāna and other allied doctrines—closely follow the arguments contained in the *Laghu-pūrvapakṣa* and *Laghu-siddhānta* of the *Śrī-bhāsya*. Vāda 9, which is concerned with demonstrating the ineligibility of the Advaitin to be a party to philosophical debate is based on the opening sentence of the *Mahā-siddhānta* of the *Śrī-bhāṣya*. Vādas 10 to 30 which are devoted to the discussion of the nature of the perception and difference, the Advaitin's theory of the illusoriness of the universe, the nature of consciousness (*anubhūti*), the relative validity of scripture and perception and other allied doctrines closely follow, with the exception of two Vādas (18 and 19), the order of the arguments found in the *Śrī-bhāṣya* commencing from the *Mahā-siddhānta* upto the topic known as the '*Śruti-ghatta*'. The 31st Vāda which relates to the discussion of the doctrine of Jīvanmukti marks the divergence from the order of the *Śrī-bhāṣya*. According to the order of the *Śrī-bhāṣya* the interpretation of the *Śruti* texts should have been taken up for discussion after the 30th Vāda; instead of this the doctrine of Jīvanmukti follows, while this doctrine is discussed in the *Śrī-bhāsya* in the *Samanvyaādhikaraṇa*. Vedānta Deśika himself seems to be aware of this fact as he attempts to give an explanation at the outset of the 31st Vāda for changing the order of the topics.[2] The Vādas that follow subsequently do not strictly adhere to the same order as that of the *Śrī-bhāṣya* though most of the Vādas are based upon

[1] See also *Śatabhūṣaṇī*, Introduction, p. 5.

See Appendix I for an enumeration of the sixty-six topics in the order in which they appear in the text.

[2] See Vāda 31. samanvyaädhikaraṇa bhāṣye pareṣām sayūthya kalaham upakṣipya jivanmukta pakṣaḥ pratikṣiptaḥ, tadevātra pūrvā-para sangateḥ vyākurmaḥ.

the arguments presented briefly in the *Śrī-bhāṣya*. Thus, for instance, in the *Śrī-bhāṣya*, in connnection with the disscussion of the interpretation of the scriptural texts in support of the nirguṇa Brahman which follows immediately after the *sphota-vāda*, the relative validity of the saguṇa and nirguṇa texts is taken up, while this topic is dealt with in Vāda 52 of the *Śatadūṣanī*. Again, in the *Śrī-bhāṣya* the issues regarding the doctrine of Avidyā appear in one place in a logical order, while these are scattered in different places and found in a different order in the *Śatadūṣaṇī*. The theory that Brahman is not the locus of nescience is discussed in Vāda 19, while the theory that Jīva is its locus is dealt with in Vāda 40. The discussion of the issue whether consciousness is indeterminate in the state of release would have been more appropriate if it had been taken along with other topics relating to the nature of consciousness (Vādas 20 to 28); instead of that, it is taken up after the consideration of the issue whether an Advaitin is eligible for the study of the sacred texts (Vāda 50), with which it has apparently no connection.

One possible explanation for the lack of sequence in the arrangement of topics is that the work must have been composed on the basis of the debates Vedānta Deśika had with the Advaitins. It is possible that the debates might have been focussed mainly on the *Laghu-siddhānta* and the *Mahā-siddhānta* of the *Śrī-bhāṣya* which contain the criticism against the Advaitins and in defence of which the arguments must have been developed further to render the refutation of Advaita complete. Some of the topics that do not find a place in the *Śrī-bhāṣya* must have sprung up as side issues for discussion during the course of the debate. The *Guru-paramparā*, which gives a biographical account of the Ācāryas of the Vaiṣṇava school including Vedānta Deśika, tells us that a debate went on for seven days at Śrīrangam between Vedānta Deśika and the pandits belonging to the Advaita school. The arguments were daily recorded by Perarulāla Jīyar, a direct disciple of Deśika. On the eighth day when the opponents were defeated, Perarulāla Jīyar handed over the whole matter to Vedānta Deśika who revised it, arranged the arguments in a proper order, and passed it on under the title of *Śatadūṣaṇī*.[1] According to another biographical account given in the *Vaibhava-Prakāśikā* to which a reference has been made earlier, Vedānta Deśika himself is believed

[1] See *Guruparamparā-Prabhāva*, p. 136.

to have composed the work after the debate was over summarising the arguments advanced in the debate.[1] Whatever it might have been, it appears from the order in which the Vādas are presented that the work must have been based mainly on the arguments advanced in the debate. Otherwise the work would have been more coherent, the Vādas being interrelated and gripped with a central idea. This remark in no way affects the value of the work as a *Vāda-grantha*. Though there is no logical sequence in the arrangement of the topics, the work is complete and comprehensive so far as the criticism of Advaita doctrines is concerned. It exhibits fully the author's mastery of the art of disputation as may be seen from the exposition of the arguments given in the subsequent chapters.

## VIII *Substance of the Work*

The sixty-six Vādas, though each one of them deals with a specific controversial issue, may be grouped under the following eight broad headings: 1. Pramāṇas 2. Perception and Difference, 3. The nature of Consciousness (*Anubhūti*), 4. The Individual Self and the Absolute 5. The Nirguṇa Brahman, 6. Universe, 7. The doctrine of Avidyā, 8. Sādhana and Mukti.[2]

The discussion regarding the 'Pramāṇas' is confined to the controversial issue whether the pramāṇas that are not absolutely real could be an evidence of what is real (Vāda 30). The Advaitin's view is that pramāṇas, even though illusory in character, can reveal what is ultimately real. The main argument adduced in support of it is that such a thing is found possible in our ordinary experience when a rope, for instance, which is mistaken for a snake, causes fear. This view is critically examined in all its aspects and the conclusion reached is that what is not real can never reveal what is

[1] See *Vaibhava Prakāśika*, Stanza 47.

[2] See *Śatabhūṣaṇī*—Samskrit Introduction, pp. xi-xii. Shri Anantakrishna Sastri has grouped the Vādas into the following ten headings: (1) Sūtra Svārasya-bhanga Vāda (2) Avidyā (3) Falsity of the world (4) Meaning of the first Vedānta-Sūtra (5) Brahma-vicāra and Sādhana-Catuṣṭaya (6) Tvam-Padārtha (7) Tat-Padārtha (8) Criticism relating to Mahāvākya (9) Jīvanmukti (10) Other topics not related to Advaita.

This categorisation does not have any logical sequence. Nor is it fully correct as some of the Vādas shown under the broad headings do not have a direct bearing on it.

real. It is also pointed out that if the pramāṇas do not have a real existence, metaphysical discussion cannot be carried on (Vāda 9). On the same ground, it is also held that scripture too cannot be claimed as the ultimate authority in spiritual matters in so far as there is nothing to distinguish it from the so-called non-authoritative sacred texts of the Buddhists (Vāda 14). Nor is it possible to claim a superior validity to scripture over perception in case a conflict arises between the two, as scripture, like perception, has for its source avidyā—a defect (Vāda 29).[1]

The discussion on 'Perception and Difference' centres round the important epistemological issue, viz., whether perception reveals pure 'Being' or difference. The *prima facie* view that comes up for criticism here is that perception is of the one real, difference being subsequently superimposed thereon. The nerve of the argument put forth in support of this claim is that difference being a relative notion is dependent for its cognition on the knowledge of its counter-correlate and substrate while 'Being' is not so. Secondly, the concept of difference when subjected to logical examination does not stand the test and as such it is not real. Both the aspects of the problem are discussed at great length with particular reference to the examination of the dialectic on difference. The conclusion reached is that difference is real and is logically intelligible and it is also revealed in perception (Vādas 12 and 13). In this connection, the theory of determinate and indeterminate perception is also discussed (Vāda 11) and the correct definition of the *nirvikalpaka* and *savikalpaka* perception as understood by the Viśiṣṭādvaita school of thought is pointed out.[2]

The discussion on the 'Nature of Consciousness' is mainly confined to an examination of the Advaitin's contentions that consciousness is identical with Reality, that it is indeterminate in character, that it is a self-luminous, homogeneous whole which is neither produced nor destroyed, and lastly that it is identical with the very self in us. The arguments, mostly in the form of inferences, that are put forth in support of these contentions are critically examined and refuted by showing the logical fallacies involved in them and also their opposition to the ordinary experience on the one hand and scriptural texts on the other. The criticism is mainly based on the theory that consciousness is that which involves the duality of the subject

[1] See Chapter I.

[2] See Chapter II.

and the object and, as such, it is the characteristic feature of the self. It is determinate in character. Although it is self-luminous, it is not absolutely unknowable. It is not one, but many and is subject to change in the form of contraction and expansion. (Vādas 10, 20, 21-25).[1]

The discussion on 'The Individual Self and the Absolute' covers the most important ontological issue, viz., whether or not the individual self is identical with the Absolute. The Advaitin who answers it in the affirmative maintains that the individual self is the Absolute conditioned by nescience (*avidyā*) and with the removal of *avidyā* the finite self becomes identical with the Absolute. The true self then is one only, and not many. The plurality of the individual self may be due to the reflection of the Absolute in the internal organs—the product of *avidyā*—comparable to the reflection of the single moon in the waves; or it may be due to the Absolute which is pure consciousness being conditioned by the internal organs in the same way as cosmic ether is conditioned by pot etc. These arguments are discussed in great detail and set aside on the ground that they are directly in conflict with our experience and secondly that they do not have the support of scriptural texts. The conclusions reached are that the entity denoted by the notion 'I' is the individual self, that it is the knower, that it is different from individual to individual and lastly that it is not identical with the Absolute, though, it is organically related to it (Vādas 26, 27, 36 and 37).[2]

The discussion on 'Brahman' is confined to the fundamental ontological issue whether Brahman is *saguṇa* or *nirguṇa* in character (Vāda 52). This issue is examined at great length with particular reference to the Advaitin's contention that the Upaniṣadic text referring to Brahman as *Satyam*, *Jñānam* and *Anantam* conveys an impartite and non-relational sense, *akhaṇḍārtha* (Vāda 38). It is pointed out that neither the scriptural texts in general nor the *smṛti* texts nor the *Vedānta-sūtras* teach the doctrine of nirguṇa Brahman (Vādas 48 and 66). It is also urged that if Brahman is devoid of all characteristics, it cannot be conceived as blissful (*ānanda*) and eternal (Vādas 57-58).[3]

The discussion on the 'Universe' bears on three important issues: (i) the illusory character of the universe, (ii) the relationship of the universe to the Brahman, and (iii) the concept of causality. Regarding the first, the various arguments of the

[1] See Chapter III. [2] See Chapter IV. [3] See Chapter V. Section i.

Advaitin to prove the illusoriness of the universe are examined and are shown to be untenable (Vādas 15, 16 and 17).[1] Regarding the second issue, the question is raised whether or not Brahman is the material cause; and if so, in what sense. *Pariṇāma-vāda* is upheld as against the *Vivarta-vāda* of the Advaitin, which is shown to be defective (Vādas 53-54).[2] As regards the last point, the famous dialectic of the Advaitin on the concept of causality is critically considered and it is proved that the concept is logically intelligible (Vāda 55).[3]

The discussion of the doctrine of Avidyā which is very comprehensive is concerned with the demonstration of its untenability from different points of view. First, its very nature (*svarūpa*) is unintelligible. Secondly, its description as something inexplicable is a self-contradiction. Thirdly, it cannot be established by any pramāṇas. Fourthly, neither Brahman nor the Jīva can be its locus. Fifthly, its function as obscuring the true nature of the Reality is unintelligible. Sixthly, the removal of nescience by true knowledge is untenable. Lastly, the very conception of its cessation is a riddle (Vādas 19, 35, 39-44).[4]

The last heading 'Sādhana and Mukti' covers mainly the issues arising out of the interpretation of the first sūtra of Bādarāyaṇa. The most important of these refers to the question whether the *sādhana-catuṣṭaya* accepted by Śamkara does invariably precede *Brahma-jijñāsā*. The view of the Advaitin is subjected to a detailed critical examination and it is shown that the discrimination between eternal and non-eternal, etc., is possible only after the study of the Vedānta, but not prior to it. What therefore precedes *Brahma-jijñāsā* is the study of the *Pūrva-Mīmāmsā* (Vāda 8).[5] To establish this theory, the relationship between the *Pūrva* and *Uttara-Mīmāmsā* is discussed elaborately and it is proved that the two constitute one integral whole (Vāda 3). The place of karma in the philosophic discipline is also considered and it is established that the performance of karma is obligatory on every individual and is the direct means to *vedanā* or the knowledge of Brahman (Vāda 6). The issue whether knowledge alone is the means to *mokṣa* is also discussed and it is pointed out that knowledge generated by the Upaniṣadic texts cannot be the means to *mokṣa* in so far as it does not remove avidyā (Vāda 4).[6] In

[1] See Chapter VI. Sections 1 to 3.
[2] Chapter VI. Sections 4 and 5.
[3] Chapter VI. Section 6.
[4] Chapter VII.
[5] Chapter VIII. Section 1.
[6] Chapter VIII. Section 4.

this connection the theory of *Jīvanmukti* and the state of Individual self in the state of *mokṣa* are also discussed (Vādas 31 and 51).

These are some of the important topics that have been discussed in the *Śatadūṣaṇī*. In the following pages an attempt is made to give an exposition of the arguments on these various topics as contained in Vedānta Deśika's *Śatadūṣaṇī* in the order in which they have been set out above under the eight headings.

CHAPTER ONE

# PRAMĀṆAS AND THEIR VALIDITY

A STUDY of the pramāṇas is an indispensable prolegomena to all metaphysical investigation. The exponent of every system has to show that the theory propounded by him is well grounded on the valid means of knowledge. In the absence of any valid proof in support of his theory, it is bound to be rejected as non-authoritative.

The adherents of the orthodox schools of Indian Philosophy have generally accepted that perception (*pratyakṣa*), inference (*anumāna*) and scripture (*āgama*) are the three important pramāṇas. Of these, scripture has been admitted to be the final authority in spiritual matters.

## I *Scripture as a Pramāṇa*

The metaphysical position held by the Advaitin presents some difficulties with regard to the pramāṇas and their validity. According to him Brahman alone is absolutely real and everything else is illusory. Pramāṇas, then, are not absolutely real. The first question that naturally arises out of this position is whether such pramāṇas, particularly the revealed scripture, can be evidence leading to and guaranteeing the knowledge of reality. If a pramāṇa is not real, can it tell us anything about the absolute reality? Secondly, if scripture too is illusory in character, how can it be claimed as the ultimate authority in spiritual matters?

Regarding the first question the Advaitin answers that although a pramāṇa is illusory it can yet reveal what is absolutely real. There are numerous instances of what is real being revealed by what is not real. The shell-silver, which is only illusory, causes joy. The rope-snake produces fear. The objects experienced in dreams are not real; and yet they produce effects which are far more real than the dream-objects. In all these cases the effects are definitely of a higher grade of reality than their causes. It is, therefore, possible that scripture, though it is illusory, can yet reveal the Absolute.[1]

Vedānta Deśika examines the above argument in great detail. The main point of criticism, which is based upon the Viśiṣṭādvaitic theory of knowledge, is that in the instances cited by the Advaitin, it is not the alleged illusory objects but their cognitions that produce the effects in question. The cognitions, on this view, are real. In the case of the shell-silver, it is the cognition which apprehends the shell as silver that causes the joy in the individual. Similarly, the cognition which apprehends a rope as a snake is the cause of fear. In the case of the dream too, it is the experience of the objects in the dream that is the cause of the real effects. The experience itself is real, because it is not denied by the waking experience. On the contrary, the objects seen in the dream are sublated by waking consciousness and hence they are not real.

It may be asked whether the cognition can be real while its corresponding object is not real. This is possible, contends Vedānta Deśika. What is needed for a cognition to be real is that it should have a reference to an object (*sālambanatva mātra niyamāt*) and it is not necessary that the corresponding object should exist at that time. The mere appearance of an object is sufficient to serve the purpose of a content of the cognition.[2] In the instances under consideration, there is the appearance of the objects to the respective cognitions owing to the defects of the object, the sense organs etc. These objects, since they are sublated later on by the succeeding cognitions are regarded as non-real. But the cognitions as such are not sublated and hence they are real.

An objection may be raised. In the instances cited above, the mere cognition as such cannot produce the effects. If that were the case, the effects should have been produced even by some other cognition. On the contrary, it is only such cognition as is qualified by a particular object, say shell-silver or rope-snake, that produces the effects in question.[3] A qualification may be of two kinds, qualification *per proprium* (*viśeṣaṇa*) and qualification *per accidens* (*upalakṣaṇa*). The former is a

[1] *S.D.*, Vāda 30. See also *Śrī-bhāṣya* I. 1. 1. p. 49 (Ananda Press Edn.), Cp. *Brahma-siddhi*, pp. 13-4; See also *S.B.*, II. 1. 14.

[2] *Śrī-bhāṣya*, I. i. i. p. 50. arthasya pratibhāsamānatvam-eva hy-ālambanatve apekṣitam.

[3] Cp. *Advaita-siddhi*, pp. 405-06 (Nirṇaya Sāgara Edn.).

distinctive mark which is syntactically related to the predicate and the latter is that which, while present, distinguishes without syntactical relation to the predicate. In either sense, an illusory object has to be admitted as a qualification of the cognition. If that be admitted, it would follow that an illusory object is the cause of a real effect.[1]

The above objection is met in more than one way. It is no doubt true that a cognition by itself does not give rise to the effects in question. Nevertheless there is no room for the possibility of their being effected by some other cognition since the cognitions themselves are diversified in their nature (*vicitra-śaktitvāt*). This diversity of cognitions is not so much due to the respective objects as to the accessories of knowledge (*śāmagrī vaicitrya*). In other words, the relation of the cognitions to the respective objects is determined by the different accessories of knowledge.[2] It cannot be said that an object too constitutes an accessory of knowledge. This is true in the case of the perceptual knowledge where the object serves as the basis of sense-contact (*indriya samprayogādhāratā*). But in the case of inferential cognition of the objects of the past and future, there is no possibility of an object being an accessory of knowledge. As regards an illusory object, it has no existence before it is manifested by knowledge and, as such, it cannot serve as the basis for the sense-contact. The shell-silver is not, therefore, the cause of joy in the capacity of its being a qualification *per proprium* (*viśeṣaṇa*) of the cognition.

The cognition qualified *per accidens* by the object, say shell-silver, may be considered as the cause of joy. Even then, shell-silver would not be the cause. There are three factors, the shell-silver, the cognition of shell-silver and the effect viz., joy. The shell-silver by itself does not produce the joy. On the contrary, it is the cognition of the shell-silver that gives rise to joy. The cognition of the shell-silver is, therefore, the cause of joy. The object is only its *upalakṣaṇa*. What is only an *upalakṣaṇa* of the cause cannot itself be the cause of the effect as it would result in undue extension. In other words, the object is only concomitant with the effect by its being an *upalakṣaṇa* of the cause and as such causality does not pertain to it.[3]

[1] *S.D.*, Vāda 30. See also Śrutaprakāśikā on *Śrī-bhāṣya*, Vol. 2, p. 920 (Mad. Edn.).

[2] *S.D.*, sāmagri vaicitryādeva tattadviṣayatva niyamopi samvidaḥ.

[3] Ibid., Vāda 30, na hi kāraṇopalakṣaṇam-api tat-kārya kāraṇambhavati, ati prasangāt.

Further, an *upalakṣaṇa* by itself does not denote the *upalakṣya*. On the other hand, it denotes it through the knowledge that cognises it (*sva-jñānena*). In other words, it is not the mere *upalakṣaṇa* but its knowledge that gives rise to the knowledge of the *upalakṣya*. Causality, therefore, pertains only to the knowledge.

Considering the nature of the cause and effect,[1] an illusory object cannot have the status of being a cause. A cause is a prior state of the effect. To be a cause is to be invariably an antecedent factor (*niyata-pūrva-bhāvitva*). *Pūrva-bhāvitva* means an existence prior to the effect (*pūrvakāla-sattvam*). Neither that which belongs to the future nor that which does not exist at all can be considered as a cause. An illusory object has no real existence in a spatio-temporal order and as such it cannot be regarded as a cause.[2]

The foregoing criticisms against the Advaitin have been levelled by accepting the view of the opponent that the objects of illusion such as shell-silver, rope-snake etc., are not real and that they are the qualifications *per accidens* (*upalakṣaṇa*) of the respective cognitions. From the standpoint of a Viśiṣṭādvaitin an object is not even an *upalakṣaṇa* of the cognition. An *upalakṣaṇa* is that which is not syntactically related to the *upalakṣya* and yet causes the cognition of the latter. According to the Viśiṣṭādvaitic theory of knowledge, a discussion of which is taken up later,[3] knowledge which is always related to an object manifests either by itself or through another knowledge that cognises it.[4] An object, therefore, cannot be considered as an *upalakṣaṇa* of the cognition in the strict sense of the term.

Even if it be admitted that an object is an *upalakṣaṇa* of the cognition, it is not illusory for the Viśiṣṭādvaitin. The object of illusion is not wholly non-real (*sarvathā mithyā*) because it exists in some other place and at some other time. On this view, if the shell-silver be an *upalakṣaṇa* of the cognition, then the real object only would be the cause of the real effect. Vedānta Deśika, therefore, comes to the conclusion that what is not real can never reveal what is real. Even

[1] A detailed discussion of the theory of causality is taken up in Chapter VI, Section 6.

[2] *S.D.*, Vāda 30.

[3] See Chapter III.

[4] *S.D.*, Vāda 30, svenaiva vā svaviṣaya jñānāntareṇa vā saviṣaya jñāna svarūpa prakāśaḥ.

granting that it is possible as it is supposed to be found in some cases of our ordinary experience, it does not necessarily follow that the real Brahman is made known by a pramāṇa that is not absolutely real because it is neither seen nor established by concomitance (*adarśanātanvayā-vyatirekā-siddheḥ*).

So far, the criticism has been directed against the analogies put forth by the Advaitin in support of his theory. There is yet another argument in favour of his theory which is more significant than the earlier one. The scripture, the Advaitin argues, is not absolutely unreal like the sky-flower. Prior to the onset of the knowledge of the Brahman, it is viewed as something real.[1] It is only after the dawn of the Brahman knowledge that it is understood to be illusory, when only it ceases to be a means to the knowledge of Brahman. As long as Brahman-knowledge has not arisen the sacred texts are real for all practical purposes and as such they are capable of generating knowledge of Reality.

The above argument does not hold good, contends Vedānta Deśika. Although scripture which is illusory in character may be capable of generating the knowledge of Brahman, it cannot establish that the content of that knowledge is real. If the knowledge based on scripture is itself illusory, the content of that knowledge would equally be illusory. This is explained by an illustration. A person mistakes the mist for smoke and on that basis infers the presence of fire. Here the inferential cognition of the fire, which is based on the false probans, is erroneous and consequently the content of that cognition viz., fire too becomes false. In the same way if the knowledge of Brahman were to be derived from illusory scripture, the content of that knowledge viz., Brahman would also be illusory.[2]

It may be argued that the content of Brahman-knowledge is real, although the knowledge itself is illusory in as much as it is never sublated by anything else. This argument is untenable, contends Vedānta Deśika. There is the teaching of the Mādhyamikas for whom Reality is void and it denies

[1] Cp. *S.B.*, I. 1. 4, & II. 1. 14.

dehātma pratyayo yadvat-pramāṇatvena kalpitaḥ; laukikam
tadvadevedam pramānam tvātma niścayāt

See also *Bhāmati*, p. 244 (T.P.H.).

[2] Vāda 30.

See also *Śrī-bhāṣya*, p. 51.

even the existence of Brahman.[1] It cannot be said that the sacred texts of the Mādhyamikas are non-authoritative as they are based on a defective source. For the Vedānta texts are equally non-authoritative as they have been held by the Advaitin himself to be the product of nescience, which is a defect (*doṣa*). It may however be possible to account for the authoritativeness of the Vedas on the basis of the empirical reality (*vyāvahārika vyavasthā*); but as it will be shown presently this will not go far to establish the superiority of the Vedānta texts to that of the Mādhyamikas. Vedānta Deśika, therefore, concludes that the real Brahman is ascertained only through the scripture that is absolutely real and not otherwise.

## II *Authoritativeness of the Sacred Texts*

If scripture be illusory can it be claimed as the final authority? This is the second question raised against the Advaitin's theory of pramāṇas and their validity. It is an important issue for the Vedāntins as scripture is the sole authority of knowing the nature of the ultimate Reality. Naturally Vedānta Deśika discusses it in detail and attempts to show that the Advaitin cannot claim the Vedic texts as more authoritative than the Buddhist texts.

Mīmāmsakas and the Vedāntins alike recognise that scripture is authoritative whereas Buddhist texts are non-authoritative. This distinction is made on the ground of certain factors such as eternity, beginninglessness and defectlessness. Scripture is authoritative because it is eternal, beginningless and free from defects. The Buddhist texts, on the contrary, are held to be non-authoritative because they do not possess any of these qualities.[2] Vedānta Deśika urges that such a distinction does not hold good in respect of the Advaitin. For him scripture cannot be eternal as it is regarded as the product of nescience. If it were eternal, then there would be eternal bondage.

[1] *S.D.*, Vāda 30.

śūnyameva tattvamiti mādhyamika vākyenaca sākṣācca bādho dṛśyate.

[2] *S.D.*, Vāda 14.

Vedānta Deśika raises twelve alternatives and mentions twelve factors as the possible grounds for determining the authoritativeness of the Vedas and the non-authoritativeness of the Buddhist texts. Of these only three which are important, are mentioned here.

Nor can it be claimed to be beginningless as it has its origin in avidyā. If it be argued that the supposition is only as beginningless then on that very ground the Buddhist texts too would be beginningless since the Buddhists also claim that their teachings which have come down in succession from the stream of consciousness known as the Omniscient are beginningless.[2]

Nor is it possible for the Advaitin to hold that scripture is free from defects since it is admitted to be the product of nescience. If it were admitted that scripture does not have a defective origin in nescience then the position would come nearer to that of the Viśiṣṭādvaitin. Thus, the very fact that the source is defective would prove its non-authoritativeness. If scripture be *kalpita*, how then could it be relied on as the final authority?

The Advaitin may contend that scripture is real from the empirical standpoint and hence is authoritative. Even this will not improve the situation. For the Buddhists also acknowledge an empirical reality in respect of their sacred texts.[2] And the denial of these texts as non-authoritative would not find any justification. In other words, it is not possible for the Advaitin to claim on the ground of the mere acceptance of the empirical reality that the Vedic texts are authoritative and the Buddhist texts are non-authoritative. If this position is welcome to him in so far as non-authoritativeness itself is indeterminable (*anirvacanīa*) in his system, then he cannot claim himself to be an *āstika*. It is then absurd, contends Vedānta Deśika, to proceed with the investigation of truth and to strive for the attainment of release.

## III *Pramāṇas and Metaphysical Discussion*

If the pramāṇas are not admitted to be absolutely real it is impossible even to carry on any metaphysical discussion.[3]

[1] *S.D.*, Vāda 14.

[2] Ibid.

The Buddhists admit what is known as *samvṛti-satyatva* which is said to be synonymous with the *vyāvahārika-satyatva* recognised by the Advaitin.

See *Mādhyamika Kārika*, XXIV, 8.

dve satye samupāśritya buddhānām dharma deśanā; loke samvṛti satyam-ca satyam-ca paramārthataḥ.

[3] *S.D.*, Vāda 9.

The aim of a discussion is the establishment of truth and the repudiation of false theories. It is also meant to establish one's own conclusions by refuting the position taken up by the opponents. This can be accomplished only when it is shown that one's position is grounded on the pramāṇas whereas the position held by the opponent does not find the support of the pramāṇas. This again is possible only when the pramāṇas have real existence. The Advaitins do not acknowledge the reality of the pramāṇas and in the absence of the real means to establish their theories they cannot carry on any metaphysical discussion.[1]

The Advaitin may, however, argue that the discussions may be carried on by the pramāṇas that have come into usage by the mere acceptance of their existence (*sattā-bhyupagama-mātreṇa*).[2] Thus, it has been said by the author of the *Iṣṭa-siddhi*—" True, there is the usage, hence we make use of them, but we do not find their origin ".[3] This will not do, contends Vedānta Deśika. For Buddhists also acknowledge such a kind of empirical reality in respect of their pramāṇas. Why then should their pramāṇas be regarded as non-authoritative? Vedānta Deśika, therefore, urges that unless the pramāṇas themselves are absolutely real, no metaphysical investigation can be carried on and consequently no truth can be established by them.[4]

[1] Ibid.

See also *Vedārtha-samgraha*: adhikaro-anupāyatvāt na vāde śūnya vādinaḥ.

[2] Cp. *Khaṇḍana-khaṇḍa-khādya*, pp. 31-2 (Chowkamba Edn.).

[3] *Iṣṭa-siddhi*, p. 2.

satyam prasiddhirasti ata eva vyavaharāmaḥ kintu
nāsyāmūlam paśyāmaḥ

[4] There is an elaborate statement of the *pūrvapakṣa* on this subject in defence of the Advaitin's position which is mainly drawn from Śrī Harṣa's *Khaṇḍana-khaṇḍa-khādya*, but there is no refutation of it by Deśika except a few words he says at the outset of the Vāda. There are two explanations for the absence of the refutation of the pūrvapakṣa. One explanation, which has been suggested by Mahācārya, the commentator of the *Śatadūṣaṇī*, is that it is the intention of Deśika to show through the arguments of the pūrvapakṣin himself that he is eligible for debate like the Mādhyamikas even without the acceptance of the reality of the pramāṇas and thereby establish indirectly that the Advaitin like the Mādhyamikas is not eligible for the debate since both accept only empirical reality of the pramāṇas. If otherwise the criticism were levelled direct against the pūrvapakṣin, the latter would become eligible for debate in so far as such a criticism could be levelled only against one who has entered the debate, but not against one who is indifferent to it. This explanation does not appear to be very convincing. When the *prima facie* view has been stated in detail it is but proper that it should have been criticised in detail. Vedānta Deśika also states at the beginning of the vāda, after quoting the view of Ramanuja, that it will be

## IV *Scripture and Perception*

In cases of conflict between scripture and perception, which is to be regarded as of greater validity? The Advaitin maintains that in cases of such a conflict, scripture is stronger than perception and as such the former is more authoritative than the latter. The reason for holding such a view is obvious. According to the Advaitin non-dualism is the purport of scripture.[1] Perception, on the contrary, apprehends a world of plurality and difference and as such there is a conflict between the two.[2] How is this conflict to be overcome? Whenever there is a conflict between two cognitions based on two different sources of knowledge, either both of them or one of them should be considered as invalid. It is not possible to deny both. For there is no room for a third alternative other than the cognition being either real or non-real. Thus it follows that in cases of conflict between two cognitions one of them should be sublated. What is weak is sublated by that which is strong. How are the strength and weakness of the two conflicting cognitions to be determined? This is to be decided on the basis of the principle which determines the relation of the sublated to the sublater. The sublated one is that which affords room for being non-authoritative and hence admits of being accounted for in another way (*bādhyam*); while that which affords no room for being held non-authoritative and cannot, therefore, be accounted for otherwise is the sublater (*bādhakam*).[3] How are we to ascertain whether a particular cognition is authoritative or not? This is to be decided, says the Advaitin, from the nature of the source of the cognition. If the source of a particular

explained in detail (*etacca vistarāt upapādayāmaḥ*). Obviously he had the intention of answering the *prima facie* view. It is therefore possible that the last portion of the Vāda containing the criticism might have been lost. Vāda 15, for instance, is incomplete and similarly the present Vāda also may be incomplete.

See Caṇḍamāruta on Vāda 9, p. 188. (Śāstra Muktāvali Series).

[1] *Śaṁkara Bhāṣya* on V. S. I. 1. 4.

[2] The author of the *Brahma-siddhi* holds that there is no opposition at all between perception and scripture since the former too like the latter reveals non-difference. See *Brahma-siddhi*, p. 39. This view is discussed in the next chapter.

[3] *S.D.*, Vāda 29.

See also *Śrī-bhāṣya*, I. 1. 1. p. 18.

sāvakāśatvāt anyathā siddham bādhyam; anavakāśatvāt ananyathā siddham bādhakam.

cognition is defective then that cognition is to be held non-authoritative; otherwise, it is authoritative. Now as for scriptural knowledge its source is absolutely free from defects. In the first place, scripture is not assigned to an authorship and as such there is not the least suspicion of its being the product of one's delusion, deceit or negligence or of the incapacity of the agent. Secondly, it is transmitted down from generation to generation in the same order without the possibility of any portion of it being either lost or added to. Thirdly, the *Upabṛmhaṇas* such as the *Purāṇas* and *Itihāsas* are fully in support of scripture and as such it cannot be suspected of any bias by any one who studies it. These are the three possible kinds of error in respect of verbal testimony and as scripture is free from them, the knowledge that is derived from it is authoritative and is also superior in validity to perception. Perception on the contrary is capable of imperfection as it has for its source the impression of difference (*bheda-vāsanā*) which is found to be a defect. Scripture is thus of greater force than perception and it is, therefore, reasonable to conclude that the knowledge of non-dualism which arises from the defectless scripture sublates the cognition of difference which is the product of a defective source.[1]

Against this theory Vedānta Deśika points out that it is wrong to assume that the alleged conflict between perception and scripture cannot be overcome except by negating the former by the latter. The conflict could be overcome by interpreting the scriptural texts in such a way as is not opposed to perception. In fact, when scriptural texts are in direct conflict with perception, the former should be interpreted in conformity with the perceptual experience and with due regard to their context.[2]

Perception is considered to be non-authoritative on the ground that it rests on a defective source, viz., the cognition of difference, while scripture which is free from defects is authoritative. This argument is untenable, contends Deśika. In so far as scripture is also held by the Advaitin to be a product of nescience (*avidyā*) it is no better than perception.

[1] *S.D.*, Vāda 29.

Some of these arguments are found in the Tarkakāṇḍa of *Brahma-siddhi*. See *Brahma-siddhi*, pp. 39-40.

[2] *S.D.*, Vāda 29.

How is it known that the impression of difference (*bheda-vāsanā*) is a defect? Is it known by any other means that the impression of difference like that of defective sight is the cause of an altogether perverse view? If it be regarded as a defect because it is in direct conflict with the import of the scriptural text, then the argument would involve a vicious circle. The defectiveness of the cognition of difference is proved by the fact that scripture has for its purport non-difference. The fact that scriptural import is non-difference is established only when it is known that the cognition of difference is a defect.[1]

Further, if in some cases the cognition of difference be a defect, it does not follow that it is always so in respect of everything. In that case such a contingency would arise even in respect of non-difference. For the knowledge of the sacred texts cannot arise except with the knowledge of the difference involved in the words, the sentences and their meaning etc. The knowledge of non-difference too is dependent upon the cognition of difference like perception and therefore the distinction made between perception and scripture as the sublated and the sublater respectively does not hold good.

It may be argued that scripture although it is based on a defect yet sublates perception in so far as it generates the cognition which dispels all plurality apprehended through perception and is thus later than perception (*param*). According to the principle of the Mīmāmsā known as the *apaccheda-nyāya* [2] what comes later is stronger than the earlier.[3] Against this it is pointed out that the defectiveness of the source of scripture having once been recognised the circumstance of its being later is of no avail. This is explained in the *Śrī-bhāṣya* by an illustration. If a man is afraid of a rope which he mistakes for a snake, his fear does not cease because another man, whom he considers to be in error himself, tells him, 'This is no snake, do not be afraid'. That scripture is founded

[1] Ibid., śāstreṇa nirviśeṣatve siddhesyāt bhedavāsanā; doṣastaddoṣa bhāve ca siddhesyān-nirviśeṣadhīḥ. See also *Śrī-bhāṣya*, I. 1. 1. p. 48.

[2] *Apaccheda-nyāya* is the principle of the later sublating the earlier. It is so called since it is formulated in the Pūrva-Mīmāṁsā in connection with the expiatory rites consequent on different priests letting go (*apaccheda*) their hold of the tucked up waist cloth of the priest in front, while going round the sacrificial fire. See *Pūrvamīmāmsā-Sūtra*, 6. 5. 54.

[3] See *Brahma-siddhi*, p. 40.

āmnāya eva balavan tadvirodhe paurvā parye pūrva daurbalyam prakṛtivat; pūrva-bādhena notpattiḥ-uttarasya-hi siddhyati iti.

on something defective is known at the very time of studying the sacred texts (*śravaṇa*) for the recollection (*manana*) which follows hearing consists in repeated attempts to cognise oneness of Brahman, a cognition which is destructive of all plurality apprehended through the hearing of the Veda.[1]

Vedānta Deśika, therefore, concludes that whenever scriptural texts conflict with perception, the former should be interpreted without opposition to the latter. Perception is the foundational and basic factor of all experience. It offers subsistence to inference and scripture (*upajīvya*) and as such it is of greater force than scripture which depends on perception (*upajīvaka*).

There is one objection to the above conclusion. It is argued that the fact that perception offers subsistence to inference and scripture (*upajīvya*) does not make it stronger than the other sources of knowledge. For we find the sublation of the perceptual cognition of the flame of the lamp as one by the inferential cognition that proves that there is a succession of different flames *jvālābhedānumāna*. The flame of the lamp, as long as it burns appears to the perception as one and the same; but on the ground of the observation that the different particles of the wick and the oil are consumed in succession, it is inferred that there are many distinct flames succeeding one another. Thus the inferential cognition even though it is mediate sublates the immediate perceptual cognition. Hence what is an *upajīvya* need not be stronger than what is an *upajīvaka*.

Vedānta Deśika controverts this argument. In the instance under consideration there is no opposition between the *upajīvya* and *upajīvaka*. The cognition of the oneness of the flame is not the *upajīvya* of the inference referring to the difference of the flame of the lamp. On the contrary, it is the perception which cognises the concomitance between the particles of the wick and the oil and the flame of the lamp that actually constitutes the *upajīvya* of the inference and this particular perception is not sublated by the inference proving difference of the flame. Thus the illustration in question does not prove the fact that the *upajīvaka* is stronger than the *upajīvya*. Vedānta Deśika, therefore, concludes that in cases of conflict perception is definitely stronger than scripture.

[1] See *Śrī-bhāṣya*, I. 1. 1. p. 48.

## CHAPTER TWO

# THE NATURE AND CONTENT OF PERCEPTION

THE discussion on the relative validity of perception and scripture leads to the consideration of an important epistemological issue regarding the nature and content of perception. If perception cognised a world of plurality and difference, it would no doubt conflict with the scripture in so far as its purport is non-dualism. Does perception really cognise difference? Such a question has been raised by some Advaitins and an answer is given in the negative. Perception, it is contended, does not cognise difference; on the contrary it apprehends an undifferentiated and indeterminate Being (*nirviśeṣa-sanmātra-grāhi*) and as such there is no conflict at all between perception and scripture since both have the same content. Perception is of the one real, difference being superimposed thereon.[1]

The arguments adduced in favour of the above theory are two-fold. First, it is held that difference is not established by any of the pramāṇās (*pramāṇā-nupapattiḥ*); secondly, it is pointed out that the concept of difference is not logically intelligible and as such it is illusory and cannot be regarded as the content of true perception (*prameyā-nupapattiḥ*). Both these arguments have been developed on an elaborate dialectic. Quite naturally Vedānta Deśika discusses them in great detail and attempts to prove that difference is real and is also the content of perception.[2]

[1] See *Brahma-siddhi*, p. 39.

āhurvidhātṛ pratyakṣam na niṣedhṛ vipaścitaḥ;
naikatva āgamastena pratyakṣeṇa virudhyate.

Both Rāmānuja and Deśika seem to have this in view when they discuss this subject.

See *Śrī-bhāṣya*, p. 21.

See also *Darśanodaya*, p. 326.

[2] *S.D.*, Vādas 12 and 13.

sanmātra pratyakṣa bhanga vādaḥ and bhedadūṣaṇa nistāra vādaḥ

I *The Advaitin's View*

The *prima facie* view that comes up for criticism in the *Satadūṣaṇī* is as follows. We say that the pot is real and the cloth is real, and so on; the reality that is constant in all these is the true content of perception. When the true content of perception is thus one, there is no room for difference. Let us assume that difference too is perceived. Then perception would have two functions, positive and negative, the former relating to the proper nature of what is perceived (*svarūpa*) and the latter to its difference from others (*bheda*). Does perception apprehend both *svarūpa* and *bheda* or only one of them? If it apprehends both, it should do so either simultaneously or in succession. It cannot apprehend them simultaneously. For the apprehension of mere *svarūpa* is immediate since it depends on no other factor, while the apprehension of *bheda* is not so, as it depends on the knowledge of what is different (*āśraya*) and that from which it is different (*pratiyogi*). Nor is it possible to apprehend them in succession, as there is no sequence in a single act of cognition. Perception which is momentary, apprehends what is in sense-contact, say the *svarūpa* and subsides with it; it does not continue for another moment to grasp difference. If perception cannot apprehend both *svarūpa* and difference, it should cognise only one of them. Difference cannot be cognised through perception, because it is apprehended along with the counter-correlates which are remote in space and time. Hence it follows that perception apprehends the mere *svarūpa* and nothing else (*svarūpa mātra grāhi pratyakṣam*). If perception cannot establish difference much less can the other *pramāṇās* prove it since they all depend on perception.[1]

Regarding the nature of difference the Advaitin puts forth the following dialectical arguments.[2] What is difference? Is

[1] *S.D.*, Vāda 12.

The entire argument has been strikingly summed up in one stanza by Yāmuna in his *Samvit-siddhi.*

yaugapadya kramāyogād-vyavaccheda vidhānayoḥ;
āikyāyogācca bhedho na pratyakṣa iti yo bhramaḥ.

The arguments have been drawn mainly from *Brahma-siddhi*, pp. 43-4.

See also *Tattva-śuddhi*, pp. 5-6.

See also *Tattvapradīpika*, pp. 165-6.

[2] The dialectic on difference is found in almost all the important treatises of Advaita. Maṇḍana appears to be the earliest thinker to refute difference; Śrī Harṣa and Citsukha followed it later. Our author has mainly drawn the arguments from Maṇḍana's *Brahma-siddhi.*

it the nature of a thing or is it an attribute of it?[1] If it were the nature of the thing, the illusion of shell-silver would not arise. The shell is mistaken for silver because the difference between the two is not cognised. If according to the present position the cognition of shell itself makes known the difference of it from silver, how can there be the apprehension of silver in the shell? Again, if difference were the nature of the thing, it would follow that the object and the so-called difference are synonymous. Consequently, such usage as 'the pot is different' etc., would be redundant as it would amount to saying that the pot is qualified by pot. Difference, therefore, cannot be the nature of the thing.

Nor can it be an attribute of the object. If it were an attribute, then is this attribute different from its substrate or not? If it were not different, then the attribute and the substrate would become identical and in the absence of any attribute whatsoever there cannot be a difference of attributes. If the attribute be different from the substrate, then is that difference between substrate and the attribute the very nature of the substrate or an attribute of it? If it be the latter, we are launched on an infinite regress (*anavasthā*).

Further, our knowledge of difference is bound up necessarily with that of the differents. That is, the cognition of differents would not arise if there were no prior knowledge of the differents as differents; and this cognition of differents would not arise as such without the apprehension of the difference. We are thus involved in a vicious circle (*anyonyāśraya*).

The concept of difference is thus unintelligible and it is reasonable, therefore, to hold that difference is only an appearance and not a reality. In the words of Bradley, "It is a makeshift, it is a device, a mere practical compromise most necessary but in the end most indefensible".[2]

## II *Nature of Difference*

Vedānta Deśika examines in detail the dialectic on difference. The cognition of difference, he contends, can never be denied

See *Brahma-siddhi*, pp. 47-8.

*Khaṇḍana-Khaṇḍa-Khādya*, pp. 111-2 (Pandit Reprints)

*Tattvapradīpika*, Chapter II, pp. 165-8.

[1] Śrī Harṣa raises four alternatives—difference as (*a*) *svarūpa*, (*b*) *anyonābhāva*, (*c*) *vaidharmya* (*d*) something else (*anyadeva*).

[2] *Appearance and Reality*, p. 33.

as that would amount to the denial of one's own words. It almost stands opposed to perception which, as it will be shown presently, establishes difference.

The Advaitin raises two alternatives to refute difference. Vedānta Deśika asks whether these alternatives have been raised after accepting or rejecting in general the difference between the nature of the thing and its attribute? If it be the former, it would be a futile attempt to refute difference. If it be the latter, there would be no room for the alternatives.

It may be said that difference is accepted as *presented* but denied as *real*. In other words, the alternatives are in respect of the difference that is spoken of in the empirical world, while the criticism of it refers to the difference that is contended to be ultimately real. This will not do, since the difference in question (*vimarśa-bheda*) is not admitted by the Advaitin to be ultimately real. If that were admitted, it would result in the contradiction of his own position.

It may be argued that the alternatives are raised in view of the difference admitted in the system of the opponent. But even then the position will not improve, since difference is established in the system of the opponent. If difference were not proved to be real even in the opponent's system, then there would be absolutely no room for the alternatives in respect of difference. Vedānta Deśika, therefore, urges that if the alternatives are raised, then it follows that difference is real; if they are not raised, even then difference is real. In other words, if difference is not refuted, it stands established as real, since it is admitted to be real in the system of the opponent. If it is refuted, then the refutation is possible only by raising the alternatives, which consequently would lead to the acceptance of difference.[1]

Further, the arguments advanced against difference may be directed against the concept of non-difference and whatever difficulties present themselves in respect of the former do occur in the case of the latter as well. Thus, it may be asked whether non-difference is the nature of the thing or its attribute. If it be the very nature of the thing, nowhere would the illusion of difference arise. When the object is perceived, its *svarūpa* is also known; since the *svarūpa* of the object itself is non-difference, that being cognised, how can there be the super-imposition of difference?

[1] *S.D.*, Vāda 13.

If, on the other hand, non-difference be an attribute of the thing, difference would become established since the concept of substrate and attribute necessarily involves difference. Again, is this non-difference between the nature of the thing and its attribute the very nature of the substrate or an attribute of it? If it be the latter, it leads to an infinite regress. If it be the former, old difficulties follow. Thus, Vedānta Deśika contends that it is possible to refute even the concept of non-difference by adopting the same dialectic put forth by the Advaitin against difference.[1]

Coming now to the question whether difference is the nature of the thing or its attribute, Vedānta Deśika replies that in some cases it is the nature of the thing and in some cases it is an attribute of the object. Difference is defined as that which gives rise to the empirical usage, viz., that it is different (*vyāvṛtta vyavahāra hetuḥ*). Such a usage is found sometimes in respect of the very nature of an object and sometimes in respect of the attribute of an object.

We say 'x' is different from 'y'. On what ground do we distinguish between 'x' and 'y'? The answer is obvious. We distinguish between the two on the basis of the attribute which the one possesses and which the other does not. In so far as this attribute gives rise to the judgment that 'x' is different from 'y', it may be treated as difference of 'x' from 'y'.

The question arises whether or not the attribute that stands for the difference is different from the substrate. It should be admitted that it is different; otherwise there is no meaning in saying that attribute is the difference. If that be the case, what is this difference again? Is it a quality of that attribute or the very nature of it? Vedānta Deśika answers that it is not a quality of it in which case it would lead to an infinite regress. It is, on the contrary, the very nature of the attribute. The attribute which stands for the difference of two objects stands also for the difference of itself from its substrate. There is no need to postulate another quality to account for the difference of the attribute from its substrate. If that were so, the fallacy of an infinite regress would become unavoidable. There is absolutely no contradiction in admitting that one and the same thing accounts for others as well as for itself. Knowledge, for instance, reveals objects as

[1] *S.D.*, Vāda 13.

well as itself. Similarly, colour reveals itself as well as the thing that has colour. Likewise an attribute that stands for the difference of its substrate from other objects can also account for its own difference from its substrate.[1]

In view of the above explanation Vedānta Deśika refutes the other objections of the Advaitin against difference. It was contended that if difference were the nature of the thing, the shell-silver illusion would not arise. This is not correct, argues Vedānta Deśika. The illusion of silver is due to the non-apprehension of the attribute or the essential characteristics of the shell, viz., shellness (*śuktitva*).[2] It is not the mere shell itself but its essential characteristic, viz., shellness that is different from the silver. Hence, even though the shell is apprehended, the illusion of silver does take place because the shellness which constitutes the difference of the shell from the silver is not yet cognised. In view of this, difference is also defined as that which when apprehended does not give rise to illusion (*bhrānti pratipakṣopalambhatvam*). When on cognition of a certain attribute in a substance, there is no possibility of the superimposition of certain others on that substrate, that attribute stands for the difference of the substrate from other substrates.

It was also pointed out that if difference were the nature of the thing, then in such empirical usage as " the pot is different " it would follow that pot is qualified by a pot. This objection is untenable because the term *bhinna* has an altogether different connotation from that of the term ' pot '. That which is the cause of the judgment of difference or that which when apprehended does not give rise to illusion is the meaning of the term ' *bhinna* ' and as such it cannot by synonymous with the term, ' pot '.

Is not our cognition of difference bound up with the knowledge of the correlates? The cognition of difference arises when we know the differents as differents; we can know the differents as such when the difference between them is cognised. Thus, there is a vicious circle.

Against this objection Vedānta Deśika points out that it is tenable only if we regard the cognition of differents as a process distinct from the cognition of difference. This is not the case. When there is an apprehension of differents there

[1] *S.D.*, Vāda 13.
*Śrī-bhāṣya*, I. 1. 1. p. 28.

[2] The explanation given here is based on the theory of Akhyāti.

is at the same time the cognition of difference too. In other words, when we perceive two objects we perceive them as different.

### III *Perception and Difference*

This raises the question whether perception cognises difference. The Advaitin's contention, as has already been pointed out, is that perception apprehends mere 'Being'. Difference is a relative notion and as such its cognition is dependent upon the knowledge of its substrate and counter-correlate while 'Being' is not so. Perception which is momentary is capable of cognising only 'Being' while difference is imposed on it later by thought.

This argument does not hold good, contends Vedānta Deśika. As pointed out by Rāmānuja, even if perceptual cognition lasts one moment, it is possible within that moment to cognise both difference as well as Being (*svarūpa*) in as much as both are capable of being known by the same sense organ.[1]

Whenever we perceive an object we see the object (*vastu*) along with its particular structure or form named *samsthāna*. *Samsthāna* is defined as *svā-sādhāraṇa rūpa*. It is that inseparable quality or attribute (*rūpa*) exclusively belonging to the object (*asādhāraṇa*) and is capable of being known.[2] The *samsthāna* of the object itself is regarded as the generic character (*jāti*) in the Viśiṣṭādvaita System unlike that in the Nyāya System, for we do not see anything other than the structure as recurrent in the individuals of the same class that are perceived. Thus, for instance, when we see a cow, we perceive at the first instance the triangularly shaped dewlap which constitutes the exclusive characteristic of the cow. This particular structure in the from of the dewlap is *jāti* or the generic character of the cow-class, because it is observed to be common among the other cows as well. Thus, we find the empirical usage in the form 'This is possessed of dewlap'. 'Even this (cow) is possessed of dewlap' etc. The *jāti* itself constitutes the difference of the object from others because it is only on its apprehension that the empirical usage that the object is different takes place. Difference, as has already been explained, is that which gives rise to the judgment of

[1] *Śrī-bhāṣya*, I. 1. 1. p. 28.

[2] See *Śruta-prakāśikā*, Vol. 2, p. 698.

difference. The judgment of difference in respect of cow is made only on the apprehension of the generic character of the cow. *Jāti* which constitutes the difference of the object from others, is apprehended along with the *svarūpa*, since both are capable of being perceived by the same sense organ; difference is, therefore, as much the content of perception as the *svarūpa* is.[1]

How can that which does not require its counter-correlate for its apprehension be called difference? Vedānta Deśika replies that there is no need for the knowledge of the counter correlate when *jāti* is known as such; on the contrary, when the same is known in the capacity of its being the difference, the knowledge of the counter-correlate is required.

The knowledge of the counter-correlate is not required when the generic character of an object is apprehended. Nevertheless, the apprehension of the generic character is regarded as the perception of difference because the judgment that the object is different is made only on the basis of the cognition of the generic character. The generic character itself constitutes the difference of the object from others. The generic character of a cow, for instance, means just the exclusion of everything else; as soon as that character is apprehended, all thought and speech referring to other creatures belonging to the same wider genus which includes buffaloes and so on, ceases. It is through the apprehension of difference only that the cognition of oneness comes to an end. In such usage as 'this is different from that,' where there is a specific reference to the counter-correlate, the knowledge of the counter-correlate is required. In fact, the empirical usage that it is different takes place with reference to the object that is different from the one we are perceiving.[2]

Vedānta Deśika therefore concludes that through perception we do apprehend difference as marked by generic character etc. constituting the structure of the thing. When we perceive an object we see it as characterised. In so far as perception reveals a thing as characterised, it is maintained that perception, even though it be momentary, cognises both difference and the *svarūpa* of the thing.

[1] *S.D.*, Vāda 12.

[2] *Śrī-bhāṣya*, p. 29.
See also *Śruta-prakāśikā*, p. 709.

## IV *Indeterminate and Determinate Perception*

Vedānta Deśika next proceeds to show that even the perception produced by the first contact of the sense organs with the object has for its content an object qualified by characteristics. The Advaitin generally recognises two types of perception, the indeterminate perception (*nirvikalpaka pratyakṣa*) and determinate perception (*savikalpaka pratyakṣa*). The former, it is held, reveals the mere 'Being' devoid of all characteristics, while the latter reveals the object with its characteristics. Against this, Vedānta Deśika urges that even the indeterminate perception also has for its object only what is marked by characteristics, for it is on the basis of indeterminate perception that the object distinguished by generic character etc., is recognised in the act of determinate perception. In the determinate perception there is the recognition of the generic character being common to all the objects of the same class. This is possible only when the object with its generic character etc., is already apprehended in the state of indeterminate perception.

Is it not a self-contradiction to assert that what is called *nirvikalpaka pratyakṣa* apprehends an object qualified by characteristics? The Viśiṣṭādvaitin replies in the negative. The apprehension of a mere 'Being' without any characteristic whatsoever is in the first place not observed to take place (*grahaṇa adarśanāt*) and secondly it is untenable (*anupa-patteśca*). It is never found to take place because all cognitions are in terms of 'This is such and such'. Nothing can be apprehended apart from some particular form or structure of the object, as for instance, the triangularly shaped dewlap in the case of the cows. It is, therefore, not possible even to postulate such a kind of apprehension on the basis of reasoning, as it is in direct conflict with experience. In view of this, it is necessary to restrict the import of the term *nirvikalpaka*. The term can be understood as devoid of some characteristics. As Śrī Rāmānuja points out "Indeterminate perception is the apprehension of an object devoid of some qualifications but not all qualifications." [1]

The real distinction between indeterminate perception and determinate perception is that in the former there is the

[1] *Śrī-bhāṣya*, I. 1. 1. p. 27.
nirvi-kalpakam nāma kenacidviśeṣeṇa viyuktasya grahaṇam na sarvaviśeṣarahitasya.

apprehension of the first individual among a number of objects belonging to the same class while in the latter there is the apprehension of a second, third and other individuals. On the apprehension of the first individual, say a cow, one is not conscious of the fact that the special shape which constitutes the generic character of the class "cows" extends to the other individuals also, while the cognition of this arises in the case of the perception of the second and third cow. In the indeterminate perception there is only the apprehension of the generic character and there is no awareness that this character is common to the other individuals of the same class as there is no perception of the other individuals. But in the perception of the second individual and so on, the generic character is recognised as common to the whole class. Thus, what was indeterminate in the perception of the first individual is made determinate in the perception of the second and the subsequent individuals. It is on this basis that the distinction between the indeterminate and the determinate perception has to be maintained but not on what those terms may literally mean. In view of this, Vedānta Deśika gives the following definitions: *Savikalpaka* perception is the apprehension involving recognition because of its being produced by the sense organs influenced by *saṃskāra*; *nirvikalpaka* perception, on the other hand, is the apprehension which is produced by the mere sense organs without the association of *saṃskāra*.[1] Thus, in the perception of the first individual the cognition is of the form 'this' and in the perception of the subsequent individuals, because they belong to the same class, it is of the form 'such it is'. Thus, perception, whether it be determinate or indeterminate, reveals an object qualified with some characteristic. In the words of Śrī Rāmānuja, "perception never has for its content an object that is devoid of all characteristics."[2]

[1] *S.D.*, Vāda 11.

samskāra sahakṛta-indriya janyatayā sapratyavamarṣam jñānam savikalpakam; samskāra nirapekṣa kevala-indriya-janya-jñānam nirvikalpakam.

See also *Nyāya Pariśuddhi*, pp. 81-82 (Chowkamba Edn.)

[2] *Śrī-bhāṣya*, I. 1. 1. p. 27.

ataḥ pratyakṣasya na kadācidapi nirviśeṣa viṣayatvaṁ.

## CHAPTER THREE

# THE NATURE OF CONSCIOUSNESS

THE present chapter is devoted to a discussion of the theory of consciousness (*anubhūti*) as advocated by the Advaitin. According to Advaita Vedānta consciousness is an independent and eternally existing Reality. It is pure contentless knowledge which is neither produced nor destroyed. It manifests everything else but is itself not manifested by any other entity (*svayamprakāśā*). Such a knowledge is identical with the Reality. It is, in other words, Brahman itself. The consciousness that is apparent in the usual distinction of knower, known and knowledge is not real but is only empirical (*vyāvahārika*). It is the psychosis of the inner organ (*antaḥkaraṇa vṛtti*) and is regarded as knowledge because of its being a determinant of consciousness.[1]

Both Rāmānuja and Vedānta Deśika have devoted great attention towards the criticism of the above theory in so far as it is in direct opposition to common experience. Knowledge for the Viśiṣṭādvaitin, as for any other realist, implies on the one hand a subject to which it belongs, and on the other, an object to which it refers. Knowledge as such is always found to be a function of the subject. It always and necessarily pertains to the self, which is a permanent spiritual entity. The Viśiṣṭādvaitin, therefore, does not admit that consciousness is identical with Reality.

## I *Advaitin's Theory of Consciousness*

Before going into a detailed discussion of this theory of knowledge, let us state briefly the view of the Advaitin. The Advaitin contends that the existence of a transcendental consciousness which is undifferentiated and indeterminate in character cannot be doubted as it is self-evident or self-proved

[1] See *Vedānta-paribhāṣā*, p. 8. (T.P.H.).

(*svataḥ-siddha*).[1] It is the basic experience on which is dependent all determinate knowledge and as such it needs no further proof in repect of itself. If such a foundational experience or consciousness were not admitted, then knowledge itself would not be established, and consequently nothing would be manifested in the universe. Though such an experience is not clearly manifest in the waking state, it is apparent in the states of dreamless sleep (*suṣupti*), trance (*samādhi*) and release (*mukti*), where consciousness manifests itself in its true nature.

As regards the nature of consciousness, the Advaitin points out that it is self-luminous (*svayam-prakāśā*). That is, it reveals every other object but itself is not revealed by any other entity. If it were manifested by anything else, it would no longer be consciousness. Its essential nature, therefore, consists in its being self-luminous. In terms of modern philosophy, consciousness is a pure subject and it can never be an object.[2] Thus, it is stated in the form of a syllogistic argument: " Consciousness is self-luminous, because it is consciousness; if consciousness were the object of another knowledge, it would not be consciousness, as in the case of a pot ".[3]

Consciousness which is self-luminous is eternal (*nitya*), because it is neither produced nor destroyed. Whatever is produced must admit itself a prior non-existence. Even granting that there is a prior non-existence of consciousness, how is it known? It cannot be apprehended through that very consciousness itself, because the two are incompatible. While there is the prior non-existence, consciousness is not produced and as such there is nothing to cognise it; when

[1] *S.D.*, Vāda 10.

Cp., *Iṣṭa-siddhi*, p. 1.

The pūrvapakṣa on this subject stated in the *Śrī-bhāṣya* as well as in the *Śatadūṣaṇī* has been mainly adopted from the *Iṣṭa-siddhi*. See *Tattvaṭīkā* (Vol. II, p. 557. Mad. Edn.)

atra " yānubhūtirajāmeyā-nantātmānanda vigrahā; mahadādi jaganmāyā citra-bhittim namāmitām " ityukta krameṇa uparitana upanyāsaḥ.

[2] Cp., Gentile's theory of the pure subject which cannot be made an object. *Theory of Mind as Pure Act*, pp. 6-7.

[3] *S.D.*, Vāda 20.

anubhūtiḥ svayaṃ prakāśā, anubhūtitvāt, anubhūteranubhāvyatve ghatādivat ananubhūtitva prasanga iti.

Cp., *Iṣṭa-siddhi*, p. 1.

See also *Tattvapradīpikā*, p. 11.

consciousness is produced, its prior-non-existence would not be there to be cognised. Nor can the prior non-existence of consciousness be apprehended through some other knowledge. The cognition of the non-existence (*abhāva*) necessarily presupposes the knowledge of its counter-correlate. The counter-correlate of the prior non-existence of consciousness is the consciousness itself. But consciousness as has already been pointed out, cannot be an object of another cognition. The prior non-existence of consciousness cannot, therefore, be proved. Hence consciousness is unproduced.[1]

The fact that consciousness is not produced implies that it cannot undergo any transmutation (*vikāra*). Thus it is argued: " Consciousness is immutable (*nirvikārā*), because it is not produced; whatever is mutable is produced; as for instance, the pot ".[2]

As consciousness is unproduced it does not admit of any plurality. Plurality is the characteristic feature of objects which are produced. To put it in the form of a syllogistic argument: " Consciousness is not manifold (*na nānā*) because it is unoriginated; whatever is manifold, is originated, as for example, the pot ".[3] The plurality of consciousness that is found in our ordinary experience is not real in so far as it is conditioned by the different objects as well as the different finite selves. This is comparable to the single moon which appears to be many when reflected in the waves.

Consciousness does not also admit of any difference within itself. It is undifferentiated in character, because it is consciousness; whatever admits differentiation is invariably found to be an object. Besides the qualities (*viśeṣas*) are objective and cannot be attributed to consciousness which is a pure subject.[4]

The transcendental consciousness which is self-luminous, eternal, and immutable is the very self (*ātman*) in so far as it

[1] *S.D.*, Vāda 21.

See also *Śrī-bhāṣya*, pp. 23-4.

Cp., *Iṣṭa-siddhi*, p. 1.

na ca svataḥ-siddhasya prāgabhāvādayaḥ svata anyato vā siddhyanti, ato ajā.

[2] *S.D.*, Vāda 22.

[3] *S.D.*, Vāda 23.

[4] *S.D.*, Vāda 24.

is sentient (*ajaḍa*), unlike an object. True knowledge, in other words, is identical with the Reality.[1]

The main contention of the Advaitin regarding the nature of consciousness or *anubhūti* are: (1) Consciousness is self-proved (*svataḥ-siddha*); (2) it is not an object of another knowledge (*avedya*); (3) it is eternal having neither a beginning nor an end (*nitya*); (4) it is immutable (*nirvikāra*); (5) it is not many but one; (6) it is undifferentiated in character (*nirviśeṣa*); (7) and lastly it is the very self (*ātman*). Vedānta Deśika subjects each one of them to a critical examination, devoting a separate vāda for each issue. The criticism is mainly based on the Viśiṣṭādvaitic theory of knowledge, viz., that consciousness is that which involves the duality of the subject and the object and as such it is not a pure subject but a function or an attribute of it. Though it is self-luminous, it is not absolutely unknowable. It is not eternal in the sense the Advaitin understands, as it is a transitory function of the subject. It is not one but many and is also subject to change in the form of contraction and expansion. Lastly, it can never be identical with the self in as much as consciousness is its attribute only.

## II *Transcendental Consciousness*

The question whether any such consciousness devoid of all characteristics (*nirviśeṣa*) exists is taken up for consideration. Vedānta Deśika at the very outset points out that such a consciousness does not exist at all. All that we know of is a consciousness which manifests itself as related to a subject on the one hand and an object on the other. A consciousness other than this is as unreal as the horns of the hare.

Granting that there is such an unqualified consciousness, what is the proof for its existence, asks Vedānta Deśika. If it is said that consciousness itself is a proof (*siddhiḥ*) and as such there is no need for any other proof, then it is asked, proof of what and to whom? The term 'proof' is a relative notion like that of 'son' and therefore these two questions arise. The Advaitin may say that consciousness is the proof of itself and for itself. If it is further questioned as to what

[1] *S.D.*, Vāda 25.
samvid-ātmā ajaḍatvāt, yaduktasādhyam na bhavati taduktasādhanam-api na bhavati, yathā ghataḥ iti.

the self is, the Advaitin would reply that it is consciousness, as the two are regarded identical by him. The argument thus involves a vicious circle. Vedānta Deśika, therefore, urges that on the basis of self-proof it is impossible to prove the existence of an undifferentiated consciousness.[1]

Vedānta Deśika further proceeds to show that neither the different states of experience in general nor any of the pramāṇas prove the existence of an indeterminate consciousness. In the waking state consciousness always manifests itself as related to a subject and an object. All states of experience, as Rāmānuja points out, have for their object something that is marked by some characteristics as is evident from the following judgment: 'I saw this'.[2]

Nor in the other states does consciousness manifest itself as indeterminate. Taking into consideration the state of deep sleep, Vedānta Deśika asks whether or not there is any experience in that state? If there be any experience, it will present itself as qualified by attributes; if there be no experience, what is it that manifests itself as indeterminate?

A more detailed study of the state of deep sleep will make the point clear. It is an admitted fact that there is no experience of any object in the state of deep sleep. If there were an experience of it, one should have had the recollection of it soon after waking from sleep. Nor is there any experience to the effect that consciousness exists as devoid of objects and its substrate because it would conflict with the experience that follows after sleep in the form: 'I was not aware of any thing all this time'. This judgment clearly indicates that knowledge or consciousness was not present during deep sleep. If knowledge existed then, it would have been recollected soon after sleep. What was experienced should have been remembered unless there be some factors that obliterate all traces of experience (*samskāras*) as for instance, the dissolution of the body or the death-pain. The very fact that there is no recollection of it goes to show that knowledge does not exist during the state of deep sleep.

[1] *S.D.*, Vāda 10.

[2] *Śrī-bhāṣya,* I. 1. 1. p. 26.

**idamaham adarśam iti kenacit viśeṣaṇa viśiṣṭa viṣayatvāt saraveṣām anubhavānām.**

The Advaitin argues that the judgment, 'I was not aware of anything all this time' refers to the manifestation of the consciousness as a witness of *ajñāna* or ignorance. This is untenable, contends Vedānta Deśika. The negation of knowledge (*jñāna-pratiṣedha*) as implied in the judgment in question cannot testify to its existence.[1] On the basis of the judgment in question it is not possible to prove the presence of consciousness during deep sleep as the witness of *ajñāna*. All that we can say is that the entity denoted by the concept 'I' persisted during deep sleep and it did not experience anything in that state except a good sleep (*sukha-svāpa*). What is denoted by the notion of 'I' is itself the very self.[2] Knowledge which is a *dharma* or attribute of the self does not function during deep sleep but is present in a quiescent form. If this were not admitted the recollection that follows soon after sleep cannot be accounted for satisfactorily. Recollection is possible only when there is the trace of what has been experienced. If during deep sleep, *ajñāna* and consciousness alone were present, as the Advaitin says, the question would arise as to where does the *samskāra* inhere? Pure consciousness cannot be the repository of the *samskāra* since that would conflict with the view that it is immutable and indeterminate. Besides, consciousness cannot be a witness. As it will be shown in the next chapter, only the subject or the self as a knower can be a witness. Thus it is difficult to prove that in the state of deep sleep consciousness manifests itself as devoid of all characteristics.[3]

The same explanation holds good for other states of experience such as swoon, trance and release. Knowledge in general always and necessarily manifests itself as related to a subject and having reference to an object.

Vedānta Deśika next proceeds to show that even the pramāṇas do not prove the existence of an indeterminate knowledge. Perception, as has been pointed out in an earlier chapter, reveals an object as qualified by some characteristics.

[1] This criticism is based on the view that *ajñāna* means absence of knowledge and not a positive entity, as the Advaitin holds. The latter view is refuted by the Viśiṣṭādvaitin. (See Chapter VII).

[2] This issue is discussed in detail in the subsequent chapter on the Nature of the Individual Self.

See Chapter IV, Section I.

[3] *S.D.*, Vāda 10.

na svāpādyavasthāsvapi nirviśeṣa prakāśa siddhiḥ.

Even the so-called indeterminate perception has for its content a qualified entity.[1]

Nor does inference establish it. Any inferential argument put forth to prove the inderminate character of consciousness would render it determinate. Inferential argument proceeds on judgment. In a judgment the predicate always adds something to the subject and as such it makes it determinate.[2]

Verbal testimony also cannot prove it. Verbal testimony can have the denotative function either in the form of words or in the form of a sentence (*vākya*). In neither way does it point to an indeterminate consciousness. Words convey their senses not in isolation but in relation to other words and as such no word by itself conveys any meaning.[3] Even granting that words by themselves convey their meaning, the situation does not improve. For a word (*pada*) is a combination of two elements—a root and a suffix and as these elements have different meanings, it necessarily follows that the word conveys only a sense affected with qualities.[4]

As regards verbal testimony in the form of a sentence, the position does hardly improve. A sentence which is an aggregate of words expresses some special combination of senses (meanings of words) and hence has no power to denote anything devoid of all characteristics. Thus the author of the *Śrī-bhāṣya* sums up the position in the following pithy statement: " As to verbal testimony, it is specially apparent that it possesses the power of denoting only such things as are characterised by qualities ".

Vedānta Deśika therefore, concludes that it is a false assumption to hold that the indeterminate consciousness is self-proved since there is neither a cognition of it nor the support of any other pramāṇas, either inference or verbal testimony.

[1] See Chapter II, Section 4.

[2] See Section VII for a detailed discussion of the syllogistic argument to prove the indeterminate character of consciousness.

[3] There are two views regarding the function of words. According to one view, known as *anvitā-bhiḍāna vāda*, held by the Prabhākaras, words convey their own sense not in isolation but as in relation. As such no word by itself gives any clear meaning but only in combination with other words. According to the other view, known as *abhihitā-nvaya vāda*, held by the Bhattas, words primarily signify their own senses; but in this respect they serve only as causes of recall (*Smāraka*) and as such they have no prāmāṇya.

See *S.D.,* Vāda 10.

[4] *Śrī-bhāṣya*, p. 26.

na nirviśeṣa vastuni śabdaḥ pramāṇam.

### III *Consciousness and Self-Luminosity*

We now come to the consideration of the second issue regarding the self-luminosity (*svayamprakāśatva*) of consciousness. The function of knowledge is to reveal an object. When knowledge reveals an object, it does not require to be revealed by another knowledge. On the other hand, knowledge reveals itself as well as the object. In other words, it is self-luminous (*svayam-prakāśa*). It means that consciousness does not require to be manifested by another knowledge at the time of revealing an object (*viṣaya prakāśana velāyām*). This is the meaning of *svayam-prakāśa* that is generally accepted by most of the thinkers including the Viśiṣṭādvaitin.

The Advaitin, however, does not accept the above meaning of self-luminosity. According to him consciousness is self-luminous in the sense that it can never at any time become the object of another knowledge. To put it in the words of Citsukhācārya, " Self-luminosity is the capability of being called immediate in empirical usage, while remaining at the same time a non-object of knowledge ".[1]

This meaning of self-luminosity, Vedānta Deśika contends, is in direct conflict with experience. Our experience shows that the knowledge of one person may become the content of the cognition of another. For instance, the experience of another individual is the object of the inferential knowledge based on the person's friendly or unfriendly appearance. Even in the case of the same individual, his past states of experience become the object of his cognition as expressed in the judgment, 'at one time I knew, etc.'. If knowledge were not admitted to be the object of another knowledge there would be an end to all empirical usage depending on speech. All emprical usage takes place through mutual understanding, that is, through the understanding of each other's thoughts. As Rāmānuja points out, " Unless it were admitted that there is the inferential knowledge of thoughts of others, there would be no connection between the words and their meanings and this would imply the termination of all empirical usage depending on speech ".[2]

[1] See *Tattvapradīpikā*, p. 9.
avedyatve saty-aparokṣa-vyavahāra-yogyatā.
See also *Nyāyamakaranda*, p. 135.

[2] *Śrī-bhāṣya*, p. 30.

The Advaitin contends that if consciousness were the object of knowledge, it would be no better than an object. Hence the essential nature of consciousness should consist in its not being an object of knowledge.

Vedānta Deśika refutes this contention. The essential nature of consciousness does not consist in its not being an object of cognition; on the contrary, it consists in that it manifests its own object by its own being or that it manifests itsef to its own substrate.[1]

The conception of self-luminosity, in other words, does not necessarily imply that consciousness is a pure subject without in any form being an object, but on the contrary it means that knowledge when it manifests an object does not require itself to be manifested by anything else; and when it manifests, it also manifests itself to its own substrate, the self.

If consciousness possesses one of these characteristics, it does not cease to be consciousness even if it becomes an object of another consciousness. A pot is not regarded as conciousness not because it is the object of knowledge, but because it does not possess any of the characteristics of consciousness mentioned above.

If consciousness were not the object of knowledge in any sense of the term, it would become a non-existent like the sky-flower. A sky-flower is not an object of knowledge and it is not consciousness. It may be argued that the sky-flower is not knowledge because it is a non-existent and not for the reason that it is not an object of cognition. On the same ground, it is replied that a pot too is not knowledge not because it is the object of knowledge but because it is opposed to knowledge (*ajñāna avirodhitvāt*). Vedānta Deśika thus comes to the conclusion that *ananu-bhāvyatva* or not being an object of knowledge does not constitue the determinant of consciousness, as the Advaitin holds.[2]

It is not possible to prove that consciousness is not an object of knowledge in the strict sense of the term. Thus, in the premise, ' Consciousness is self-luminous ' does the term *anubhūti* denote something or not? If it denotes something and if that

[1] *S.D.*, Vāda 20.

sva sattayaiva svāśrayam prati prakāśamānatva rūpasya sva sattayaiva sva viṣaya bhāsakatva rūpasya vā kasyacit anubhūti lakṣaṇasya svānubhava-siddhasya anapagamāt.

See also *Śrī-bhāṣya*, p. 31.

[2] *S.D.*, Vāda 20.

4

be the Reality or Brahman, then that becomes manifested in so far as it is the object of knowledge, conveyed by that term. If it be said that the nature of Brahman which is illuminating itself is only restated by the term, even then the manifestation of it is inevitable in as much as it is the object of that cognition conveyed by the restatement. To avoid all these difficulties it cannot be said that the term denotes nothing, in which case it would have no meaning. Thus in some form or other consciousness should be admitted to be an object of knowledge even though it be self-luminous in character. Thus, the author of the *Śrī-bhāṣya* sums up the position: "The contention that something which is an object of consciousness cannot be consciousness is unsound ".[1]

## IV *Is Consciousness Eternal?*

The next issue to be considered is whether consciousness is eternal. The Advaitin's conception is that consciousness is unproduced because its prior non-existence is neither known by itself nor through another consciousness.

Vedānta Deśika rejoins that the prior non-existence of knowledge is apprehended through itself as well as through another knowledge. Thus, the following cognition, 'I was not aware of anything all this time', apprehends its non-existence in the previous state. The competent non-cognition (*yogyānupalabdhi*) is the pramāṇa in support of the cognition of prior non-existence of knowledge as well as of any other object.[2] It may be asked as to how the non-cognition which is past is helpful in establishing the prior non-existence of an object. This is possible, replies Vedānta Deśika, because of the absence of recollection of the cognition of the object. If knowledge were present during deep sleep, we should have had its cognition in so far as it is capable of being known (*yogya*) and consequently we should have had a recollection of it soon after waking from sleep. But there is no remembrance of it after waking up from sleep and this proves the non-existence of knowledge during deep sleep. It cannot be

[1] *Śrī-bhāṣya*, p. 31

ato anubhāvyatve ananubhūtitvam iti upahāsyam.

[2] *Anupalabdhi* (non-cognition) is accepted by some as a separate *pramāṇa*, the sixth one, while by some as part of perception (*pratyakṣa*). This is the means through which non-existence or negation (*abhāva*) is apprehended.

said that the non-recollection is due to the extinction of the *samskāra* or latent impression. Only such factors as intense pleasure, intense pain and long interval are capable of extinguishing the *samskāra* and in the absence of these it is absurd to speak of its extinction. Nor can it be argued that deep sleep itself extinguishes the *samskāra*. If that were the case there would be no recollection of what was experienced on a previous day.

The prior non-existence of knowledge is also cognised through another knowledge. This is possible since knowledge can be the object of another knowledge. If one's knowledge were not the object of cognition of another, there would be an end to all empirical usages depending on speech. We come to know of the non-existence of knowledge by means of inference. In fact, it is on the basis of the presupposition of the absence of knowledge about a particular fact, we proceed to instruct a person on it. Again, when a preceptor teaches his pupil, he does it on the supposition that the pupil does not possess the knowledge of that which is taught to him. This absence of the particular knowledge of a thing or fact is the prior non-existence or the *prāghabhāva* of knowledge. This is known, as has been explained, by means of knowledge. The prior non-existence of knowledge of the future which exists in oneself is known through competent non-cognition, while the prior non-existence of knowledge of the past is known through recollection or by means of inference. Thus, it is possible to prove the non-existence of knowledge and in view of that it is not logically unintelligible to hold that consciousness is originated.[1]

As regards the contention that consciousness is eternal and therefore it is neither produced nor destroyed, it is pointed out that destruction and origination are possible even though consciousness is eternal. Origination and destruction are the particular states of consciousness. When knowledge flows through the channel of sense organs to the object and it apprehends the object, knowledge becomes produced. When the knowledge of the object ceases to exist, it is destroyed. Thus, the author of the *Śrī-bhāṣya* says, " In view of the expansion and contraction of knowledge through the sense

[1] *S.D.*, Vāda 21.
*Śrī-bhāṣya*, I. 1. 1. p. 33.
tasmāt na prāgabhāvādi asiddhyā samvidaḥ anutpattiḥ upapattimatī.

organs, there is the designation of orignation and destruction ".[1] In so far as these states do not affect in any way the essential nature of consciousness, consciousness even though it be eternal, admits both a beginning and an end.

## V *Is Consciousness Immutable?*

On the basis of the foregoing conclusion Vedānta Deśika proceeds to refute the theory that consciousness is not subject to transmutation. Since knowledge is originated, it is futile to argue on that ground that it does not undergo any transmutation.

In the judgment 'knowledge is *nirvikārā*', what does the term *nirvikārā* mean? It can be understood in three ways. It may mean not having an upper limit or in other words, not being subject to destruction (*uttarā-vadhi-rāhityam*). Secondly, it may mean, which is a more appropriate sense, the mere absence of particular states which are named differently (*avasthā-viśeṣa-rāhityam*). Lastly, the word *nirvikārā* may even refer to the absence of mere transformation (*avasthāmātra rāhityam*).

Vedānta Deśika contends that in none of these senses it is possible to understand the immutability of consciousness. Taking the first alternative, the argument put forth by the Advaitin becomes inconclusive in respect of avidyā. Avidyā, according to the Advaitin, is not originated and yet it has an end since it is removed by right knowledge. It cannot be argued that avidyā itself is illusory and hence its destruction too is illusory. For the Advaitin even the destruction of the pot is illusory and there would be nothing which could be truly regarded as having an end or destruction. In view of this it would not be possible to prove the negative concomitance (*vyatireka-vyāpti*) viz., whatever has an end has a beginning. If the destruction of the pot has an empirical reality, this is true of avidyā as well. Nor can the Advaitin argue that what is implied by the probandum is the absence of *real* end (*pāramārtha-vikāra*). For there is no object which can be regarded by him as having a *real* end.

To overcome this difficulty the syllogism may be expressed in a different form: " Consciousness does not have an end which

[1] *S.D.*, Vāda 21.
**tamimam-indriya-dwāraka-jñānaprasaram-apekṣya-udayā-stamaya vyapadeśaḥ.**

is *absolutely real*, because it is unoriginated; whatever is unoriginated does not have an end that is absolutely real, as for example avidyā". Even this does not solve the difficulty, contends Vedānta Deśika. The syllogism suffers from the defect of the non-established probandum. The absence of an end that is *absolutely real*, which is the probandum of the syllogism, is a non-existent for the Advaitin. If he admits such a thing, it would lead to the denial of one's own theory (*apasiddhānta*).

The second alternative is also untenable because the argument is inconclusive in respect of avidyā. The Advaitin himself maintains that avidyā which is unoriginated transforms itself into different states that are designated as *mahat*, *ahamkāra* etc. Consciousness also assumes different states known as *smṛti*, *anubhūti* etc. This is proved by experience and it would be difficult to deny them. It cannot be said that the different states of consciousness are illusory in character because for the Advaitin there is no such state that is truly *real*.

For the same reason the third alternative is not valid. It also results in the denial of one's own theory. The Advaitin himself admits illusory transformation in respect of consciousness. If this were not admitted, the illusion of the universe, the need to overcome it and for this purpose the study of the sacred texts would all be meaningless.

The Viśiṣṭādvaitin also admits that Brahman is unoriginated and immutable. Nevertheless the criticisms levelled against the Advaitin do not apply to his own theory. The Viśiṣṭādvaitin does not say that the knowledge which is evident to ordinary experience, which admits changes in the form of origination and destruction and which is the attribute of the self, is identical with Reality (Brahman). Nor does he accept that the transcendental consciousness devoid of a substrate and unrelated to objects is Brahman. According to the Viśiṣṭādvaita Vedānta, Reality is a qualified entity. Brahman is associated with *cit* and *acit*, the sentient individual selves and the non-sentient matter. The changes such as origination and destruction belong to the latter, and these do not in any way affect Brahman. Brahman is no doubt omniscient but His knowledge is not subject to contraction and expansion, unlike the knowledge of the individual self. It is in this sense that the immutability or *nirvikāratva* of the Reality is understood in the Viśiṣṭādvaita system. In other words, the concept of immutability is intelligible in respect of a qualified Brahman but not in the case of a transcendental consciousness which is identical with Reality. Vedānta Deśika, therefore, concludes that it is impossible to establish by means of reasoning that consciousness is immutable. In fact, consciousness, as is evident from our ordinary experience, assumes different states which are called by such names as *anubhūti*, *smṛti*, *buddhi* etc. All these are synonymous with *jñāna* or knowledge. These cannot be dismissed aside as false states of consciousness.[1]

### VI *Is Consciousness Manifold?*

The argument that consciousness is not manifold is also untenable. What does the term 'manifold' (*nāna*) mean? Taking the premise as a whole, viz., 'Consciousness is not manifold' the words '*not manifold*' can be interpreted in five ways. It may either mean that consciousness is not different from anything; or it is not different from the knowledge-class; or it is not different from the *svarūpa* of knowledge or it is not different from another consciousness; or it may simply mean that there is no consciousness of a similar kind.

Vedānta Deśika examines each of the above alternatives. To take the first alternative, it is not possible to say that consciousness is not different from anything. It is, as a matter of fact, different from the external objects. Śamkara himself admits the distinction between consciousness and objects.[3] If there were no distinction between the two, it would follow that they are identical, a position which is philosophically unsound.

Nor is it sound to say that *samvit* is not different from samvit-class or that it is not different from its own nature. Both the alternatives are acceptable to the Viśiṣṭādvaitin and as such the argument does not accomplish anything new.

The fourth view is of some importance and is to be examined in detail. The contention that consciousness is not different from another consciousness raises the issue whether or not another consciousness does exist. If it exists, it is not sound to argue that consciousness is not different from

[1] *S.D.*, Vāda 22.

[2] *S.D.*, Vāda 23.

[3] See the opening sentence of Śamkara's *Adhyāsa-bhāṣya*.

another consciousness. If it does not exist, the proposition itself falls to the ground.

It may be argued that there is only one consciousness, but the same as a result of its being conditioned by an adjunct assumes the form of another consciousness. In view of this it is said that consciousness is not different from the *svarūpa* of knowledge just as the moon is not different from the reflected moon.

Even this will not hold good, contends Deśika. Avidyā is unoriginated according to the Advaitin and yet it is distinct from another consciousness, and as such the probans becomes fallacious. If nescience and the other consciousness (*samvidantara*) are not distinct, it would follow that they are essentially one—a position which is unacceptable to the Advaitin. The analogy of the moon and its reflection does hardly serve the purpose. The reflected moon which alone is illusory cannot be admitted to be identical with the original moon which is real.[1]

As none of the alternatives stands logical examination, the proposition that consciousness is not manifold falls to the ground. Consciousness, on the contrary, should be admitted to be manifold. As Rāmānuja points out, the difference of knowledge is proved by means of the difference of the objects of cognition which is established by valid knowledge in the same way as the difference of acts of cutting is proved by the difference of the objects cut.[2] If all cognitions were identical then a single cognition which has for its object a pot only, should manifest the object of another cognition as well. But this is not the case in as much as there is the distinction of the known and the unknown. Hence it should be admitted, Vedānta Deśika urges, that cognitions which are reciprocally related to objects are by their nature manifold in the same way as the acts of cutting, operating on different objects, are reciprocally different.

It may be asked how knowledge, which is eternal, can admit in itself difference? This is possible, contends Deśika. Knowledge though it is eternal assumes contraction and expansion in respect of its objects in accordance with the

[1] *S.D.*, Vāda 23.

[2] *Śrī-bhāṣya*, I. 1. 1. p. 34.

abādhita pratipatti-siddha dṛśyabheda-samarthanena darśana bhedopi samarthita eva, çhedya-bhedāt çhedana-bhedavat.

Karma of the individual.[1] It is in view of such changes which only consist in the respective objects becoming the content of experience conforming to Karma, that the difference in the act of knowing as well as the relationship of knowledge to the respective objects (*pratiniyata viṣayatā*) are accounted for. The Advaitin cannot adopt the same explanation, since consciousness has been admitted by him to be eternal, immutable and self-luminous. It may be argued that *māyā* obscures it and as a result of this variegated experience takes place. But as it will be shown later,[2] this theory is hardly satisfactory.

## VII *Is Consciousness Undifferentiated?*

The theory that consciousness does not admit of any differentiation is also untenable. The Advaitin puts forth two arguments, both in the form of inference, in support of this theory. The first argument is that consciousness is undifferentiated because it is consciousness. To express the same negatively, whatever is differentiated is not consciousness, as in the case of a pot. The second argument which is more significant than the first is based on the contention that the characteristics which are objective in so far as they are knowable (*dṛśya*) cannot be attributed to consciousness which is pure subject.

Vedānta Deśika refutes both the arguments. Taking the first argument, it is asked whether in the premise ' consciousness is *nirviśeṣā* ', the term *nirviśeṣā* denotes anything more than what is implied by the term ' consciousness ' or not. If it be the latter, it would amount to saying that consciousness is consciousness which is tautologous. If it be the former, then the predicate adds something to the subject in which case consciousness becomes determinate. It may be argued that the term ' indeterminate ' implies that consciousness is devoid of all characteristics including indeterminateness itself as a quality of consciousness. This will not do, contends Deśika. In a judgment, the predicate should be amitted to be related to the subject in some way or other. If it is not related in any way, then the judgement has no meaning. According to Indian Logic, there would follow the fallacy of non-relationship

[1] *S.D.*, Vāda 27

nityāpi samvit taṭtat-karmānurūpam teṣu teṣu
viṣayeṣu saṃkocaṃ vikāsamca bhajate.

[2] See Chapter VII.

between the subject and the probandum (*ananvitanigraha-sthānam*). If, on the contrary, the probandum is admitted to be related to the subject, it would inevitably follow that the subject is determinate. Hence it is not possible to assert that consciousness is devoid of all characteristics.[1]

The second argument is refuted by pointing out that it is not possible to deny all characteristics in respect of consciousness. The Advaitin himself admits, to distinguish his own theory from that of the Vijñānavādins, that consciousness is eternal. Vedānta Deśika asks whether or not eternity is denied as a characteristic of consciousness. If it be denied, then it would conflict with his own position. If it were not denied, the argument would be inconclusive.

The Advaitin may however argue that eternity as a characteristic of consciousness is illusory and as such even if it be attributed to consciousness it will not involve any logical difficulty. In that case Vedānta Deśika replies that the Advaitin's attempt to establish that consciousness is eternal against those who deny it is futile. If the eternity of consciouness is illusory, then there would be no need to refute the view that consciousness is not eternal. To avoid these difficulties if eternity is regarded as the very nature of consciousness then the Advaitin should have no dispute with the Buddhists in so far as they also admit it as the *anubhūti-svarūpa*.

Further, if the term *anubhūti* refers to the knowledge current in the empirical world, then there is the sublation of it by perception, because it is evident that such knowledge is manifold, being qualified by an object, a substrate and many other qualities involved in it. If, on the other hand, it refers to the nature of Brahman evident in scripture, even then the inference stands contradicted by the very scriptural texts which point out that Brahman is qualified by countless attributes. Thus, it is not possible to prove conclusively by means of inference that consciousness is devoid of all determinations.[2]

## VIII *Consciousness and the Self* (*Ātman*)

We come to the last and most important issue, viz., whether consciousness is identical with the self. One of the arguments

[1] *S.D.*, Vāda 24.
ato na kathañcidapi sarva viśeṣa śūnyatvam pratijñātum śakyate.

[2] *S.D.*, Vāda 24.

put forth by the Advaitin to prove their identity is that consciousness is *ajaḍa*. Vedānta Deśika refutes the argument on the ground that consciousness and self are of different nature and as such the two cannot be identical. According to the Viśiṣṭādvaita Vedānta knowledge can, unaided, reveal the external object. What it thus manifests is never for itself but always for another. That is "it can only *show* but cannot *know*". It is only the self that can *know* what is revealed or manifested by consciousness while it cannot reveal anything but itself. Knowledge is like a lamp which can reveal the presence of an object as well as its own, but cannot see either, its revelation of things being always for another. It is thus a function of the self, an attribute of it and as such cannot be identical with its substrate.[1]

On the basis of the above theory, the inferential argument of the Advaitin is subjected to a critical examination. What is the meaning of the term *ajaḍa*? If it means, as the Viśiṣṭādvaitin understands, the manifestation for itself (*svasmai bhāsamānatvam*) then consciousness cannot be regarded as identical with the self on that ground. Consciousness manifests not for itself but for the self.

The word *ajaḍa* may be understood in the sense of manifestation without depending upon another knowledge (*samvidantara nirapekṣa prakāśa*). To whom does consciousness manifest itself? Does it manifest itself for itself or to something else? The former is untenable since consciousness does not manifest for itself but for the self (*ātman*). Nor is the latter tenable as in that case it would be contrary to its nature of being *ajaḍa*. Manifestation to another is the characteristic feature of an object but not of the self.

The word *ajaḍa* may also mean knowledge (*jñāna*). Knowledge is of the nature of manifestation (*prakāśarūpa*). *Prakāśa* or manifestation is a relative notion and the question naturally arises as to whom it manifests? Does it manifest to oneself or to somebody? As has been shown above neither is possible. It cannot be said that it does not manifest to any body at all. In that case, it would cease to be *prakāśa* or knowledge. Thus, it is difficult to prove that consciousness is self on the ground that it is *ajaḍa*.[2]

[1] See Prof. Hiriyanna's article on "Rāmānuja's Theory of Knowledge" in the proceedings of the Indian Philosophical Congress, 1925.

[2] *S.D.*, Vāda 25.

Let us consider the meaning of the term 'self' (*ātman*) and see whether consciousness can be identical with it. It may mean a knowing subject (*jñāta*); or it may be understood in the sense of that which manifests itself for itself (*svasmai-bhāsamānatvam*) or it may also refer to that which is self-luminous (*svayam prakāśatvam*). These are the three important views regarding the meaning of the term *self* and in none of these senses, Vedānta Deśika contends, can consciousness be regarded as identical with the self.

To take the first view, a knowing subject or *jñāta* is that which is the locus of consciousness (*jñānāśraya*).[1] If consciousness be the self in this sense, then it would amount to saying that consciousness is the locus of consciousness which is a self-contradiction in so far as the substrate as well as that which inheres in it are opposed to each other.

As regards the second alternative, it is found on the analysis of experience that consciousness manifests itself to its substrate only and not for itself. The term *svasmai* signifies that which is the self should be the recipient of the manifestation (*prakāśaphali*). To be a recipient of manifestation is to have an empirical usage independent of the manifestation. This is not admitted by the Advaitin in respect of consciousness. The view that *phalitva* is superimposed on consciousness does not solve the difficulty.

The last alternative regarding meaning of the term 'ātman' does not favour the Advaitin's theory. That consciousness is a self-luminous entity is acceptable to the Viśiṣṭādvaitin. On this ground, the identity of consciousness and the self is hardly established.

The inferential argument may be stated in a different way to avoid the above logical difficulties. Ātman is consciousness, because it is ātman; that which is not consciousness is not ātman, as for instance, the pot. Even this inference, Vedānta Deśika urges, is not free from defects. If what is affirmed in the above premise is that the substrate is identical with the attribute, then it involves a contradiction in as much as the two are incompatible. If mere *jñānatva* be predicated of the self, the position is acceptable to the Viśiṣṭādvaitin and as such nothing new is accomplished by the inference.

[1] *S.D.*, Vāda 25

jñātṛtvam hi jñānāśrayatvam.

Vedānta Deśika, therefore, concludes that consciousness is not the very self. On the contrary, it is only an attribute of the knowing subject.

All these criticisms, it may be argued, apply to the so-called common sense view of consciousness or the empirical knowledge which admits a duality of subject and object and not to the transcendental absolute consciousness which is the very Reality. We also admit, the Advaitin may say, that the *vṛtti-jñāna* or the knowledge of the psychosis is non-eternal, mutable, manifold and determinate. Against this argument Vedānta Deśika urges that there is no such transcendental absolute consciousness devoid of all differentiations in so far as it is not established by any of the pramāṇas.[1] Hence the only consciousness that we know of is that which is related to a subject on the one hand and has a reference to an object. Such a knowledge can never be the same as the self or the Reality.

[1] Vāda 33.
tasyāḥ sarva-māna-anāghrātatvena kha-puṣpāya-māṇatvāt.

CHAPTER FOUR

# THE NATURE OF THE INDIVIDUAL SELF

WITH the refutation of the theory that consciousness is identical with the self, we are presented with the problem as to what the self is? According to Viśiṣṭādvaita Vedānta, the individual self or the *jīvātman* as it is called, is an eternal spiritual entity. It is the very *Ego* or the entity denoted by the notion of 'I' (*ahamartha*). Thus, it is not mere knowledge, but a knowing subject (*jñātā*). There are many such jīvas each with its own individuality. It is also a separate entity distinct from Brahman, a 'spiritual monad' of Brahman.

The Advaitin holds a different view which is in direct conflict with the above doctrine. He does not admit that the 'Ego' or the notion of 'I' is the true self in so far as it is only a product of illusion. Nor does he admit that the self is the knower (*jñātā*) in as much as knowership involves change, while the self must be immutable. Further, the true self is one only and cannot be many. The so-called knowing self or the jīva is either a reflection of the Brahman in avidyā or the limitation of Brahman by avidyā. The plurality of the self is thus due to avidyā. True self is identical with the Absolute or the Brahman (*Ātmāca Brahmā*).

Thus, there are four issues involved in the doctrine of the individual self. The first one which is psychological in character refers to the question whether the 'Ego' is the self? The second issue, which is epistemological in nature, relates to the question whether the self is a knower. The third and the fourth are ontological issues and refer to the questions whether the individual self is one and whether it is identical with the Absolute. Vedānta Deśika discusses each one of these issues at great length and refutes the Advaitin's views with a view to defending the Viśiṣṭādvaitin's doctrine.[1]

[1] See Vādas 26, 27, 36 and 37.
**ahamarthātmatva samarthana vādaḥ; jñātṛtvādhyāsa bhanga vādaḥ; ātmādvaita bhanga vādaḥ; jīveśvaraikya bhanga vādaḥ.**

I *The 'Ego' is the Self*

Regarding the first issue, the Advaitin contends that the notion of 'I' or the 'Ego' (*ahamartha*) is not the true self. His main argument is based on the view that the self is eternal. What is eternal should persist in all the states. The notion of 'I' does not satisfy this condition; it does not persist during deep sleep as well as in the state of release. If it were present in the state of release, it would follow that even in the state of *mokṣa* there is ignorance. During the state of bondage the notion of 'I' is found to be co-terminous with nescience and if that were admitted to persist in the state of release, ignorance would continue even in the state of release. The *ahampadārtha* is, therefore, a product of illusion and as such it cannot be regarded as the self. Consciousness alone is the self.[1]

The criticism of the above contention which is very elaborate is mainly directed to show that the notion of 'I' persists both in the states of deep sleep and release. Let us first analyse the sleep experience. Soon after waking from sleep we make the judgments, 'I slept happily', and 'I was not aware of anything all this time'. Obviously this is a case of recollection of the previous state of experience. To whom does this experience belong? Does it belong to the entity denoted by the notion 'I' or does it belong to something else? If it be the former, it follows that the notion of 'I' persists in deep sleep. If it be the latter, then the Ego that recollects the past experience would not be the same as that which experienced the sleep. It is true that the notion of 'I' is not manifest in deep sleep, but nevertheless its existence cannot be denied. The notion of 'I' is present both prior and subsequent to deep sleep. Obviously it must have persisted even during deep sleep. The time, for instance, that lapsed during sleep is not experienced, but nevertheless it is not denied. We infer it on the basis of its being present prior and subsequent to sleep. Same is the case with the notion of 'I'.

Further, the recollection of an experience is dependent upon the residual impression (*samskāra*) of the experience. If the entity denoted by 'I' were not present during sleep, wherein does the *samskāra* inhere? Neither consciousness nor *avidyā* can be its repository since there is no proof either of *avidyā* or consciousness being present in sleep. Even granting

[1] *S.D.*, Vāda 26.

that they persist in sleep, the residual impression cannot inhere in either of them. If the impression inheres in consciousness, it would conflict with the immutable and indeterminate character of consciousness. If, on the other hand, *avidyā* be its repository, it would become the knowing subject since the residual impression can inhere only in a knowing subject. Moreover, the *samskāra* residing in some particular entity cannot be the basis of the recollection by some other entity.[1]

What is the proof in support of the existence of consciousness and ignorance in the state of deep sleep? The judgments, 'I slept well' and 'I did not know anything all this time' do not prove it. They only refer to the persistence of 'I' as associated with sound sleep. The latter judgment does not contradict the persistence of 'I' in sleep. It only negates the experience of external objects. In other words, it simply refers to the absence of knowledge of anything (*jñānā-bhāva*). Nobody recollects after sleep that for such and such a time 'I did not exist'. On the other hand, the cognition is to the effect that 'though I was present I did not know anything'. If, on the basis of the negative judgment the existence of the notion of 'I' during deep sleep be denied, it is possible on the same ground to deny even consciousness as the witness of ignorance. If consciousness persists in sleep because it is self-manifest, the same explanation holds good in respect of the notion of 'I'. It is not, therefore, possible to deny the existence of the notion of 'I' during deep sleep. To say that 'I' alone slept previously and even then 'I' did not persist in sleep is a self-contradiction.[2]

The Advaitin contends that the Ego does not persist in deep sleep but nevertheless, it can recollect the sleep experience. Consciousness endures in sleep as the witness of *ajñāna* and happiness (*sukha*). The same is called (*sākṣi-pratyakṣa*). *Sākṣin* is the consciousness qualified *per accidens* by the internal organ, whereas the Ego is the consciousness qualified *per proprium* by the internal organ.[3] As there is thus an identity between the *sākṣin* and the the Ego (*aham-pratyaya* ) the ignorance and happiness experienced by the *sākṣin* during deep

[1] *S.D.*, Vāda 26.

[2] Ibid.

ato na kathañcidapi suṣuptau ahamarthābhāvo vaktumapi śakyaḥ.

[3] *Vedānta Paribhāṣā*, p. 29.

sleep is recollected by the Ego in the form 'I slept well' and 'I was not aware of anything all this time'.

The above theory is not sound, contends Vedānta Deśika. What is the nature of the pleasure that is experienced in deep sleep? It cannot be ordinary sensual pleasure because the sense organs are not admitted to be functioning in that state. If the pleasure be that which constitutes the essential nature of the self, then there is no need of its being experienced by the witness-self in so far as it is self-manifest. Nor is there the manifestation of *ajñāna*. The presence of *ajñāna* during the state of deep sleep is only inferred by the absence of the recollection of *jñāna* at the time of waking up from sleep just as the time that lapsed during sleep is inferred. *Ajñāna* is not, therefore, witnessed by consciousness.

Vedānta Deśika further argues that the conception of *sākṣin* itself is untenable. What is the nature of *sākṣitva*? Is it the act of knowing (*kartṛtvam*) or is it the direct awareness (*sākṣātkāratvam*)? Or is it something else? It cannot be the act of knowing in as much as the Advaitin does not admit any real cognisership in respect of the Self or Brahman.

Nor is the second alternative tenable. A witness or *sākṣin* is one who knows about something by personal observation (*sākṣitvam-ca sākṣāt jñātṛtvam*). A person who himself directly does not know cannot be a witness. In our ordinary experience too we do not speak of mere knowledge as a witness. This view is also in consonance with the meaning offered by the learned grammarian, Pāṇini. Thus, it is said that *sākṣin* means one who knows in person (*sākṣāt draṣṭari sam-jñāyām*).[1] Pure consciousness cannot, therefore be the witness of *ajñāna* and pleasure. The conclusion to which we are led to is that it is not the pure consciousness but the notion of 'I' that endures in deep sleep.

The notion of 'I' endures even in the state of release. Its continuance in the state of release does not cause ignorance to the self (*ajñatva*). For the notion of 'I' manifests itself in the state of release in its true nature. What manifests in its true form does not cause ignorance.[2] If that were the case,

[1] *S.D.*, Vāda 28.
See *Srī-bhāṣya*, I. 1. 1. p. 45.
sākṣāt jñātary-eva sākṣi śabdam.

[2] *S.D.*, Vāda 26.
yathāvasthita svarūpa prakāśaḥ na ajñatvādi hetuḥ.

then the persistence of consciousness too in deep sleep would cause ignorance. Further, if the notion of 'I' did not persist in the state of release, then no one would attempt to study the *mokṣa śāstra* in as much as release would bring about the destruction of 'I'. No one would cherish one's own destruction.

Further, if the notion of 'I' were not the self, how could the cognition of 'I' in the body, the non-self, be called the delusion of self in the body (*dehātma-bhrama*)? According to the position held by the Advaitin it should be named as *deha-ahamkāra-bhrama*, that is, the delusion of the body as *ahamkāra*. The Advaitin may say that there is the illusion of the self and the *ahamkāra* as identical and hence the *deha-ahamkāra-bhrama* is itself called *dehātma-bhrama*. But this does not hold good because the illusion of the self as identical with *ahamkāra* is itself unfounded.[1]

The notion of 'I' is generally identified with the *ahamkāra* or the ego which is the product of the *mahat-tattva*, the evolute of *prakṛti*. In view of that, it may be said that the entity denoted by 'I' is not the self. This is not sound, argues Vedānta Deśika. For on the same ground it may as well be said that *samvit* or consciousness is *mahat* in as much as it is synonymous with *buddhi*. The empirical ego is quite distinct from the notion of 'I'. The former is that which causes attachment to the body, the non-self, while the latter is the pure self. The self-hood indicated by 'I' cannot be rejected as it is involved even in the very thought of renunciation. Vedānta Deśika, therefore, concludes that the entity denoted by 'I' which is the knowing subject is the true self.[2]

## II *Self is the Knowing Subject*

Self, we have said, is the knower (*jñātā*) and not pure consciousness. Can knowership be attributed to the self without affecting its immutable character? The Advaitin's contention is that cognisership involves change and as such it cannot be the property of the self which is immutable. Cognisership, on the other hand, belongs to the internal organ (*antaḥ-karaṇa*). The self only appears to be the knower or cogniser because

[1] *S.D.*, Vāda 26.

[2] Ibid.

siddham anāropita jñātṛtva viśiṣtaḥ ahamartha eva ātmā iti.

of the superimposition of the property of the internal organ on it. The manifestation of cognisership is an illusion because it takes place in him alone who has the illusion of the body as the self as in the case of the cognition, 'I am fat'.[1]

The above argument is subjected to a critical examination. The criticism is two-fold. First, the superimposition of the cognisership on the self is in no way possible. Secondly, the admission of the cognisership in respect of the self does not affect its immutable character.

Cognisership cannot be a superimposition on consciousness or the self. Superimposition is possible only in respect of a substrate (*adhiṣṭāna*) which is real. What is the substrate on which cognisership is superimposed? Apparently it must be consciousness, since for the Advaitin there is nothing else which is real. But this does not hold good, argues Vedānta Deśika. Whenever there is a superimposition, the substrate and the superimposed object are found in apposition. Thus, in the case of shell-silver illusion, 'This is silver', *silver* is found in apposition to *this*. If consciousness be the basis for the superimposition of cognisership on it, the latter should be found in apposition to the former in the form, viz., 'Consciousness is the cogniser'. This is not actually the case.

Further, superimposition is possible either when there is some similarity between two things or where the distinction between the two objects is not distinctly apprehended. In the case of the consciousness, as it is devoid of all determinations, it does not admit similarity with any other object and consequently the question of non-apprehension of distinction does not arise at all.

The Advaitin may account for the superimposition of the congnisership on consciousness in a different way. Just as the white crystal when placed near a china rose appears to be red and iron ball hot, likewise consciousness too, because of the reflection of the *ahamkāra* in it or of its contact with it, appears to be the congniser.

Even this position is unsatisfactory, contends Vedānta Deśika. Redness and heat are really found in the china rose and the iron ball respectively. Because of the reflection of the red flower in the white crystal and of the contact of the

[1] *S.D.*, Vāda 27.

fire with iron ball, the appearance of the redness and the heat as the qualities of the crystal and the iron ball respectively is perfectly intelligible. In the case of the cognisership, however, since real cognisership is not admitted either in respect of consciousness or in respect of *ahamkāra*, the position is totally different.[1]

It may be argued that consciousness becomes reflected in the particular psychosis of the internal organ and as a result of this there is the manifestation of the cognisership. Even this is inadmissible. The reflection of an entity that has no form (*nīrūpasya*) in that which is also devoid of form is impossible just as there cannot be any reflection of sound, odour, taste etc.

Another explanation is put forth by the Advaitin. *Ahamkāra* which possesses capacity for action (*kriyā-śakti*) and whose nature is to manifest things, manifests consciousness as if possessing its action, that is, as abiding within itself, just as the mirror manifests the face as abiding within it. It is, therefore, that the delusion in the form of 'I know' arises.

Even this is untenable. Consciousness which is ever luminous needs no manifestation. Even if it is to be manifested, non-intelligent *ahamkāra* cannot manifest it directly in the same manner as consciousness manifests other things.[2]

Further, does the *ahamkāra* that has not been manifested reveal consciousness or the *ahamkāra* that has been manifested? If it be the former, *ahamkāra* would become real in so far as it can manifest consciousness by its being self-existent, i.e., without depending for its existence on consciousness. If it be the latter, unless the consciousness itself were manifest, *ahamkāra* would not be manifested. If the unmanifested consciousness be manifested by *ahamkāra* then there would be the denial of the self-luminosity of consciousness.

After having shown that the superimposition of cognisership is unintelligible, the other contention of the Advaitin is taken up for criticism. Cognisership, it is argued, like motion involves change because it is a particular act of knowing which involves action (*kriyāviśeṣa kartṛtvarūpa*). Hence it is the property of the internal organ which is possessed of action. Because of its proximity to the self which is

[1] *S.D.*, Vāda 27.

[2] Ibid.,
*Śrī-bhāṣya*, p. 41.

essentially consciousness, it appears to be of the nature of knowledge. Thus, cognisership is an adventitious property of the self.

The entire argument, Vedānta Deśika contends, is based upon the wrong assumption that cognisership involves change. In what sense does it involve change? It cannot be in the sense of the transformation from one state to another, as in the case of a lump of clay, since no such transformation is admitted in respect of the self. Nor is it in the sense that the word *jñāta*, in so far as it admits a root meaning, involves change. If that be the case, then consciousness too involves change in as such as it is connected with such words as *asti*, *bhavati* etc., which admit a root meaning. If the words *asti* and *bhavati* do not involve change as they are eternal, the same may be said of cognisership too. If it be argued that knowership is found to be accidental then it can as well be said that *astitva* too is found to be accidental. If on the strength of scriptural texts *astitva* is regarded to be eternal not involving any change, then it may also be pointed out that scriptural texts establish that cognisership too is eternal.[1]

Thus it is difficult to prove either on the strength of scriptural texts or by means of reasoning that cognisership is an adventitious property of the self. The Viśiṣṭādvaitin, therefore, strikes at a compromise by holding the view that knowledge is the essential attribute of the self. The function of such knowledge is to reveal objects through the respective sense organs. Whenever it functions it is said to have been originated. When it does not function, it is said to have been destroyed. What is meant by the origination and destruction of consciousness is its manifestation and non-manifestation. The self is overlaid with the previous deeds (karma) and this accounts for the expansion or contraction of knowledge. Knowledge is eternal and by its very nature it is pure and is capable of revealing everything. Nevertheless it does not manifest things always because of the fact that its functions are subjected to karma. This is explained by the analogy of the diamond encrusted with dirt. The lustre of the gem is not produced by the mere removal of dirt. It is already there as unmanifest on account of its being covered by the dirt; as soon as the latter is removed it shines itself in its true

[1] See *Br. Up.*, VI. 3. 30.
na vijñātuḥ vijñāteḥ viparilopo vidyate.

nature. So also knowledge in the self is not originated but is always there. When karma is overcome knowledge shines forth in its true nature. As long as there is karma, the contraction and expansion of knowledge takes place and in this sense we speak of origination and destruction of knowledge. As these states do not directly belong to the self, the immutable character of the self remains unaffected. Whenever knowledge reveals an object there arises the cognition 'I know'. This cognisership belongs to the self. It is not, therefore, a mere superimposition but is real.

### III *Plurality of the Individual Self*

True self, according to the Advaitin, is one only. If this be the case, naturally the question arises, regarding the plurality of the individual selves or jīvas. The individual selves as far as our experience goes are many and they appear to be real. How are we to account for the plurality of the jīvas? The Advaitin answers that the one self appears as many and so the plurality of selves is not ultimately real. The self appears as many because of the difference of the bodies, the internal organs etc. This is explained on the analogy of the reflection of the single moon in the waves. Just as the single moon appears as many being reflected in the waves, likewise the self appears as many being reflected in the numerous internal organs. This is the theory of *bimba-pratibimba-vāda* associated with the name of Prakāśātman, the author of the *Vivaraṇa*.[1]

There is another view known as *avaccheda-vāda*, which is associated with the author of the *Bhāmatī*, Vācaspati Miśra, who holds that the plurality of the individual selves is conditioned by the adjuncts.[2] The individual self is not the reflection of the pure consciousness in the internal organ, but it is the pure consciousness itself conditioned by the internal organs. The illustration offered to explain this view is the cosmic ether (*ākāśa*) which is one and all-pervasive and which is conditioned by pots etc. In either of the views, the plurality of the self is only illusory.

The following inferential argument is put forth to prove the illusory character of the plurality of selves. "The bodies in question possess my own self as their selves because they

[1] See *Pañcapādikā Vivaraṇa*, pp. 64-6 (V.S.S.).

[2] See *Bhāmatī*.

are bodies just like my own body in question ". " The self of all is myself, because it is sentient like my own self." Again, it is argued, " The plurality of the bodies in question is not dependent on the plurality of selves, because of the difference of the bodies, just like the different bodies of *Saubhari*. If this were not accepted, there would follow the prolixity of assumptions ".[1]

There are two possible objections against this theory. We find different types of individuals in our ordinary experience and the difference in respect of them is made only on the basis of the different characteristics they possess. Thus, we call one a wise man and another a fool. One is considered happy while another unhappy. From these distinctions it follows that the selves are many. In view of this Akṣapāda says, " Selves are established as many ".[2] The Sānkhyas also point out that there are many selves because of the fact that birth, death, sense organs etc., are distinct in each individual.

The second objection refers to the difference of experience from individual to individual. If the self of 'A' is the same as the self of 'B' then the experience of 'B' should be had by 'A' as well. But this is not the case, as far as our ordinary experience goes. Hence the self should be admitted as many.

As regards the first objection the Advaitin contends that it is not established that there is opposition between the characteristics in question. What is understood by an opposition is that the qualities do not exist together (*sahānavasthāna*). That the qualities do not exist together can be known when the difference between the substrate (in which the qualities inhere) is established; that there is difference between the substrates can be known only when the difference of the qualities is established. The argument thus involves a vicious circle.

As regards the other objection it is argued that the experience of each individual is determined by the nescience of the individual as well as his internal organ which experiences pleasure and pain and hence there is no possibility of one individual having the recollection of the experiences of the

[1] *S.D.*, Vāda 36.

[2] These arguments have been mainly drawn from *Nyāyamakaranda*. See pp. 4, 32 (kṣetrajña bheda nirāsaḥ).

other. This is the case as far as ordinary human beings are concerned. In the case of Prahlāda and Vāmadeva, the Advaitin admits that they can have the recollection of the experiences of all.

Further, the Advaitin argues that the recollection of the experiences of other individuals by oneself is acceptable to him. The experience of another is also the experience of oneself, because the self of another is identical with one's own self. It is not possible to establish the difference of another from oneself. Perception cannot prove it. For all that we know in perception is that an individual exists there and it cannot prove that that individual is different from oneself. Nor can it be inferred by such characteristic features as appear in his face. As has been already pointed out, it is not possible to prove that the characteristics are mutually opposed.

It may be argued that if the selves are identical, the distinction between the bound and the released selves would be unintelligible. This cannot be, contends the Advaitin. According to those who hold that *ajñāna* is located in the Absolute, there is no one who has been released. There is only one self who being bound by one *avidyā* is deluded and the same is released when that *avidyā* is removed. On this view the release of such persons as Śuka and Vāmadeva has to be understood as illusory as the release of the dream persons.[1] As for those who hold that *ajñāna* is located in the jīva, release consists in the cessation of *ajñāna* of that particular jīva. Though one jīva is released, the other jīvas continue to be in bondage since the *ajñāna* located in them continues. Brahman, however, is eternally free and has neither bondage nor release.

Vedānta Deśika first examines the soundness of the syllogistic arguments put forth by the Advaitin. In the inferential premise, "The bodies in question possess for their selves *my own* (*mayaiva*)". What is meant by the expression *my own*? Does it mean the entity denoted by the Ego-notion or the consciousness that is associated with the 'I' or something that supersedes both and stands as their witness (*sākṣin*)?

[1] This is the view of the Eka-jīva-vādin associated with the author of *Vedānta Siddhānta Muktāvali* (Prakāśānanda).

See p. 16 (Benares Edn.)

ata evājñānasya jīvopādhitvāt tasya caikatvāt tadupādhika ātmā jīvo bhavanneka eva bhavatītyeka jīvavādino vadanti.

The first alternative will not do, because the Advaitin does not admit that the entity denoted by 'I' is the self and as such the argument becomes fallacious in so far as one's own body (which is the illustration of the syllogism) is devoid of a self. Nor does the second alternative hold good. Samvit or consciousness is not admitted to be the self by the Viśiṣṭādvaitin and the argument is, therefore, defective for the opponent. Nor is the third alternative correct because the conception of *sākṣin* as understood by the Advaitin is proved to be untenable.[1]

Similarly in the case of the other argument viz., "The self of all is my own self, because it is sentient", what is it that is sought to be established here? If the identity of the individual selves is sought to be established, the argument falls to the ground. As it will be shown presently there cannot be any identity of the individual selves in so far as there is mutual opposition between the characteristics possessed by the different individuals. Thus, it is not possible to prove on the basis of the inference the identity or the oneness of the self. It is also possible to put a counter argument. The self of 'A' is different from the self of 'B' because 'A' can never at any time recollect the experience of 'B', as for instance, the pot. The probans is supported by one's own experience.[2]

It is argued that there is no opposition between one individual being wise and the other ignorant as it is not possible to establish that there is opposition between these two characteristics. Against this argument Vedānta Deśika asks whether the opposition in question is denied after having accepted opposition in general in some other case or is it denied without admitting the opposition anywhere. If it be denied everywhere it would be absurd even to argue with the opponent in so far as there is no opposition (according to the position held by the Advaitin) between one's own view and that of the opponent. If opposition is accepted in some other instances, it is hardly possible to disprove it in the present instance.

It was pointed out that the experience of other individuals cannot be recollected by oneself because of the variegated nature of the *avidyā* located in each individual self or because

[1] *S.D.*, Vāda 28.

[2] *S.D.*, Vāda 36.

of the difference of the limiting adjunct. This will not do, contends Deśika. The theory of *avidyā*, as will be shown in a subsequent chapter,[1] is riddled with contradiction and hence on that ground the difference in the experience of the different individuals cannot be accounted for. As for the difference of adjuncts (*upādhi*), it cannot constitute a hindrance to the recollection of the experience of one individual by another as in the case of *Saubhari*, the Purāṇic personality. The different bodies assumed by *Saubhari* had different internal organs and yet the experience of one body was recollected by the other. Hence, it is not the mere difference of the adjuncts in the form of internal organs but the different selves etc., that actually account for the difference of the experience in each individual. If difference in experience be determined on the basis of the difference of *antaḥkaraṇa*, then why not the same be determined on the basis of the difference of external sense organs? Actually that is not the case, for we only recollect what we have seen or experienced.[2]

The contention that the experience of another is one's own because the self in both is the same does not hold good since the experiences of two individuals are quite different. That the other individual is different from oneself is established by inference, if not by perception. The apprehension of otherness is definitely possible by means of inference based on such factors as joy etc., which are not present in oneself.

Unless the difference of the individual self is admitted to be real, the distinction between bondage and release cannot be accounted for satisfactorily. According to those who hold that Brahman is the locus of *ajñāna*, there is no individual who has been released. And even the release of such persons as Śuka, Vāmadeva etc., is also illusory. If such a theory be admitted then the release of the preceptors who teach Advaita would be illusory and as such they would hardly attract any aspirants for the release. How can then the preceptor persuade the disciples to study Vedānta for the sake of attaining release? Such a view would lead to the conclusion that there was never any release of any self nor was there at any time bondage. Such a position would also lead to the theory that there is eternal bondage which is never removed and in the

[1] See Chapter VII.

[2] *S.D.*, Vāda 36.

absence of the removal of bondage, the sacred texts which are meant for the purpose of imparting the means of overcoming bondage are meaningless.

On the view that *ajñāna* is located in the jīvas, Brahman would be free from bondage; but the distinction between bondage and freedom would stand unaccounted for. For everything other than Brahman is illusory and as such bondage would only mean what is illusory while freedom means what is real. Such a distinction is philosophically unsatisfactory. Hence it should be admitted that there are many individual selves distinct from each other.[1]

## IV *The Individual Self and Īśvara*

After having set aside the view that the individual selves are identical, Vedānta Deśika takes up for consideration the theory of the identity of the individual self and the Absolute. The self in us, the Advaitin contends, is identical with the Absolute (*Īśvara*). What is the ground on which the finite self is held to be identical with the Absolute, asks Vedānta Deśika. Is it established by means of perception or inference or scriptural texts? These are the three pramāṇas which could establish the theory of the identity of the self and the Absolute.

Perception does not prove it because in perception we always apprehend ourselves as other than *Īśvara*. It is not necessary that Īśvara should be known directly in order to apprehend ourselves as different from Him. The knowledge of Īśvara as given to us by the scriptural texts is sufficient for the purpose of knowing the self as different from Him.

Is there an apprehension in the form 'I am not the Lord'? There is such an apprehension in respect of him who is weak. Even if one does not have such a cognition, there is at least the cognition in oneself of such characteristics as are contrary to those of Īśvara. The individual selves are subject to karma, possess unfulfilled desires and are tortured by the three-fold misery. They are, therefore, seeking some means of overcoming the bondage. Thus, it is evident through perception that the individual selves are not identical with Īśvara.[2]

Nor is it possible to establish the identity of the self and Īśvara on the strength of reasoning. Just as in one's own

[1] *S.D.*, Vāda 36.

[2] *S.D.*, Vāda 37.

body the self is found to be different from Īśvara, in the same way the selves in the other individuals are different from Īśvara in so far as the former possess such characteristics as are different from the latter. This is evident, as has been shown above, from one's own experience. Thus, the inferential argument viz., the jīva is identical with Īśvara because it is sentient, stands sublated. The very premise involves self-contradiction in so far as the jīva is known to be different from Īśvara.

It may be argued that there is identity between the two because the characteristics of jīva that are opposed to Īśvara are all illusory. This will not hold good. For the Advaitin himself admits that Īśvara and jīva are superimposed on Brahman in the form of cause, effect and upādhi just as the snake and the crack in the ground are superimposed on the rope; nevertheless if Īśvara and jīva are identical, then the superimposed snake and the crack in the ground would also become identical which is absurd as far as our ordinary experience is concerned. The superimposed objects are never identical, much less the substrate and the object superimposed on it.

The scriptural texts also do not establish the identity of the self and Īśvara. There are numerous scriptural texts which explicitly point out the difference of the individual self from the Absolute.[1] In some places the sacred texts also point out the distinguishing characteristics of the self and the Absolute.[2] In other contexts the texts also refer to the *Sambandha* or the relationship between the self and the Absolute which accounts for the difference.[3] Even during the state of release the

[1] See *Muṇḍaka Up.*, 3-1-2.
juṣṭam yadā paśyati anyam-īśam.
*Svet. Up.*, I. 6.
pṛthagātmānam preritāram ca matvā.
*Mund. Up.*, 3-1-1.
*Tait. Up.*, 2-5-2.
tasmādvā etasmāt vijñāna mayāt;
anyontara ātmā ānandamayaḥ.
*Gita*, 15-7.

[2] See *Muṇḍaka Up.*, 1-1-9.
yaḥ-sarvajñaḥ-sarvavit.
*Svet. Up.*, 6-8.
parāsya śaktiḥ vividhaiva śrūyate svābhāvikī jñāna balakriyā ca.
*Svet. Up.*, 6-9 and 6-10.

[3] See *Brah. Up.*, 5-7.
ya ātmani tiṣṭan . . . . . . yasyātmā śarīram.
*Svet. Up.*, 11-3.

Absolute and the self are spoken of as different.[1] Thus, it is established by the sacred texts that the self and the Absolute are different which is also in conformity with our ordinary experience.

Nevertheless if some texts refer to the identity of the self and Īśvara, then they should be understood in a secondary sense as referring to the relationship between the two in the form of the Master and the servant. If such an interpretation were not accepted, then whenever Īśvara and matter (*acetana*) are spoken of as one, it would follow that they are identical. It may be argued that matter and Īśvara are stated in apposition and as such the former in so far as it is unreal is meant to be sublated by the latter.[2] This will not do since the same interpretation can as well be applied to the statements where jīva and Īśvara are stated in apposition and as a result of it jīva would stand sublated by Īśvara.

It may be said that if the self itself be negated, release would not be a *summum bonum* (*puruṣārtha*). But this contention does not hold good for the Advaitin because he negates the existence of the entity denoted by the notion 'I' and still holds that release is the ultimate goal. On the analogy of the cosmic ether and the ether conditioned by the pot, the self and Īśvara may be regarded to be identical in the state of release. But such an interpretation will not do as it would stand in direct conflict with the texts pointing out equality (*sāmya*) between jīva and Īśvara in the state of release. If this conflict is to be avoided identity of jīva and Īśvara cannot be maintained. The two are spoken of as identical only in view of the fact that Īśvara is the inner self of the individual. This meaning is implied in the following *Vedānta Sūtra*: *Avasthiteriti Kāśakṛtsnah.*[3] In the *Mahābhārata* also it is said "The Lord is different, likewise the self which is the twenty-fifth principle is distinct; wise men say that they are one because the former resides in the latter".[4] The individual self therefore, which is a permanent spiritual entity can never be identical with Īśvara.

[1] *Tait. Up.*, 1-7.
so' śunte sarvān kāmān saha brahmaṇā vipaściteti.
*Muṇḍ. Up.*, 3-1-3.
niranjanaḥ paramam sāmyam upaiti.
*Gita*, 14-2.

[2] See Vāda 32.

[3] *Vedānta Sūtra*, I-4-2-2.

[4] See *Mahābh.*, Mokṣadharma.
anyaśca rājan sa paraḥ tathā anyaḥ pañca vimśakaḥ;
tatsthatvāt-anupaśyanti-hy ekaeveti sādhavaḥ.

CHAPTER FIVE

# THE DOCTRINE OF NIRGUṆA BRAHMAN

The most distinguishing feature of Advaita Vedānta on its metaphysical side is the advocacy of the doctrine of *nirguṇa* Brahman. The one and the only reality admitted is the pure Brahman devoid of all determinations (*nirviśeṣa*). In view of this Advaita is designated as *Nirviśeṣa Brahma Vāda.*[1] This doctrine is established mainly on the strength of the scriptural texts.

The rival schools of Vedānta which also take their stand on the scriptural texts in determining the nature of the ultimate Reality maintain that Brahman is qualified by numerous attributes. In other words, they uphold the theory that *saguṇa* Brahman is the ultimate Reality. Quite naturally the critics of Advaita have subjected the Advaitin's doctrine of *nirguṇa* Brahman to severe criticism. The criticism is mainly directed towards the examination of the scriptural texts quoted by the Advaitin in support of his theory and showing that their import is something different from what the Advaitin holds.

Vedānta Deśika does not take up in the *Śatadūṣaṇī* a detailed examination of the meaning of the scriptural as well as the smṛti texts referring to the nature of Brahman, as this has been covered by Rāmānuja in his *Śrī-bhāṣya.* He, on the other hand, devotes his attention to the discussion of some of the important issues which constitute the basis for the Advaitin's interpretation of the scriptural texts. The first issue is whether scriptural texts referring to Brahman as *nirguṇa* are more authoritative than the texts that refer to Brahman as *saguṇa.* Secondly, does a scriptural text wherein the terms are found in apposition (*sāmānādhikaraṇya*) convey an impartite and non-relational sense (*akhaṇḍārtha*)? Lastly, would it be possible to conceive a *nirguṇa* Brahman as *ānanda*, *nitya* and *advitīya*? How far do the smṛti texts in general and Vedānta-Sūtrās in particular support the doctrine of *nirguṇa* Brahman?

[1] Cp. the opening sentence of Vāda 1.

What then is the function of the sacred texts in respect of Brahman which is not characterisable in any way? Each one of these questions will be considered in the course of the present chapter.

## I *Saguṇa Śrutis and Nirguṇa Śrutis*

Śruti is the final authority in spiritual matters and hence the question whether Brahman is *saguṇa* or *nirguṇa* in character will have to be ultimately decided on the strength of the scriptural texts. But here we are faced with a difficulty. There are scriptural texts which speak of Brahman as devoid of qualities, [1] while there are also texts which openly declare Brahman to be qualified by numerous attributes.[2] How are we to overcome such a conflict? There are two ways of resolving it. One way is to accept the validity of both the texts and interpret them in such a way that the apparent conflict does not arise at all. This is the method adopted by the Viśiṣṭādvaitin. The other way of solving the difficulty is to ascribe a superior validity to one of the two conflicting texts and deny the other as non-authoritative. The Advaitin who does not agree with the former method adopts the latter. Both the texts, he contends, cannot be maintained to be equally valid in view of the fact that they refer to an existent (*siddhavastu*). Obviously one of them has to be negated as invalid. Now, of the two conflicting texts, *saguṇa* śrutis, and *nirguṇa* śrutis, which of them are of greater validity? The Advaitin's answer is that the texts which deny all qualities of Reality are later in order than the texts which refer to the Reality as

[1] See *Svet. Up.*, VI. 19.
niṣkalam niṣkriyam śāntam niravadyam niranjanam.
*Mund. Up.*, I. 1.6.
yattad-adrésyam agrāhyam agotram avarṇam acākśuḥ aśrotram tad-apāṇipādam. . .
*Ch. Up.*, 8. 1.7. Apahatapāpmā vijaraḥ.
*Brah. Up.*, 5. 8.8. Asthūlam anaṇu. . .

[2] See *Mund. Up.*, 2. 2.7.
yas-sarvajñaḥ sarvavit.
satyakāmas-satya-saṁkalpaḥ.
*Ch. Up.*, 8. 1.5.
*Svet. Up.*, 6.8.
*Tasit. Up.*, I. 1.2.

qualified, because denial presupposes that which is to be denied. Negation in view of affirmation is later and what is later, according to the principle of the subsequent sublating the earlier (*apaccheda-nyāya*) [1], is of greater force and occupies the position of the sublater (*bādhakam*). In view of this the *nirguṇa* śrutis are of greater validity than the *saguṇa* śrutis.

Vedānta Deśika controverts the above argument. He contends that the entire argument is based on the assumption that the *apaccheda-nyāya* holds good here. This is far from the truth. The *apaccheda-nyāya* holds good where the two texts that are not regularly opposed to each other follow as the earlier and later (*aniyata virodha paurvāparye-hy-apaccheda nayaḥ*). Where there is a regular opposition between the two texts coming as earlier and later, (*niyata virodha paurvāparye*), the earlier text is predominant, according to the principle known as *upakramādhikaraṇa-nyāya*,[2] and as such the question of later being stronger does not arise at all. Thus the *apaccheda-nyāya* does not apply in the case of the *saguṇa* and *nirguṇa* texts as the two are mutually opposed to each other by their very nature.

On the other hand, the principle known as *utsargā-pavāda-nyāya* offers a better solution to the problem. According to this principle, the negative text will have to be interpreted in accordance with the affirmative text. Thus, for instance, there is a scriptural text which says that animals should not be injured while another text points out that an animal (*paśu*) should be used for a particular sacrifice.[3] The conflict here is overcome by interpreting the former text to mean that animals other than those enjoined in the scriptural text for sacrificial purposes should not be injured. The same logic holds good in respect of *saguṇa* and *nirguṇa* texts. If some texts affirm that Brahman possesses qualities while others deny the same, letter should be understood to mean the denial of qualities other than those mentioned in the former (*vihita vyatirikta guṇa niśedhaḥ*). In other words, the implication of the negative texts is that Brahman is devoid of such inauspicious attributes as change, karma etc., but not that it is devoid of all characteristics. Such an interpretation, though it restricts the import of the negative texts to some

[1] See fn. 2, p. 29.

[2] This is the principle of the earlier being stronger than the later.

[3] na himsyāt sarvabhūtāni
agnīśomiyam paśum-ālabheta.

extent, maintains the validity of both the *saguṇa* and *nirguṇa* śrutis. If, on the contrary, the principle of the later sublating the earlier is adopted, it is not possible to maintain the validity of both the texts. The *apaccheda-nyāya* holds good where the later cannot arise except as contradicting the earlier, as in the case of the two cognitions, 'This is silver' and 'This is not silver'. The later cognition cannot arise except as sublating the earlier and as such what is sublated cannot be regarded in any sense as valid.[1]

It may, however, be argued that though the *saguṇa* texts are contradicted by the *nirguṇa* texts the former do not become invalid so far as they subserve those texts referring to contemplation for the purpose of definite ends. This will not do, since those very texts point out that contemplation of *saguṇa* Brahman leads to *mokṣa*, the supreme goal of spiritual endeavour. It is therefore, not possible to maintain the validity of either texts except on the basis of the interpretation offered by the Viśiṣṭādvaitin.

Vedānta Deśika, concludes that *saguṇa* śrutis are as valid as the *nirguṇa* śrutis in as much as both refer to the same Reality. Negation only refers to those qualities other than those affirmed (*vihita vyatirikta viṣayaḥ niṣedhaḥ*). As the contents of the two texts apply to different aspects of Reality, there is absolutely no conflict between them. In the absence of conflict the question of the sublater and the sublated does not arise at all.[2] Thus, it is not possible to establish on the strength of the *nirguṇa* texts that Brahman is *nirguṇa* in character.

## II *The Theory of Akhaṇḍārtha*

We now come to the second issue, viz., whether any of the scriptural texts can convey an impartite and non-relational sense (*akhaṇḍārtha*). This question arises particularly in connection with the interpretation of the Upanisadic text,

[1] *S.D.*, Vāda 52.
See also *Śrutaprakāśika*, Vol. 3, pp. 975-6.

[2] *S.D.*, Vāda 52.
See also *Tattvasāra*.
yad-brahmaṇaḥ guṇa-śarīra-vikārajanma-
karmādi-gocara-vidhi-pratiṣedha vācaḥ;
anyonya-bhinna-viṣayaḥ na virodha-gandham
arhanti tanna viṣayaḥ pratiṣedha bodhyaḥ.

'*Satyam Jñānam Anantam Brahma*'[1] which gives the definition of Brahman as 'Truth, Knowledge and Infinitude'. The main issue is whether in this text the terms in question denote the very *svarūpa* of Brahman or its characteristics. The Advaitin maintains the former view while the Viśiṣṭādvaitin holds the latter. The chief argument of the Advaitin for adopting the above view is that a sentence in which the terms are found in apposition (*sāmānādhi-karaṇya*) conveys an impartite and non-relational sense. Thus, for instance, in the judgment 'He (is) that Devadatta' the two terms 'He' and 'Devadatta' which stand in apposition do convey the idea of one individual. In other words, a sentence conveys the idea of one entity only when all its constituent terms denote one and the same thing. Accordingly, the Upaniṣadic text in question is understood to mean that Brahman is Truth, Knowledge and Infinitude and not that it is possessed of these three characteristics. The argument is also stated in the form of a syllogism: "The text under dispute refers to what is impartite and non-relational; because it is an appositional sentence just like the sentence, 'He is that Devadatta'."[2]

If all the terms denote the same sense would it not follow that they are synonyms? To this the Advaitin replies that the terms can convey one meaning without being synonyms. These terms convey a meaning which is contrary to what is ordinarily implied by them. They have a negative implication and serve to distinguish the entity denoted by them as different from things which possess characteristics other than what are ordinarily implied. In the Upaniṣadic text under question Brahman is defined as what is contrary in nature to all other things. Whatever is opposed to its nature is virtually contradicted by these three terms. The term *Satya* for instance, has the purport of distinguishing Brahman from whatever things are not real (*anṛta*). The term *Jñāna* distinguishes Brahman from things which are non-sentient (*Jaḍa*). Similary, the term *Ananta* distinguishes it from whatever is limited in space, time and object (*deśa kāla vastu paricchinna*). Thus, these terms, though they denote the

[1] *Tait. Up.*

[2] *S.D.*, Vāda 38.

vigītam vākyam akhaṇḍārtha param; samānādhi-karaṇa vākyatvāt; so'yam devadatta ityādi vākyavat.

Cp. *Tattvaśuddhi*, p. 59.

*svarūpa* of Brahman, do not become synonyms in so far as they convey the essential distinction of Brahman from everything else.[1] Brahman as defined by the Upaniṣadic text is one homogeneous being devoid of all difference.

The criticism of this doctrine is very elaborate. The main point of the criticism is that a sentence, where the terms stand in apposition, does not convey an impartite and non-relational sense but on the contrary it denotes one entity as qualified by the characteristics connoted by the terms of the sentence. This, the Viśiṣṭādvaitins contend, is the true meaning of *sāmānādhi-karaṇya.* This meaning is adopted on the basis of the definition given by the grammarians. Thus, it is defined: "*Bhinna pravṛtti nimittānām śabdānām ekasmin arthe vṛttiḥ sāmānādhi karaṇyam.*" "It is the application to one thing of several words, for the application of each of which there is a different motive."[2] To put it in terms of modern logic, *sāmānādhi-karaṇya* is that where the terms having different connotations denote one thing. Though the terms of the proposition have different connotations, they can yet denote one and the same thing. Thus, for instance, in the judgment 'blue lotus' (*nīlotpalam*), the term 'blue' has a different connotation from that of 'lotus'. The connotation of 'blue' is the quality of blueness while that of lotus is 'lotusness' and yet the two terms refer to one object viz., 'lotus'. Such terms are said to be in apposition and a sentence containing such terms is called a *sāmānādhikaraṇa-vākya.*

Keeping this point in view Vedānta Deśika critically examines the arguments of the Advaitin. Taking the syllogism, he asks the meaning of the term '*akhaṇḍārtha param*', which is the probandum of the syllogism. It is resolved into seven alternatives: (1) that which is formless (*niravayava*), (2) that which is indivisible (*acchedya*), (3) that which is devoid of all characteristics (*nirviśeṣaṇatva*), (4) that which is the substrate only (*viśeṣya*), (5) that which admits of no difference (*nirbhedārtha*), (6) that which is devoid of qualities

[1] See *Śrī-bhāṣya*, I. 1. 1. p. 19.
See also *Śruta-prakāśika*, Vol. I, p. 260.
*Nyāyamakaranda*, p. 260.
lakṣyārtha bheda-bhāve-pi vyavacchedya vibhedhataḥ;
vijñānā-nanda padayoḥ paryāya vyarthatākutah.

[2] Thibaut's translation of *Śrī-bhāṣya*, p. 79.

of positive character, (7) that which is a substance only (*eka viśeṣya*).[1]

The first two alternatives are acceptable to the Viśiṣṭādvaitin and as such the syllogism would suffer from the defect of what is already established (*siddha sādhanatā*). Besides, the illustration of the syllogism would also be fallacious; because the sentence 'He is that Devadatta', does not denote an individual who is either formless or indivisible (*acchedya*).

As regards the third alternative viz., that *akhaṇḍārtha* means *nirviśeṣaṇatva*, it is asked whether this meaning is ascertained on the strength of the denotative power of the terms in question (*śābdabodhyatva*) or on the basis of the fact that the object denoted is *nirviśeṣa* by its every nature? If it be the former, it would follow that the entity referred to is that which is qualified by the characteristic viz., *nirviśeṣaṇatva*. If *nirviśeṣaṇatva* is not an attribute but the very nature of Brahman, then there would be no need to establish it in so far as the svarūpa of Brahman is already established. If it be the latter, there would be nothing to distinguish the text referring to Brahman as *nirguṇa* from those which refer to it as *saguṇa*, because for the Advaitin all texts in general refer to Brahman which is by its nature *nirviśeṣa* in character.

The fourth alternative, that *akhaṇḍārtha* means that which is the substrate only (*viśeṣyamātra*), is also inadmissible. If the term *viśeṣyamātra* means the mere *svarūpa* of the *viśeṣya*, then the position is acceptable to the Viśiṣṭādvaitin. If something more than the *svarūpa* is implied by it, then it would hardly establish the Advaitin's position. The admission of any additional factor would make it relational.

The fifth alternative also is untenable. If *akhaṇḍārtha* is understood to mean an entity that does not admit of any difference in it (*nirbhedārtha*), even then the interpretation of the text adopted by the Advaitin viz., that Brahman is other than non-real, inert and finitude would stand contradicted.

Nor does the sixth alternative hold good. For if *akhaṇḍārtha* means that entity which is devoid of positive characteristics, then whatever arguments are used against the admission of positive qualities would equally apply against the admission of negative qualities as well. Moreover, the syllogistic

[1] *S.D.*, Vāda 38.

Cp. the alternatives raised by Citsukha in his *Tattvapradīpika*, pp. 105-06.

argument would be inconclusive in respect of the sentence 'Devadatta is dark and young'. This is also a sentence where the terms are in apposition and yet it refers to a single entity as qualified by positive characteristics such as darkness and youth.

The seventh alternative also does not hold good, for the meaning of *akhaṇḍārtha* in the sense of one substance only (*eka viśeṣya*) is acceptable to the Viśiṣṭādvaitin.

Further, does the premise of the syllogism, *vigītam vākyam*, cover the Upaniṣadic text only or all the *samānādhikaraṇa* texts other than that cited as an illustration of the syllogism? If it be the former, then the argument would be inconclusive in respect of the sentence 'Devadatta is dark and young' In this sentence the terms are found in apposition and yet they do not convey an impartite and non-relational sense. If it be the latter, then again the syllogism would stand contradicted by the sentence 'Devadatta is dark and young'. The syllogism thus does not establish the Advaitin's contention.[1]

To avoid these difficulties the syllogistic arguments may be stated in a different form. Thus, it is stated: "The text under dispute refers to what is impartite and non-relational, because it is a sentence giving the definition (*lakṣaṇa vākya*); just like the sentence 'what is very luminous is the moon'".[2]

Even this syllogism is not free from defects. In the first instance, the main thesis of the syllogism (*pratijñā*) is opposed to the probans. The probans is, 'because it gives a definition'. The sentence that defines would always imply the distinguishing characteristic of the object defined. On the contrary, the thesis of the syllogism asserts that the sentence under dispute refers to what is impartite which obviously does not admit of any kind of characteristic in respect of the entity denoted by it.

The illustration of the syllogism also does not support the view sought to be established. In the proposition, *prakṛṣṭa prakāśaḥ candraḥ*, is the term, *prakṛṣṭa-prakāśa*, meant to be

[1] *S.D.*, Vāda 38.

[2] Ibid.

vigītam vākyam akhaṇḍārtha param, lakṣaṇa vākyatvāt, prakṛṣṭa prakāśaḥ-candra iti vākyavat.

Cp., *Nyāyamakaranda*, p. 263.

See also *Tattvaśuddhi*, p. 62.

the connotation (*pravṛtti-nimitta*) of the term 'moon' or the qualification *per accidens* of the term 'moon' (*upalakṣaṇa*)? If it be the former, then the two terms would have different connotations since the term 'moon' can denote by its own connotation the actual moon and as such the object denoted would be a qualified one. Supposing the two terms have the same connotation, then there would be no need to use two terms to denote the same object. In the absence of different connotations, it would hardly be possible to call it a *samānādhikaraṇa vākya*. It is only when the terms of a proposition having different connotations denote the same object that they are said to be in apposition. As such the terms that have the same connotation do not constitute the *sāmānādhikaraṇya*.[1] If it be the latter, even then the object denoted would be a qualified one. That is, if the term *prakṛṣṭa prakāśaḥ* is understood to mean a qualification *per accidens* of the term 'moon', there would be the distinction of one term being an *upalakṣaṇa* and the other *upalakṣaṇīya* and as such what is denoted by them would only be a qualified object.

Against this the Advaitin may argue that in all definitions, the subject of the definition (*lakṣya pada*) is meant to refer to the *svarūpa* of the object, while the generic character or differentia through which it is defined is intended to distinguish the object from what is other than its own svarūpa (*svetara samasta vyāvṛttiḥ*). Thus, if one looking at the sky asks which is the moon in the sky, naturally the reply given would be that which is very luminous is the moon. Obviously, what is intended to be pointed out by the latter is not that the moon is that which is qualified by luminosity but the very moon itself. The term connoting the qualification 'luminosity' is intended to distinguish the moon from other entities in the sky such as stars, etc. Thus, the qualification only refers to the *svarūpa* of the moon itself by distinguishing it from other entities.[2]

Vedānta Deśika controverts the above argument. The definition of an object is possible only through the exclusive characteristic of the object and as such the object denoted by such a sentence would inevitably be that which is qualified

[1] *S.D.*, Vāda 38.
na hi paryāyeṇāpi sāmānādhi-karaṇyam.

[2] Cp. the arguments given in the *Tattvaśuddhi*, p. 62.

by the characteristic. If the exclusive characteristic of the object is not known, it is not even possible to understand its distinction from others (*lakṣaṇa vaiśiṣṭya pratipattau vyāvṛtterapi asiddheḥ*). Thus, for instance, it is not possible to know that the earth is different from others without knowing *gandhavattva* or odour which is the exclusive characteristic of earth.[1] Vedānta Deśika, therefore, urges that all sentences convey what is only characterised by something (*sarveṣu api vākyeṣu vaiśiṣṭyam dustyajam*). As such the Upaniṣadic text, " Truth, Knowledge and Infinitude is Brahman " also conveys the idea that Brahman is qualified by truth, knowledge and infinitude.

It cannot be argued that the distinction of several attributes predicated of one thing implies a distinction in the thing itself to which the attributes belong and as such the several terms would denote several things. This is not the case, contends Vedānta Deśika. Even though the characteristics connoted by the several terms found in apposition are different, the object denoted remains one and the same without losing its integrity. The mere fact that an object is related to several characteristics would not mean that the object itself is not an integral whole. One and the same entity may be related to several characteristics without in any way impairing its integrity. This is what is implied by *sāmānādhikaraṇya.* It aims at conveying the idea of one thing as qualified by several attributes. In other words, the true meaning of *sāmānādhikaraṇya* is not absolute identity but the relation of a thing to its attributes.

Further, if what is connoted by one term is exactly the same as that connoted by the other term, the terms would be synonymous and as such the use of more than one term to denote an object is superfluous. If it be said that it is not superfluous because there is difference in respect of their connotations (*nimitta-bheda*), then the object denoted by those terms would be a characterised entity. If, on the contrary, it be argued that all the terms denote the very *svarūpa* of the entity, then not more than one term would be required for the purpose.[2]

The Advaitin may retort that the terms even though they denote the *svarūpa* are meant for the purpose of distinguishing it from what is opposed to it (*tattat pratiyogi vyāvṛtti*

[1] *S.D.*, Vāda 38. [2] *S.D.*, Vāda 38.

*siddhyartham*). This will not do, argues Vedānta Deśika. On what basis is it ascertained that the terms in question are meant to distinguish the *svarūpa* from the characteristics opposed to it? If it be on the strength of the connotation of the respective terms, then the object denoted would be characterised. If, on the contrary, it be ascertained on the basis of the fact that the terms denote only the *svarūpa*, then even one term would do for the purpose and as such the use of other terms would be superfluous.

If the several terms of the Upaniṣadic text in question are understood in their primary sense (*mukhya-vṛtti*) then what is denoted by them is obviously a qualified entity. If, on the contrary, the terms are understood in their secondary sense (*lakṣaṇā*) as the Advaitin does, then also the difference in respect of their connotation will have to be admitted. Otherwise, the terms would become synonymous. If difference in connotation be accepted, then the object denoted would necessarily be a *viśiṣṭa* entity in so far as its qualities are connoted by them. Vedānta Deśika, therefore, concludes that the Upaniṣadic text in question refers to what is qualified by characteristics (*ataḥ sakhaṇḍa param satyamityādi vākyam*).[1]

### III *Brahman as Advitīya*

Vedānta Deśika also examines the meaning of the scriptural text which refers to Brahman as one only without a second (*ekam-eva advitīyam*) and points out that the term *advitīya* in the text does not imply a *nirviśeṣa Brahman.*[2]

What is the meaning of the term *advitīya*? It is apparently a compound word and as such it may be a *tatpuruṣa compound* or a *bahuvrīhi compound.* If it is a *tatpuruṣa compound*, then the word must mean either that Brahman is different from the second (*dvitīyāt anyatvam*), or that it is opposed to it (*tadvirud-dhatvam*) or that it does not have the second (*tadabhāva*). In none of these senses it woud follow that Brahman is *nirviśeṣa.*

If the term *advitīya* signifies different from or similar to the second, the second entity would clearly be established. If the second entity exists either as similar to Brahman or as different from it, Brahman would not be *nirviśeṣa*.

[1] *S.D.*, Vāda 38.

[2] *S.D.*, Vāda 59.

This Vāda is entirely based on the arguments given in Yāmuna's *Samvit-siddhi.*

See *Siddhitraya*, pp. 175-7 (Annamalai Univ. Edn.)

If *advitiya* means opposed to the second, then Brahman must be either a first or a third entity, for what stands opposed to the second is the first or the third.

If the term means the absence of a second, Brahman would be self-existent and as such the negative particle could not be associated with the term Brahman.

Even if the word is taken as a *bahuvrīhi* compound, it would follow that Brahman is *saviśeṣa*. According to the *bahuvrīhi* compound the term would mean that for which there is no second. When we say that it has no second, it would only follow that all other objects which in relation to Brahman could be spoken of as the first, the third, fourth and so on, would exist safely and without any danger of ever being contradicted, for all that is denied is merely the possession of a second.

If, on the contrary, everything other than Brahman is denied, then it would not be a *bahuvrīhi* compound at all. In a *bahuvrīhi* compound the negative case implied by it (that for which there is no second) would be appropriate only in the event of there being a true relation (of Brahman) with something else. It is only when the phrase, 'not having a second', is attributed to something that *advitīya* could be taken as a *bahuvrīhi*.

The phrase, the absence of a second, does not mean Brahman itself nor an attribute thereof. For it is essentially negative, while Brahman is positive. If it is an attribute it would conflict with Brahman being devoid of characteristics.

What then is the true meaning of *advitīya*? As Śrī Yāmuna strikingly explains it, "*Advitīya* is one who neither has, nor had, nor will have an equal or superior capable of being counted as a second". In other words, it implies that there is no second similar to Brahman (*sadṛśa dvitīya niṣedha param*). For instance, the statement, "The paramount ruler of the Chola country now reigning is without a second in this world", is only intended to deny the existence of a ruler equal to him; it does not deny the existence of his servants, sons, consort and so on.[1] Again, in the statement, "There is but a single sun in the sky and not two", the presence of the ray of the sun is not contradicted. Similarly, when Brahman

[1] See *Siddhitraya*, p. 117.
yathā colanṛpaḥ samrāt advitīyotra bhūtale;
iti tattulya nṛpati nivāraṇa param vacaḥ;
na tu tad-bhṛtya-tatputra kalatrādi niṣedhakam.

is declared to be without a second, the existence of his possessions is not denied but there is nothing similar to Brahman.

## IV *Brahman as Ānanda and Nitya*

If Brahman, as the Advaitin contends, is pure consciousness devoid of all characteristics (*nirviśeṣa*) it cannot be regarded even as *ānanda* in any sense of the term. If *ānanda* means that which induces an agreeable experience (*anukūla vedanīyatvam*), then Brahman would be knowable, a position which is not welcome to the Advaitin. It cannot be said that this knowability is only empirical, for the *ānandatva* of Brahman too would then be empirical and as such Brahman in reality would be other than pure bliss.

If *ānanda* means merely an agreeable experience, (*anukūla vedanatva*) then Brahman would not be pure indeterminate consciousness in so far as an element in the form of agreeableness (*anukūlatvam*) in addition to experience (*vedana*) is admitted in Brahman. If this be not admitted, then the qualification added to *vedanatva* would be superfluous.

If, on the other hand, *ānanda* means a mere agreeable attitude (*anukūlatvam*) then in so far as that is a relational notion the unity of Brahman would be affected.

Nor can we understand by *ānanda* the negation of pain (*duḥkha nivṛtti-rūpatā*) for Brahman in that case would not be positive. This is quite against the purport of the Upaniṣadic teaching. According to the Advaitin himself, the state of intuition of Brahman is regarded as a positive state like the state of dreamless sleep.

Nor can it be said that pure bliss is of the nature of consciousness itself (*jñānātmakatva*). For in the scriptural text *vijñānam ānandam brahma*, the two are stated to be distinct.

Thus, in whichever way one may look at the problem, the contention that the indeterminate Brahman is of the nature of pure bliss becomes untenable.[1]

Similarly, Brahman cannot even be conceived as eternal (*nitya*). According to Advaita Vedānta, Brahman alone is eternal; and time and avidyā, which are other than Brahman, are all non-eternal. What is this eternity which is admitted

[1] *S.D.*, Vāda 57.
ataḥ na kathañcidapi nirviśeṣa-cinmātra-vādinaḥ tad-ānandatva siddhiḥ.

in respect of Brahman? Does it mean existence in all time (*sarvakāla sattā rūpam*)? Or that which does not cease in time (*kālāvaccheda nivṛtti rūpam*)? Or being devoid of destruction? Or being non-sublated, or being immutable? Or having neither a beginning nor an end (*ubhayāvadhi rahitatvam*)? Or some other unique characteristic? [1]

If eternity means existence in all time, then avidyā too would be eternal. It is also associated with all time, and time is itself regarded as its product. If it is argued that association with all time does not mean existence in all time, then the term *sarva kāla* used to define eternity would be of no significance. Consequently, eternity would simply mean existence (*sattā*) since it is possible to distinguish Brahman from other things on that basis itself. It cannot be said that existence (*sattā*) itself is eternity since the two terms are admitted to be different. We are therefore forced to accept that eternity means existence in all time; in that case, such an eternity could be affirmed of avidyā as well.

Eternity cannot also be understood as that which does not cease in time, since such a definition would apply to time also which does not cease in time.

Nor can it be understood in the sense of absence of destruction. In that case destruction (*pradhvamsa*) would itself become eternal since that is also devoid of destruction.

Nor can eternity be regarded as that which is non-sublated (*abādhitatvam*). For the so-called real object which is not sublated, as far as our ordinary experience goes, is never regarded as eternal.

The fifth alternative, viz., that eternity is that which is immutable is also untenable. In this sense, transformation (*vikāra*) itself would be eternal in so far as it does not undergo any further transformation. If transformation be mutable, then it would lead to an infinite regress.

The sixth alternative also does not hold good. That is, eternity in the sense of that which is devoid of a beginning and an end is untenable. If it is an empirical beginning and end, since it can be admitted in respect of Brahman, it would be non-eternal. If, on the contrary, a real beginning and an end are implied (*pāramārthika*), then the world would be eternal since they are absent in respect of it.

[1] *S.D.*, Vāda 58.

Further, if eternity is the very *svarūpa*, then eternity would be identical with Brahman and the expression 'Brahman is eternal' would be unnecessary. If it be the characteristic of Brahman, Brahman would be determinate in character. Thus, it is impossible to conceive *nirguṇa* Brahman as eternal.[1]

V *Thought and Reality*

If Brahman is pure consciousness devoid of all characteristics what then is the function of the sacred texts which impart to us the knowledge of Reality? If the sacred texts refer to Brahman, then the latter would become the object of knowledge generated by the sacred texts. If not then the sacred texts would become purposeless.

The Advaitin faces this difficulty directly. No word can have any direct reference to Brahman. A word has a reference to its corresponding object on the basis of its connotation (*pravṛtti nimitta*). Connotation is intelligible only in respect of an object that has some characteristics. Since Brahman is devoid of all characteristics, words cannot have any direct reference to it. Nor is there any need for the manifestation of Brahman which is self-manifest. Nevertheless the teaching of the sacred texts is not futile. It has a negative value. It serves the purpose of removing the false notions about Reality. The words like 'Brahman', 'Self', etc., appearing in the Vedānta texts referring to Brahman do not also have a direct reference to Brahman but serve as *upalakṣaṇa* or qualification *per accidens* as in the case of the moon appearing through the tree branches (*śākhā candra*). The moon appearing through the branches of the tree does not affect the original moon but yet serves to identify it. Similarly, the words 'Self' and 'Brahman' have an indirect reference to the object of metaphysical investigation.[2]

Vedānta Deśika refutes the above theory. Reality is not without any characteristics as the Advaitin contends and hence it is not correct to argue that words do not function in respect of the *nirguṇa* Brahman in so far as the former do not have any primary import in respect of the latter.

[1] *S.D.*, Vāda 58.

See also Chapter III, Section IV for the criticism of the theory that consciousness is eternal.

[2] *S.D.*, Vāda 45.

Nor is it sound to argue that what is self-luminous does not require to be manifested by anything. As it has been shown already,[1] even that which is self-luminous can be the object of another knowledge. The contention that Reality is absolutely unknowable in the sense that it is not the content of any kind of knowledge involves a self-contradiction. If that were the case we cannot even speak of Reality. The Vedānta texts would all become purposeless. It cannot be said that they are useful in removing the false notions about Reality. How could that be possible without any reference to Reality? Even if the Vedānta texts are meant to bring into mind the nature of Reality, it would not follow that Brahman is *avedya*, in so far as the reference to Brahman is unavoidable.

The analogy of the moon in the tree-branches also does not hold good. For there is a relationship between the qualification *per accidens* and what is qualified by it.[2] The relation is one of manifested and the manifester or *bodhya* and *bodhaka*. This much is enough to prove the knowability of Reality by verbal testimony. It may be said that the reference is only indirect (*lakṣaṇa*) and not direct. Even then it would follow that Reality is knowable. Besides, a secondary implication is dependent upon the primary sense of the term. If knowability in the above sense is acceptable, why not accept it in the full sense of the term, asks Vedānta Deśika. It cannot be for the reason that the words denoting Reality do not have a connotation in view of the latter being devoid of all characteristics. For even the very svarūpa of the object can constitute the connotation of the word referring to it. Thus it is impossible to maintain that Brahman is *avedya* in the strict sense of the term.

According to the position taken up by the Advaitin the application of the term Brahman to the ultimate Reality is also unintelligible.[3] Has the term Brahman any primary import or not? If a term is devoid of primary import (*mukhya vṛtti*), then it must be considered to be ill-used or definitely fallacious from the linguistic standpoint. If a term is devoid of primary import, its subsequent operations are all arrested.

[1] See Chapter III, Section 3.

[2] *S.D.*, Vāda 45.

upalakṣya upalakṣaṇayor-api bodhya-bodhaka-
bhāva-lakṣaṇa samsparśasya sarvatra dustyajatvāt.
tāvataiva ca śabda-vedyatva siddheh.

[3] *S.D.*, Vāda 1.

If there is to be a secondary import or if there is to be an inferential development, these would be impossible as they necessarily have to be grounded on the primary import. It means language will cease to be the medium of communication. In the absence of the primary import, a secondary import is unimaginable.

If the term Brahman has a primary import, then it is asked whether the reference is in respect of something else or it is in respect of the content of philosophic enquiry.

The reference cannot be elsewhere as the connotation of the term Brahman does not apply to anything other than Brahman. Nor does the term apply to the object of enquiry, viz., Brahman. If it applies to Brahman, does it refer to the pure Brahman or the qualified Brahman? It cannot be the former as the connotation pointed out by the scriptural texts suggestive of the attributes *growing* and *causing to grow* is not applicable to what is believed to be eternal and devoid of attributes.[1] It cannot be argued that it is applicable since Brahman is the substratum and the root of all illusory manifestations, for these are not admitted in Brahman. If these be admitted, then the concept of final release would vanish into nothing as these would exist even in the state of release. It cannot be contended that the characteristics viz., *bṛhatva* and *bṛmhaṇatva* are meant as qualifications *per accidens*; for there would be no contradiction in understanding them as the attributes proper. The śruti text, "Therefore, it is called higher Brahman etc." (*tasmāt uchyate param brahma*) analysing the etymological meaning of Brahman refers to them as attributes; so does the smṛti text: "It is called Brahman because it grows and causes to grow".[2]

If the qualified Brahman is itself admitted to be the object principally referred to it involves an obvious contradiction of the Advaitin's position, if the qualities intended are the natural omniscience etc., declared by the śruti; if it is held that the pure Brahman qualified by avidyā is the primary import of the term, it is replied that this position is not sanctioned by any *pramāṇas* either perception, or inference or śrutis including smṛtis and the Vedānta-sūtras. Thus,

[1] *S.D.*, Vāda 1.

na hi nirviśeṣatāyā abhimate śuddhe bṛhati bṛmhayati-iti śrutyukta ṇimattam asti.

[2] Ibid.

bṛhatvāt bṛmhaṇatvāt ca tad-brahmeti abhidhīyate.

the author of the *Śri-bhāṣya* points out that the term Brahman refers in virtue of primary import to the supreme Lord free from all traces of blemish, full of countless excellent attributes.[1]

If Brahman is not an object of knowledge, even metaphysical enquiry in respect of it is impossible.[2] *Jijñāsa* or desire to know generally springs up when an object is understood in its generality i.e., in respect of general and superficial features and when its details or its specific features are yet to be understood (*sāmānyataḥ vedite viśeṣataśca veditavye*). In the absence of these, there will be no desire to know the object. The conditions that are necessary to bring about the quest will not be there, and there will be no specific reward or fruit either. The Advaitins do not admit that Brahman is susceptible of being the object of these two ways of knowing, a *prima facie* approach through the specific features.

Suppose it is argued that *Jijñāsa* is possible in respect of the qualified Brahman (*upahita brahma*) since that can be the object of the two approaches of knowledge. While it may be possible that an object of a lower degree of Reality may somehow be conceived as the cause of the *Jijñāsa*, it cannot be the final goal or the ultimate fruit, as the fruit anticipated would also be illusory. And since illusion is not a thing to be attained, an endeavour to attain an illusory goal is futile.

The Advaitin may contend that there is a general knowledge of the svarūpa of Brahman and the specific nature of Brahman as contradictory to *adhyāsa* is to be understood and as such enquiry can take place. This cannot be, argues Vedānta Deśika. One can speak of generic and specific provided a given entity is capable of that differentiation. But Brahman is devoid of all differentiations. Where there is no differentiation, the distinction between generic and specific cannot apply.

What then is the object of philosophic quest? If it be the tainted lower Brahman (*upahita brahma*), the quest would be a fruitless endeavour. Such a knowledge of tainted Brahman can never be admitted as an effective cure for the ills of mundane existence (*samsāra bheṣajam*). Nor can the Advaitins

[1] *Śrī-bhāṣya*, I. 1. 1. p. 2.
brahma śabdena svabhāvataḥ nirasta nikhila doṣaḥ
anavadhikātiśaya asamkhyeya kalyāṇaguṇa gaṇaḥ
puruṣottamaḥ abhidhīyate.

[2] See Vāda 2.
Jijñāsānupapatti vādaḥ.

hold that the pure Brahman may be the object of *Jijñāsa*, since by its very nature it is inaccessible to knowledge.

It may be said that although Brahman is not accessible to knowledge, yet it can be known just as the moon is identified through the tree-branches. This will not do. Unless it is admitted that Brahman and the moon are the objects of knowledge (derived from the *upalakṣaṇa*, viz., through knowledge and tree-branches respectively) the former (Brahman and the moon) cannot be taken as *upalakṣyas*. In other words, the analogy is inapplicable unless it is admitted that Brahman is an object of knowledge. If it be admitted to be the object of knowledge, then Brahman would become knowable and determinate.

## VI *Upabṛmhaṇas and Brahman*

It was shown in the previous sections that the scriptural texts in general do not support the theory of Brahman advocated by the Advaitin. We now come to the question whether smṛti texts and the Vedānta sūtras do teach such a doctrine. Vedānta Deśika examines this issue and comes to the conclusion that neither the smṛti texts nor the Vedānta sūtras are in consonance with the Advaitin's theory of Reality.

As to the smṛtis, Vedānta Deśika does not examine individually the meaning of the various smṛti texts that are quoted by the Advaitin in support of his theory for the obvious reason that Rāmānuja had already done this in his *Śrībhāṣya*.[1] He confines his attention to the general issue viz., whether smṛtis and purāṇas can be regarded as *upabṛmhaṇas* in the sense of being elucidation of the meaning of the scriptural texts in view of the position held by the Advaitin.

Vedānta Deśika argues that it is not possible to regard smṛtis and purāṇas as *upabṛmhaṇas* if Brahman is *nirviśeṣa*.

That Brahman is devoid of all determinations is taught by the scriptural texts themselves. If anything more than that is to be revealed or elucidated by smṛtis, then Brahman would become determinate. It may be pointed out that the nature of Brahman alone which has been known to some and unknown to others in the scripture is revealed in the smṛtis and purāṇas. In that case smṛtis and purāṇas would cease to be the auxiliaries to scripture (*anangatva prasangāt*). The smṛtis

[1] See the opening sentence of Vāda 48.

and purāṇas are regarded as *upabṛmhaṇas* in as much as they subserve the scripture in the form of either pointing out the specific nature of what has been obtained in the sruti or making clear what is vague. And the mere teaching of something independently would not secure for it the status of being the *upabṛmhaṇas.*[1]

The smṛtis and purāṇas cannot be considered as *upabṛmhaṇas* in the sense of the restatement of what is already said in the Vedas. For the term in question is not widely current in that sense. Besides, the restatement of what has already been said serves no definite purpose. Nor can it be understood in the sense of the description of something that has not been said already (*anukta vastvantara varṇanam*). For it would follow that even the different portions of the Vedas are the *upabṛmhaṇas* of each other in as much as they refer to different things.

Vedānta Deśika, therefore, argues that it is not possible to uphold *smṛtis* and *purāṇas* as *upabṛmhaṇas* unless it were admitted that Brahman taught in the scripture is endowed with infinite attributes and *vibhūtis*. The attributes and *vibhūtis* of Brahman which are not ordinarily known through scripture are revealed by *smṛtis* and *purāṇas* and as such the latter could rightly be called *upabṛmhaṇas* in the true sense of the term viz., manifestation or elucidation of what has already been said in scripture.[2]

## VII *Vedanta-Sūtras and Nirguṇa Brahman*

The discussion on the question whether the doctrine of Reality advocated by Advaita Vedānta is in consonance with the teachings of Vedānta-sūtras is rather elaborate. The various topics or *Adhikaraṇās* of Vedānta-sūtras bearing on Brahman are examined briefly and shown to be in direct conflict with Advaita.[3] We will only enumerate here the main points of the cirticisms without entering into a detailed discussion of the interpretation of the sūtrās by the two schools of Vedānta.

[1] See *Caṇḍamāruta* on Vāda 48

[2] *S.D.*, Vāda 48.
See also *Śrī-bhāṣya*, p. 63.

[3] See Vāda 66.
paramate sūtra svārasya bhanga vādaḥ.

Taking the first aphorism of Vedānta, "Then, therefore, the desire to know Brahman",[1] Vedānta Deśika points out that it is in direct conflict with the theory of *nirviśeṣa* Brahman. In the first instance, *Jijñāsā* or the desire to know is unintelligible in respect of Brahman which is pure consciousness, devoid of all characteristics, since it is not an object of knowledge (*jñāna-viṣaya*). Secondly, the application of the term Brahman to the object of enquiry is also untenable. Both these points have already been discussed fully in an earlier section.

The second aphorism of the Vedānta points out that Brahman is that from which the origin etc., of the universe proceeds.[2] This aphorism, Vedānta Deśika points out, is intended to define the nature of Brahman. The function of definition is to point out the essential characteristic (*asādhāraṇa dharma*) of the object. How would this be possible if Brahman is devoid of all characteristics? That definition in terms of the essential characteristic of the object is impossible in respect of *nirviśeṣa Brahman*. If it is said that Brahman is defined (negatively) through its accidental characteristics, even then Brahman would be *saviśeṣa* in so far as it is qualified *per accidens* by those characteristics.

The third aphorism says that scripture is the source of the knowledge of Brahman (*śāstra yonitvāt*). This does not hold good in respect of Brahman which is not the object of knowledge. If Brahman were admitted to be the object of knowledge, it would become a *dṛśya*.

The fourth aphorism referring to the harmony of the texts *samanvaya* does not also hold good in respect of *nirviśeṣa* Brahman. *Samanvaya* means right relation.[3] Relation necessarily presupposes difference, while Brahman is devoid of all difference.

The next topic of the *Vedānta Sūtras* known as *Īkṣatyadhikaraṇa*,[4] does not also favour the Advaitin's view. For the aphorism primarily indicates that Brahman is associated with

[1] *V.S.*, I. 1. 1.
athāto brahma jijñāsā.

[2] *V.S.*, I. 1. 2. janmādysya yataḥ.

[3] Cp. *Bhāmatī*, p. 149 (T.P.H. Edn.)
samyaganvayaḥ samanvayaḥ.

[4] This topic comprises the aphorisms I. 1. 5 to I. 1. 12 according to Rāmānuja and upto I. 1. 11 according to Śaṃkara.

the characteristic of *Īkṣaṇa* or thinking (*Īkṣaṇādi guṇa yogasya mukhyatayā abhidhānāt*).[1]

The same is the case with regard to the topic known as *Ānanda-mayādhi-karaṇa*[2] which points out that Brahman is blissful, for in the term 'Ānandamaya' the suffix *maya* is used in the sense of abundance (*prācuryārthe mayat prayogāt*).

The topics known as *Ākāśādhikaraṇa* and *Prāṇādhikaraṇa* mention *Ākāśa* and *Prāṇa* as the characteristic mark of Brahman (*linga*).[3] A characteristic mark is the essential attribute of the object. If Brahman is *nirviśeṣa*, what is its characteristic mark?

Similarly, the remaining two topics of the first pāda known as *Jyotiradhikaraṇa* and *Prāṇādhikaraṇa* also refer to what is *saviśeṣa*. The former topic points out that Brahman is light (*jyoti*) on account of the mention of the feet (*jyotiścaraṇābhidhānāt*).[4] The reference to *Caraṇa* or feet does not hold good in respect of Brahman which is *nirviśeṣa* in character. The latter topic refers to Brahman as prāṇa, on account of connection (*prāṇah tathānugamāt*).[5] It is ascertained that the sūtras refer to Brahman alone as the inner self (*Antaryāmin*) of Indra etc. This apparently implies that Brahman is *saviśeṣa* and not *nirviśesa* as the Advaitin holds.

Thus, the first pāda of the first Adhyāya is in favour of a qualified Brahman. As the sūtras of the remaining pādas have to be interpreted in conformity to the teachings of the first pāda, these too do not favour the Advaitin's theory of Brahman.

The second Adhyāya is meant to establish the teachings of the first Adhyāya on a sound basis by refuting the rival theories. Obviously its purport also must be the same as that of the first Adhyāya.

Coming to the third Adhyāya of the *Vedānta Sūtras*, Vedānta Deśika points out that the first two pādas known as

[1] *S.D.*, Vāda 66.
See also *Śrī-bhāṣya*, I. 1. 12, p. 166.

[2] See *V.S.* I. 1. 13 to I. 1. 20. (According to Rāmānuja).
I. 1. 12 to I. 1. 19. (According to Śamkara).

[3] See *V.S.* I. 1. 23 (According to Rāmānuja). Akāśaḥ tallingāt.
I. 1. 24 ata eva prāṇaḥ.

[4] *V.S.* I. 1. 25 according to Rāmānuja.
I. 1. 24 according to Śamkara.

[5] *V.S.* I. 1. 29 according to Rāmānuja.
I. 1. 28 according to Śamkara.

*Vairāgya-pāda* and *Ubhayalinga-pāda*, refer to the difference of the Individual selves (*Jīvas*) who are in bondage and the Lord who is the remover of bondage. This teaching is in direct opposition to *Advaita*.

The third pāda known as *Guṇopasamhāra-pāda* is also opposed to the theory of *nirguṇa* Brahman. For it discusses the question whether the Vidyās or the different forms of meditations on Brahman which the Vedānta texts enjoin are different or non-different in view of the infinite attributes possessed by Brahman. This question obviously implies that Brahman is *saviśeṣa* and not *nirviśeṣa*.

The last section of the third Adhyāya deals with the question of what is principal and subordinate to contemplation. This again implies difference only.

The last Adhyāya which is known as *Phalādhyāya* deals with the nature of the fruit or the ultimate goal of spiritual endeavour. The teaching of this Adhyāya does hardly fit in with the metaphysical position held by the Advaitin. The realization of a supreme end, the *summum bonum*, in the form of manifestation of its true nature in its full splendour (*sevenarupeṇa abhiniṣpattiḥ*), is intelligible only when it is held that the individual Jīvas, by worshipping the supreme Puruṣa (*Paramātman*) overcome the bondage and realize the said end, from whence there is no return, as the last *Vedānta-Sūtra* [1] expressly declares. Vedānta Deśika, therefore urges that the *Vedānta-sutras* in general do not in any way support the doctrine of the *nirguṇa* Brahman.

[1] anāvṛttiḥ śabdāt anāvṛttiḥ śabdāt.

## CHAPTER SIX

# THE NATURE OF THE UNIVERSE

THE theory of Reality as advocated by the Advaita Vedānta presents a problem which every monistic system has to face. If the Self or Brahman alone be real, how the plurality of the universe, which we perceive, is to be accounted for? This is the vexed problem of the one and the many—the hard rock on which most of the monistic systems break. A solution is offered to this problem in the Advaita system by maintaining the theory that the universe is illusory (*mithyā*). How far does this theory solve the problem is the question which is taken up for discussion in the present chapter.

### I *Dṛśyatva as the Proof of Illusoriness*

What is the ground on which the universe is characterised to be illusory? The Advaitin offers several arguments to prove the illusory character of the universe, the chief of which is the famous syllogism having for its probans cognisability (*dṛśyatva*). That is, the phenomenal world is regarded as illusory on the ground that it is presented to knowledge or objective in character (*dṛśya*). The argument is thus stated: "The universe under dispute is illusory, because it is cognised; whatever is cognised is illusory, like the shell-silver".[1] The inference is called *dṛśyatvānumāna*, because it establishes the probandum, *mithyātva* by means of the probans *dṛśyatva*.

[1] *S.D.*, Vāda 15.

vigītam mithyā, dṛśyatvāt, yadyadittham.
tat-tathā, yathā śuktirajatam-iti.

Cp. *Anandabodha's Nyāya Dipavali*, p. 1 (Chowkamba Edn.).
*Advaita Siddhi*, p. 31 (Nirnayasagara Edn.).

The theory of the phenomenality of the worldly existence is first propounded by the Vijñāna-vādins and the Mādhyamikas. This has been adopted by Gauḍapāda who establishes the illusory nature of the world of experience on four grounds: (1) it is similar to dream states, (2) it is presented, (3) the relations that organise it are unintelligble, and (4) it does not persist for all times. See *Indian Philosophy*, Vol. 2. p. 458. Except the first all the other views are examined by Deśika.

Vedānta Deśika subjects this syllogism to a critical examination. He first examines the meaning of the term *mithyā.* It is resolved into seven alternatives keeping in view the different interpretations of the Advaitins: (1) unreality (*tucchatva*), (2) being the content of apprehension otherwise (*anyathā-khyāti viṣayatvam*), (3) being different from the real as well as the unreal (*sadasad-vilakṣaṇatvam*), (4) being the counter-correlate of the negation of what is found in a particular locus (*pratipanna-upādhau niṣedha pratiyogitvam*), (5) being cognised in the same locus as its own absolute non-existence (*svātyantā-bhāva samānādhi-karaṇatayā pratīya-mānatvam*), (6) being different from the real Brahman (*satyabrahma vilakṣaṇatvam*), (7) something else (*anyadeva kiñcit*).[1]

The first two alternatives are not of importance as the Advaitin himself does not admit them. By illusoriness he does not mean either that which is totally unreal (*tuccha*) or that which is the content of apprehension otherwise.

The third alternative is of some significance. The term *mithyā* is understood in the sense of that which is neither real nor unreal but different from both. That is, the universe is illusory in the sense that it cannot be characterised either as real or as unreal. Real is that which is not sublated at any time. But the universe is sublated by the Brahman-knowledge, and therefore, it is not real. Nor is it unreal because what is unreal is never cognised while the universe is cognised. It cannot be both real and unreal because of contradiction. It is, therefore, something different from the real as well as the unreal.[2] In other words, it is indeterminable (*anirvacanīya*). This is the meaning of the term *mithyātva* or illusoriness.

This argument is untenable, contends Vedānta Deśika since for a non-advaitin *sadasad-vilakṣaṇatva* is a non-established qualification (*aprasiddha viśeṣaṇa*). That is, there is no such entity which is neither real nor unreal but something different from both. A thing must be either real or unreal and to say

[1] All these alternatives except the last one have been stated by Citsukha in his *Tattvapradīpikā* as a pūrvapakṣa. See *Tattvapradīpikā* (2nd Edn.), pp. 32-3.

[2] *Iṣṭasiddhi*, page 47.

sattve na bhrānti bādhaustām nā-sattve khyāti bādhakau; sadasadbhyām anirvācyā-'vidyā vedyaissaha bhramāḥ.

that it is different from both is a self-contradiction. There is no middle ground between the real and the unreal.[1]

Illusoriness may be understood as that which is negated even where it is found to exist. This is termed as *bādhyatva* or being sublated. The silver, which appears to be present in the shell is negated by the later cognition in the form, 'this is not silver'. The shell-silver is thus the counter-correlate of the negation of what is found to exist in shell. It is, in other words, sublated by the cognition, 'This is not silver'. It is, therefore, regarded as illusory. Similarly, the world-appearance is also negated by the Brahman-knowledge and hence it is illusory.[2]

Vedānta Deśika controverts this argument. He asks whether *bādhyatva* which is the meaning of *mithyātva* is sublated or not. In other words, is the illusoriness of the universe illusory or not? If it be illusory, it would follow that the world is real,[3] a position which is acceptable to the Viśiṣṭādvaitin. Thus the inference would suffer from the fallacy of the establishment of what is already established (*siddha-sādhanatva*). If, on the other hand, the illusoriness of the world were not illusory then it is asked whether it is Brahman or different from Brahman. If it be the former, then the position would come nearer to that of the Viśiṣṭādvaitin in so far as he maintains that the world is organically related to Brahman. If it be the latter, then in respect of this probandum only the probans in the syllogism would become inconclusive (*anaikāntyam*). In a syllogistic argument, if the probans be present in a thing where that what is sought to be established (*sādhya*) is absent, then it would not be conclusive. The probans in the present inference is *dṛśyatva*; this must be invariably co-existent with illusoriness (*mithyātva*) which is the probandum of the present syllogism. But according to the present alternative *mithyātva* means *abādhita bādhyatva* i.e., *bādhyatva* which is real; if this be established by the probans *dṛśyatvāt*, the latter, in so far as it is present in that where *sādhya* is absent, would become inconclusive.[4]

[1] *S.D.*, Vāda 60.

The Advaitins do not admit that the real and the unreal are contradictories. They are contraries and as such *sadasad-vilakṣaṇatva* is held to be logically tenable.

[2] *S.D.*, Vāda 15.

[3] For a reply to this objection see *Advaita Siddhi*, pp. 210-3.

[4] *S.D.*, Vāda 15.

Illusoriness of the universe may mean the appearance of the universe in the same locus where it does not exist at all (*svā-tyantābhāva śamānādhikaraṇatayā pratīyamānatvam*).[1] The shell-silver, for instance, does not exist in the shell but yet it appears there. It is, in other words, cognised in the same locus as its own absolute non-existence. Similarly, the universe does not exist in Brahman but it appears there in so far as it is superimposed on Brahman. In this sense it is illusory.

Against this argument Vedānta Deśika urges whether it is possible to prove the absolute non-existence of the universe in Brahman. The non-existence of the universe in the place, where it appears cannot be understood by perception. If there is no perception of it the inference, which is based on perception, is also not possible. Nor can it be proved on the strength of the scriptural texts. As it will be shown later, the purport of the scriptural texts is different from what the Advaitin means.[2]

The world may be understood to be illusory in the sense that it is different from the ultimate reality viz., Brahman (*satya brahma vilakṣaṇatvam*). This will not do, for the Viśiṣṭādvaitin also admits that the world is different from Brahman though it is inseparably related to it. Nevertheless, if it is argued that the world is illusory because it is different from reality, it is replied that it need not be so. For that which is real by its nature would not become unreal because it is different from another real entity. The pot, for instance, though it is different from another pot would not become a non-pot *aghaṭa*.[3]

It may be argued that it is evident from the scriptural texts that Brahman *alone* is real and the mere establishment of the world as different from it would prove its illusoriness. This argument does not hold good as it involves the fallacy of self-dependence (*ātmāśraya*). That is, on the strength of the scriptural text namely, Brahman *alone* is real, the illusoriness of the world is indicated; and on this ground it is further established that the world is other than Brahman.[4]

We now come to the last alternative viz., whether *mithyātva* means something else. Even this is not admissible, argues Vedānta Deśika. If *mithyātva* means something, it is asked whether or not that something can be affirmed of shell-silver

[1] This is the view of Citsukhi. See *Tattvapradīpikā*, p. 39.

[2] *S.D.*, Vāda 15. [3] Ibid. [4] Ibid.

and negated in respect of the silver found in the shop. In the latter sense *mithyātva* is a non-existent (*aprasiddha*). In the former sense, it stands in direct contradiction to perception.

The inference proving the illusoriness of the world stands sublated by perception in so far as the latter reveals to us that the world is real. Reality, Deśika point out, is that which is the object of the valid means of knowledge (*prāmāṇikatva*). Thus, Rāmānuja also defines that Reality is that which is capable of admitting an empirical usage (*vyavahāra yogyatā*). In other words, that which serves the purpose of practical life is real. In this sense the reality of the universe is evident to perception and the same is, therefore, undeniable. On this ground the inference proving the illusoriness of the universe stands sublated, just as the inference that establishes the coldness of fire is contradicted by the perception that apprehends the heat of the fire.

The probans *dṛśyatva* is also examined. What does *dṛśyatva* mean on the ground of which the universe is regarded to be illusory? Does it mean being the object of visual organ (*cākṣuṣatva*)? Or being the object of perceptual cognition? Or being merely the object of cognition? Or being different from consciousness? Or something else?

In none of the above senses does the probans in question establish the illusoriness of the universe. Taking the first alternative, there are many things which are not visible to the visual organs and yet they may be real. For the same reason the second alternative is also untenable. By adding the qualification ' perceptual ' the defect obtaining in respect of the first alternative is not overcome.

As regards the third alternative viz., being the object of cognition, it is pointed out that the probans is inconclusive. If something is illusory merely because it is the object of cognition, then Brahman also would become illusory in so far as it is the object of knowledge in some sense or other. It cannot be argued that Brahman is not the object of knowledge. For the scriptural texts and the Vedānta aphorisms indicate that Brahman is the object of knowledge. It may be said that the cognisedness of Brahman is only empirical and is not absolutely real. This is inadmissible since the cognisedness accepted in respect of the universe is also empirical and not real. As has been discussed in an earlier chapter Brahman should be admitted to be the object of knowledge in some form or other; otherwise it would involve a self-contradiction.[1]

The fourth alternative is also untenable. If *dṛśyatva* means being different from consciousness or Brahman, it is asked whether this difference is real or illusory. The Advaitin does not admit the difference to be real. It, therefore, follows that difference is illusory. Even according to the Advaitin there is an illusory difference of the world from Brahman and as such the probans is inconclusive.

We may therefore draw the conclusion that the syllogistic argument in question does not establish the theory that the world is illusory.[2]

## II *Vyāvartamānatva as the Proof of Illusoriness*

The problem may be looked at from a different point of view. Reality is that which is constant in entities that change. In other words, what is real must be unchangeable. Judged from this standpoint the objects of our experience cannot be regarded as real. They come and go; they are constantly changing. They are, therefore, illusory.

The same argument is expressed in the form of a syllogism. Pot and similar things are illusory because they are changing (*vyāvartamānatvāt*); whatever are changing are illusory as are the snake, a cleft in the ground, the water-course etc., which have for their substrate the rope. On the contrary, that which is real is unchangeable just as the rope that is the substrate of the snake etc., or like Brahman which is the substrate of everything in the universe. If that which does not persist were real then it would not be possible to make a distinction between the real and the illusory.[3]

Vedānta Deśika examines the soundness of the inference. What is meant by *vyāvartamānatva*? Does it mean (1) difference from something or other? or non-existence in some place

[1] See Chapter V.

[2] The dṛśyatvānumāna-bhanga-vāda in which the arguments given above are based is incomplete and hence the discussion on this topic is not comprehensive. Thus, for instance, the illustration given in the syllogism is not proved to be faulty.

[3] *S.D.*, Vāda 16.

ghatādayaḥ aparamārthāḥ; vyāvartamānatvāt;
yadukta sādhanam tadukta sādhyam, yathā rajvādy-
adhiṣṭāna sarpa-bhūdalana-ambudhārādi.

or other? (3) or having destruction, (4) or being sublated, (5) or being manifested in some place at sometime?

The term *vyāvartamānatva* does not mean mere difference from something or other. If this be the meaning of the term, the probans would be inconclusive in respect of Brahman in so far as it is different from the sphere of *thou* (*yuṣmad-artha*). The Advaitin himself admits the difference of the subject or the self which is the reality for him from the non-self.[1]

If the difference of the self from the non-self were illusory then it would follow that in reality they are identical. If Brahman be identical with the illusory world, Brahman itself would be illusory or the world would become real in so far as it is identical with the real Brahman.[2]

Nor can change be understood in the sense of non-existence in some place or other. The absence of a thing in a particular place cannot be the determinant of illusoriness. The shell-silver is considered illusory not because it does not exist in some other place; on the contrary, it is illusory because it does not exist in that place where it appears to exist. Otherwise Brahman itself would be subject to change because it does not exist as unreal or as an entity different from both being and non-being.

The third alternative is also untenable, because the probans understood in the present sense becomes completely divorced from the illustration mentioned in the syllogism. No one would say that the snake superimposed on the rope is destroyed. The terms *vināśa* and *bādha* have different connotations. Destruction is the dissolution of an entity, whereas sublation or *bādha* is the negation of what was cognised as not this.[3] Only when a real snake is killed by a stick, it is considered to be destroyed. If on the contrary, the illusion of snake in the rope is removed, we say it is sublated.

Nor can change be understood in the sense of that which is the counter-correlate of the negation of what is found in a particular locus. For the probans in this sense is

[1] See the opening sentence of Śamkara's *Sūtra-bhāṣya*.

[2] For the Advaitin the world is identical with Brahman as it is nothing apart from Brahman.

See *S.B.*, II. 1. 14.
ananyatvam vyatirekeṇa bhavati.

[3] *S.D.*, Vāda 16.
pratipannasya neti niṣedho bādhaḥ; vināśastu labdha sattākasya svarūpa pracyutiḥ.

non-established. We do not say that the pot does not exist in its place where it appears to exist. Just as there is the sublation of the shell-silver in the form 'This is not silver,' there is no negation of a pot in the form 'This is not a pot'.

It may be argued that 'being' or *sat* alone which is recurrent in everything is manifested as the substrate of every object. Thus, in the judgment 'cloth is there', if cloth is affirmed, the pot which is different from it becomes negated and as such the pot is illusory. Against this argument Vedānta Deśika urges that *sat* or *being* is not the ground or the locus of cloth and similar things. Nor does it recur in them. Thus, for instance, in the cognitions 'pot exists', 'cloth exists' etc., *sattva* or existence is apprehended as the very attribute of the pot and similar things, and not as their substrate. Just as in the usages 'pot moves', 'cloth moves' and 'pot is big', 'cloth is big', motion and magnitude are considered to be their activity and attribute respectively, in the same way 'being' or existence also constitutes the attribute of the objects.

There is yet another view of change viz., manifestation of a thing in some place at some time. Even this view is inadmissible since it cannot be the determinant of illusoriness. In fact, the manifestation of a thing in some place at some time would establish its reality. The non-manifestation of a thing at other times is due to the absence of the accessories that cause its cognition. If non-manifestation at any particular time be regarded as the criterion of illusoriness, then Brahman also would be illusory since it is not manifest to us owing to *avidyā* until the time of release.

The negative concomitance viz., 'that which is not illusory does not vary' is also untenable. Brahman is not illusory but nevertheless it varies in the sense that it is other than everything. Vedānta Deśika, therefore, concludes that it is not possible to establish the illusoriness of the universe on the basis of the inference having for its probans *vyāvartamānatva*.[1]

### III *Subject-Object Relation*

Besides inferences there are other arguments which are advanced to prove the theory that the universe is illusory. One of these and the most important one, is the subject-object

[1] *S.D.*, Vāda 16.

relation (*dṛk-dṛśya sambandha*). The so-called object itself is unintelligible. Much less is its relation to the consciousness or the *dṛk*. The arguments put forth in support of this contention are mainly two. The first one, which is epistemological, consists in that the concept of relation when subjected to logical scrutiny does not stand. Even granting that it is intelligible it is hardly possible to understand the nature of the relationship between the subject and the object. The second argument, which is metaphysical in character,,is based on the dictum of the unity of consciousness. The unity of consciousness implies that there can be no relation whatever between consciousness and something beside it.

As regards the unintelligibility of the concept of relation it is argued as follows. Relation necessarily involves relata. Without the relata relation is hardly conceivable. How does this relation stand to the relata. If it is nothing to the relata, then they are not related to the terms. But here we are condemned to an infinite regress since we are forced to go on finding new relations endlessly.[1] Thus, in the words of Bradley, " If we take the connection as a solid thing, we have got to show, and we cannot show, how the other solids are joined".[2]

Even granting that the concept of relation is intelligible, it is hardly possible to understand its nature. What is the nature of the relation of the subject to the object? It cannot be an external relation as the subject is not a corporeal thing. Nor can it be an internal relation. For consciousness, which is an essential property of the subject, cannot be inherent in the object. Nor can the object be inherent in consciousness since it is external to it and it appears as opposed to its nature. Nor is a relation of identity possible in as much as the two are opposed to each other and an identity between them is absurd.[3]

There are various other theories to account for the subject-object relation. These theories which mainly come from the camp of the realists account for knowledge by relating consciousness with the object by way of representation (*sārūpya*),

[1] *S.D.*, Vāda 17.

[2] *Appearance and Reality* , p. 28 (2nd Edn.).

[3] *S.D.*, Vāda 17.

Cp. *Nyāyadīpāvali*, p. 3.

The arguments given in this work are substantially the same as found in the *Śatadūṣanī*.

parallelism, causation, or a unique relation called *svarūpa sambandha*. " The insuperable difficulty in all such attempted relations between consciousness and the object is that the one or the other end of the relation is unknown and unknowable. For consciousness has in that case to perform two functions at once; it has to appear as one of the terms related and as that which is conscious of the relation. It has to assume two positions at once and this is an impossible feat. Consciousness is nothing if not all-comprehensive and universal ".[1] The object cannot be placed on an equal footing with consciousness in which case the latter would be no better than an object. It is the unique nature of consciousness not to be related to anything outside it. Thus, the relationship between the subject and the object being unintelligible, it follows that both of them cannot be equally real. Of the two, subject and object, the reality of the former is undeniable as it is self-evident, while that of the latter is doubtful in so far as its existence is dependent on consciousness or the subject. Obviously the object is illusory while the subject which is pure consciousness is real.

Vedānta Deśika subjects the above arguments to a critical examination. Even if no relationship is possible between two things, it does not follow that the relata are illusory. Thus, for instance, there is no relationship between the hare and the horns or between Meru and Mandra, the mythological mountains but nevertheless the relata in question are real. If the relata are held to be illusory on the ground that their relation is unintelligible, then both the subject and the object should be admitted to be illusory. There is no justification for holding that only one of the relata is real and the other is illusory.

Against this contention the Advaitin will no doubt urge that consciousness or the subject is not illusory because it is self-evident while the object is not so since it is dependent for its existence on consciousness. Vedānta Deśika controverts this argument by showing that on the ground of self-luminosity or the self-proof of consciousness it is not possible to demonstrate the illusory character of the object. What is the basis on which the Advaitin claims that consciousness is self-luminous, and the pot etc., are not self-luminous? The reply is that consciousness does not require another consciousness

[1] T. R. V. Murthy's article in the *Indian Philosophical Quarterly*.

in respect of its manifestations, while the object is not so as it is dependent on consciousness for its revelation. If this be the position of the Advaitin, then he must admit, Vedānta Deśika contends, that the object is related to the consciousness. If this relationship were not admitted, then it would follow that object is not dependent on consciousness for its manifestation and in view of that it would be possible to say that object too is self-evident like consciousness. Hence, it must be admitted that the object is related to consciousness. If it be admitted, then it is absurd to deny the relationship between the subject and the object. The point is that unless it be admitted that object is real and is related to consciousness it would not be possible to establish that consciousness alone is self-luminous and objects are not self-luminous. If the object were illusory, because of the unintelligibility of the relation of the consciousness to the object, then on the same ground consciousness too would become illusory. As regards the contention that consciousness, if it be related to an object, would cease to be self-luminous, it is pointed out that such a meaning of self-luminosity as not being an object of another cognition (*avedya*) is untenable. As has been discussed in an earlier chapter,[1] consciousness even though it be self-luminous can be an object of another consciousness. On such a view the relation of consciousness to another object is not at all unintelligible.[2]

What then is the relation of consciousness or subject to the object? If the name of the *sambandha* is asked, it may be designated as *viṣaya-viṣayi-bhāva-sambandha* or subject-object-relation. If a definition of it is required, it is defined as that which makes the empirical usage about knowledge being related to an object (*jñānagata vyavahāra janakatva yogyatā*). If something is evident to our experience it cannot be denied even if it cannot be specifically defined. The difference in the taste of sugar-cane juice and that of milk cannot be defined in words but all the same it is undeniable in as much as it is evident to one's own experience. The same explanation holds good in respect of subject-object relation.

The contention that the concept of relation is not logically intelligible is also untenable. The entire dialectic on the concept of relation is based upon a wrong theory of relation. A relation which relates the two relata does not require

[1] See chapter III, Section 3. [2] *S.D.*, Vāda 17.

another relation for relating itself to the relata. It can, on the contrary, relate the terms without depending on any other relation for the purpose. The point would be clear if we keep in mind the proper meaning of the term *relation*. A relation is that which brings about the empirical usage viz., that two terms or objects in question are related (*vastunor-viśiṣṭavyavahāra-janana svabhāvatvam*). While the relation that obtains in respect of the two relata could give rise to the judgment viz., the relata in question are related, it is rather superfluous to postulate another relation in order to account for the relation in question. A relation, like consciousness, is capable of accounting for itself as well as another relation. If a relation itself were held to be both of the nature of relation as well as of the relata, then it would involve a self-contradiction. Such a view is not admitted by the Viśiṣṭād-vaitin. What he holds is that wherever the objects themselves are found to be capable of giving rise to the judgment that the objects are related, there the very objects constitute the relation in as much as it brings about the judgment of relation. Wherever the relation itself is evident as in the case of *samyoga*, *samavāya*, *viṣayi-viṣayabhāva-sambandha*, there is no need of any relation other than what is admitted. The concept of relation is therefore not unintelligible and it is wrong to hold on that account that the objects are illusory.[1]

## IV *Material Causality of Brahman*

That the universe is illusory is also proved on the basis of the theory of the material causality of Brahman. The Upaniṣads say that Brahman is the material cause of the universe. This material causality of Brahman, the Advaitin contends, would be intelligible if only the universe is regarded as illusory.

The material causality of Brahman may be understood in three ways (1) Brahman itself transforms into the universe just as a lump of clay undergoes the transformation into pot etc. This is the view of *yādava prakāśa* known as *Brahma-pariṇāma vāda*. (2) Brahman associated with *cit* and *acit* in their subtle form (*sūkṣma cid-acid-viśiṣṭa*) is the material cause of the universe. This is the view of the Viśiṣṭādvaitins. (3) Brahman is the basis of the illusory appearance of the

[1] *S.D.*, Vāda 17.

universe. This is the view of the Advaitins, known as the *Vivarta-vāda*. The Advaitins reject the first two views and uphold the last one as the only possible explanation of the material causality of Brahman.[1]

The view held by *yādava prakāśa* is untenable because it would conflict with the scriptural texts that declare that Brahman is immutable. That is, Brahman which is immutable in character cannot undergo any transformation. It cannot be said that one part of Brahman transforms while the other part remains immutable or that at a particular time it is subject to transformation while at other times it is immutable, since Brahman is admitted to be partless and not to be delimited by time.[2]

To overcome these difficulties it is held that Brahman associated with *cit* and *acit* or spirit and matter in their subtle form (*sūkṣma cid-acid-viśiṣṭa-brahma*) is the material cause of the universe. According to this view what actually transforms is *acit* or matter while Brahman which is the basis of the matter remains unaffected by the change. If this be the position, the Advaitin contends, material causality would apply only to matter and not to Brahman. In other words, it is not Brahman but matter that would be the material cause. To avoid this difficulty if it be said that Brahman along with *cit* and *acit* is the material cause, then Brahman would become subjected to change. Further, if the universe, the effect, is brought forth by the combination of the *cit*, *acit* and *Īśvara*, then in all the effects these three elements should be present, just as in the piece of cloth produced by white, black and red threads all the three colours are found together. To cite another illustration, a piece of wood lying in the salt mine contains in it predominantly the salt element. In the same way, if the universe be the product of Brahman the nature of Brahman should also be predominant in the objects of the universe. But this is not the case. Hence, Brahman as qualified by *cit* and *acit* cannot be admitted as the material cause.

The analogy of the clay and the pot offered in the Upaniṣads to explain the material causality indicates that the *svarūpa* of an object alone can constitute the material cause.

[1] See *Saṃkṣepa-śārīraka*, II, 61.
vivarta vādasya hi pūrvabhūmiḥ vedānta vade pariṇāmavādaḥ.

[2] *S.D.*, Vāda 53.

But the scriptural text, on the other hand, points out that Brahman is immutable. The only way of reconciling the two texts is to admit that the universe is an illusory manifestation of Brahman. In other words, Brahman itself appears as the universe. This is explained on the analogy of the rope appearing as the snake. The rope does not transform itself into a snake. On the contrary, it only appears as a snake due to *ajñāna*. The rope is regarded as the cause of the appearance of the snake in so far as it is the basis or substrate of the illusory snake. In the same way, Brahman which is the basis or the substrate of the world-appearance is said to be the material cause of the universe. Such a view accounts for the material causality of Brahman in conformity with the illustration cited in the Upaniṣads, without at the same time contradicting the scriptural text referring to the immutable nature of Brahman.[1]

Vedānta Deśika examines the above theory in detail and attempts to defend the Viśiṣṭādvaitic view that Brahman as qualified by the individual selves and matter in their subtle form is the material cause of the universe. It is no doubt true that if Brahman as qualified by *cit* and *acit* be the material cause, causality would pertain to the latter. Nevertheless Brahman can be regarded as the material cause in so far as it is the basis of that which undergoes change (*vikārā-śraya*). While the matter is the substrate of change directly, Brahman is the substrate of it only indirectly, that is, through matter. Such a position is held by the Advaitin too. *Māyā* for the Advaitin is the direct substrate of the illusory manifestation of the universe and yet Brahman is said to have the illusory manifestations since it is the basis or locus of *māyā*. Likewise though the transformation mainly belongs to the matter (which according to the Viṣiṣṭādvaitin is the body of Brahman), yet it is possible to say that Brahman transforms it as much as in the *ādhāra* or basis of matter. On such a view Brahman would not be subject to any change. This is illustrated by the analogy of a boy growing into a youth and a youth attaining manhood. In the above instance, the different states such as youth, manhood etc., indicating the changes actually belong to the body, and the self which is the basis of the body is in no way affected by them. Nevertheless in such a usage as the boy grows into a

[1] *S.D.*, Vāda 53.

youth, the terms youth etc., are used to include the self as the latter is the basis of body. Vedānta Desika points out that the causality of Brahman also should be understood in the same sense. The different states involving changes do belong to Brahman and yet the immutable character of Brahman remains unaffected. *Avasthā* or a state is a characteristic which is accidental (*āgantuka*) and which is inseparably related to that which is the substrate of it. Accordingly there is no defect whatsoever in admitting the different states in respect of Brahman. A characteristic that is only accidental does not affect the true nature of that to which it belongs. The states of boyhood and youth are not the permanent characteristics of the self; they are only accidental in the sense that they are passing states. Hence even if they belong to the self, the true character of the self is not affected in any way.[1]

Nor is it necessary that if an effect is produced by a combination of certain factors, that the qualities present in the causal factors should also be present in the effect. When a boy grows up into a youth, the characteristics found exclusively in the body as well as the self do not come together. Nor in the case of the cloth made out of the white, black and red threads, there is an admixture of those qualities. As in the divided states, even in the combined state, the whiteness, blackness etc., pertain severally only to those threads of the concerned colours.

Vedānta Deśika further proceeds to show that the explanation offered by the Viśiṣṭādvaitin about the material causality of Brahman has the full support of the scriptural texts. The scriptural text referring to the causality runs thus: *tad-dhe-dam tarhi avyākṛtam-āsit tannāmarūpābhyām vyākriyate.*[2]

In this text does the word *avyākṛtam* refer to the pure Brahman or to the *viśiṣṭa* Brahman? Obviously the reference is not to the pure Brahman because the word *avyākṛta* is not current in respect of Brahman in the same way in which the term 'Brahman' itself is. That it does not refer to pure Brahman is also evident from the meaning of the subsequent words viz., *nāmarūpābhyām vyākriyate*. Apparently what is meant here is that the entity denoted by the word *idam* is devoid of manifestation in the form of name and form in the

[1] *S.D.*, Vāda 53. [2] *Brah. Up.*, I. 4. 7.

state of dissolution. What then is the meaning of *idam*? This term, Deśika points out, refers to the spirit and matter (*cit* and *acit*) as it is evident from experience. The first part of the text would, therefore, mean that *cit* and *acit* when they assume the subtle form, are said to be devoid of change or transformation in the form of whole and parts. Hence, it follows that even in the state of dissolution the individual selves and matter do exist in their subtle form. How does it follow from this that Brahman as associated with the subtle matter and spirit exists in the state of dissolution? This is established on the strength of the other scriptural texts referring to the causality of Brahman. Thus, the text *tama ekī bhavati* suggests that *tamas* or matter assumes the subtle form in the state of dissolution. That the *tamas* is the body of Iśvara is evident from such texts as *yasya tamaḥ śarīram.* Again, there are scriptural texts referring to causality which clearly point out that Brahman exists even in the state of dissolution. Hence, it is ascertained that the word *avyākṛtam* in the text under consideration refers to Brahman qualified by the individual selves and matter in their subtle or unmanifest form. The analogy of the clay and the pot is given to illustrate that the qualified Brahman alone is the material cause. Hence, even though the terms *Brahman* or *Ātman* denote the *svarūpa* of Brahman as the material cause, these have to be understood to mean the *viśiṣṭa Brahman* as the material cause so that there may be no conflict with the text referring to the immutable character of Brahman.[1]

The Advaitin also admits Brahman exists during the state of dissolution as associated with the subtle *avidyā*. Thus in both the systems Brahman is the material cause only indirectly. Nevertheless the view of causality advocated by the Viśiṣṭādvaitin is sounder than that of the Advaitin in so far as the former maintains the reality of the universe in conformity to our perceptual experience. Besides, the Viśiṣṭādvaitin's theory does not conflict with the scriptural texts teaching that Brahman is immutable. Thus, if the material causality of Brahman is to be accounted for without conflicting with the scriptural text referring to the immutable character of Brahman, the only way left is to maintain that Brahman as associated with *cit* and *acit* in their unmanifest form is the material cause of the universe.

[1] *S.D.*, Vāda 53.

Vedānta Deśika sums up the position as follows: Material causality consists in the association of an entity with a different state (*avasthāntara-yogitvam*). The illustration of the clay and the pot is intelligible in that sense only. In the case of the appearance of the rope as the snake etc., the rope cannot actually be called the material cause since the different states of appearance do not really belong to the rope. Similarly, the supposition of Brahman as the cause of the superimposed universe is untenable as it is opposed to wordly experience and scriptural teaching. The theory of material causality of Brahman as advocated by Advaita Vedānta is unintelligible.[1] The Universe cannot, therefore, be regarded as illusory in order to account for the material causality of Brahman.

## V *Māyā as the Material Cause of the Universe*

Some Advaitins who do not subscribe to the view that Brahman is the material cause maintain that *māyā* is the material cause of the universe. This view is maintained on the strength of the Upaniṣadic text *māyāmtu prakṛtim vidyāt*. The meaning of this text according to the Advaitin is that *māyā* is the material cause, the word *prakṛti* being understood as material cause. The term *māyā* is current in the sense of illusoriness. Hence, it follows that the material cause of the Universe is illusory in character. If the cause be illusory then its effect also must be of the same nature. Accordingly, the Universe which is the product of *māyā* is also illusory.

Vedānta Deśika criticises the above view. He points out that the meaning of the text has been twisted to suit the theory of the Advaitin. If we take into consideration the context in which the Upaniṣadic text appears, it does not follow that either *māyā* is illusory or the world which is its product is illusory. In the text in question illusoriness is not attributed to *prakṛti*. On the contrary, *māyā* has been first stated and then it is asserted that it is *prakṛti*. In other

[1] *S.D.*, Vāda 53.

> **avasthāntara yogitvam upādānatvam-ucyate;**
> **mṛtpiṇḍa-ghata-dṛṣṭāntaḥ tatraiva-hy-upapadyate,**
> **sarpa-bhūrandhra mālādi rūpā-vasthāntarānvayaḥ;**
> **rajjau na vidyate tasmāt nopādānatvam-iṣyate.**
> **Ittham adhyasta viśvasya brahmopādāna bhāṣaṇam:**
> **lokaveda viruddhatvat svayameva nirudhyate.**

words, *Māyā* is the subject while *prakṛti* is the predicate and the latter is attributed to the former.

Let us take the whole context into consideration. The scriptural text preceding the one in question runs: *Asmātmāyī sṛjate viśvam etat tasmiścānyo māyayā sanniruddhaḥ.* In this passage both the terms *māyin* and *māyā* are used but their meaning is not pointed out. Obviously the subsequent text is intended to explain the meaning of these terms. Thus, it is stated "know *māyā* to be the *prakṛti* and the wielder of *māyā* (*māyin*) to be the supreme Lord".[1] Hence the word *māyā* refers to the *prakṛti* which is well known in the Upaniṣads as the material cause of the universe, while the word *māyin* means that supreme Lord who is the basis or *adhiṣṭāta* of *prakṛti* and the individual selves constituting the universe.[2]

Now it may be argued that if the term *māyā* refers to *prakṛti*, then it would follow that *prakṛti* is illusory in so far as the term *māyā* means what is illusory. This will not do, contends Deśika. Since it is not possible to establish conclusively that the term *māyā* in the present context means illusoriness, it is even possible to apply the term *māyā* to what is illusory in a figurative sense and as such it cannot be ascertained that *prakṛti* which is denoted by the term *māyā* is illusory in the strict sense of the term. Further, the word *māyā* does not mean an illusory thing. On the contrary, it means that which is an instrument or means of wonderful creation (*vicitra sṛṣṭyupakaraṇa*). The term *māyā* is not always used only in the sense of what is illusory. It is also widely current in the sense of what is real. Thus, in the following passage, "whatever dust particles were found on the earth, were counted by the *māyā* of devatas", the term *māyā* is used in the sense of that which is an instrument or means of counting. What serves as a means or an instrument of counting cannot be illusory. Considering the context as well as the etymology, it is only proper to say that *māyā* here means a specific type of knowledge.[3] There are many such instances where the term *māyā* is used in a sense other than that of being illusory.

Even granting that *māyā* is the material cause and that it is illusory, it need not follow that the effect too is illusory.

[1] *Svet. Up.*, 4. 10. [2] *S.D.*, Vāda 54.

[3] Ibid.

māyā vayunam jñānam-iti naighaṇṭukānusārāt
arthaucityāc-ca jñāna viṣayatvam-eva tatrocitam.

According to the principle set forth in the section called *vilakṣaṇādhikaraṇa*,[1] the effect could be of a different nature from its cause. Vedānta Deśika, therefore, urges that even though the material cause be illusory, the effect of it need not be illusory. As a matter of fact, the material cause is not illusory, but real. This has been proved already in the earlier section of this chapter. This is also established by the scriptural texts teaching *sadvidyā*.

## VI *The Theory of Causality*

We considered in the foregoing sections that the universe cannot be proved to be illusory on the basis of its material cause (*upādāna kāraṇa*). Now we come to another issue viz., whether the universe as a product or as an effect of something (*kārya*) can be regarded as real. The Advaitin points out that the universe as an effect is also illusory. The argument put forth by him in favour of this view is that all effects, whether established by scripture or by perception, are illusory because the concepts of cause and effect do not stand a logical examination (*sarvam kāryam mithyaiva vikalpāsahatvāt*). To prove that the causal relationship is logically untenable, the Advaitin adopts a dialectic. Vedānta Deśika subjects the dialectical arguments to a critical examination and establishes that the theory of causality is logically intelligible.[2]

The following is the Advaitin's dialectic on the theory of causality. What is an effect? Is the effect produced out of the cause related with it or unrelated? If the former, the cause and the effect being but two relata connected together by relation, there is no reason why the effect should be produced by the cause and not the cause by the effect. If the cause produces the effect without being related to it then anything might produce anything.

Further is the effect totally different from the cause or not? If totally different, then difference being common to all, objects which are different from one another would produce one another. If the effect be non-different from the cause, then there would be nothing to distinguish the effect from the cause. It may be argued that the cause is that which

[1] See *V.S.*, II. 1. 4.

[2] See Vāda 55. kāryānyathānupapatti-bhanga vādaḥ.

invariably exists prior to the effect, while the effect is that which invariably exists subsequent to the cause and as such there is a distinction between the two. If that be the case, how can it be said that the effect does not exist at the time prior to its non-existence?

Again, is the effect derived from a material cause which has undergone any transformation or from one that has not undergone any transformation? If it be the former then it is asked whether or not these transformations are produced from some other transformations. If this question is pursued further we are condemned to an infinite regress. If it be the latter, then the effect would abide all the time the material cause continues.

Further does the effect exist already in the cause or not? If it does not exist in the cause how can it be produced from it? What is blue can never be produced from what is yellow. If the effect exists already, then it cannot be considered to have been produced. It may be said that the effect which potentially existed in the cause is only made manifest by producing it. If that be the case, it is asked whether the manifestation does exist already or not? In either case old difficulties recur. If the manifestation is already manifest, then is that manifestation manifest or not? The issue would lead to an infinite regress. If it is always manifest, then it would follow that the effect too is always manifest.

Again, is the effect produced from a positive entity or from a negative entity? It cannot be either; for an effect, say, a pot cannot be produced from its cause, the lump of earth, without effecting some change in it. If a change is effected in it, it would no more be called a positive entity. On the other hand, if the effect is brought forth from a being which is not positive i.e., from what does not exist, then the effect would itself be unproduced. Thus, any attempt to understand the causal relation logically would involve a self-contradiction. Effects are, therefore, illusory and the universe too in so far as it is regarded as an effect, is illusory.[1]

Just as what is produced illusory, likewise what is subject to destruction (*nāśa*) is also illusory. That is, whatever is destructible is neither real nor unreal but something different

[1] *S.D.*, Vāda 55.

from both. The universe is non-eternal (*naśvara*) and hence is admitted to be illusory.[1]

Vedānta Deśika subjects the above arguments to critical examination. It was asked by the Advaitin whether the effect when it is produced is related to the cause or unrelated to it. Vedānta Deśika replies that the effect is unrelated to the cause; nevertheless it does not follow that all that is unrelated to the cause should be the effect, because mere unrelatedness itself does not cause the production of the effect. The special powers associated with the causal entities are responsible for the production of the particular effects.[2] This fact can be established by concomitance. That is, in the presence of special factors in the causal entities the effect is produced, while in their absence no effect is produced. If the relatedness of the cause to effect were a requisite factor (*anga*) to the production of the effect, then it would amount to the acceptance of what is not required (*anangāngikāraḥ*); or it would amount to the rejection of what is considered to be a requisite point for the explanation of causal relationship (*yuktāngatyāga*).

As regards the question whether the effect is different or non-different from the cause, it is replied that the effect is produced as different from the cause. The pot, for instance, is produced as different from the stick and the potter's wheel. If it be admitted that the effect is non-different from the cause, then it would amount to the rejection of what is an essential condition of causal relation. The relation of the cause to the effect is only based on their difference. If, therefore, it is held that the two are non-different, then it would result in the acceptance of what is not an essential condition to the causal relation or the rejection of what is an essential condition.

It is again asked by the Advaitin whether the effect is produced from the cause that undergoes modification or from that which does not? If by *vikāra* or modification is meant an association of an entity with any accidental characteristic (*āgantuka dharma*), then it is admitted that the effect is

[1] *S.D.*, Vāda 55.

naśvaratvācca jagataḥ mithyātvam nipuṇa dhiyām svadhyavasānamiti.

[2] Ibid.

tattad-vastūnām pratiniyata śaktīnām pratiniyata kāryārambhakatvasya anvayavyatireka siddhatvāt.

produced from a modified cause, for any change in the cause, even the proximity of an accessory condition, would be a modification. If modification is understood in the sense in which the effect is regarded as a modification, it is said that the effect is produced by an unmodified cause. It cannot be said that if an effect be produced from an unmodified cause any and every effect might spring from any and every unmodified cause, for an effect is produced from an unmodified cause subject to time factors and in relation to accessory factors.[1]

When a material cause passes into the state of an effect, there are certain parts of it which remain unchanged, even when that effect undergoes change into other objects called effects; and there are some characteristics which are found only in certain effects. Thus, when gold is changed into a bangle and the bangle into a necklace, the quality of gold continues to be the same both in the bangle and in the necklace, but the special form of the bangle does not pass into that of the necklace.

As regards the question whether the effect does exist or not in the cause, Vedānta Deśika answers that in the sense of a substance (*dravya*) the effect exists in the cause. On this ground it cannot be said that the effect is not something produced or effected (*sādhya*). For an effect is called so because of the new state assumed by the cause (*avasthāntarāpatti*). It is only in this sense that the Viśiṣṭādvaitin adopts *Satkāryavāda*. An effect in the sense of an effect-state (*karyāvastha*) does not exist in the cause. The objections that if the effect-state did not exist in the cause it could not be produced and that similarly anything could be produced from anything are untenable; for the effects are produced by specific powers which manifest themselves as effects subject to spatial and temporal conditions.

A question was also raised whether the effects are produced from a positive or a negative entity? What is the implication of this question, asks Vedānta Deśika. Does it mean whether the effects like pot etc., are produced from the substance that exists or from a substance that does not exist? Vedānta Deśika replies that the substance persists in the effects produced from a particular substance. Only the states and conditions change

[1] *S.D.*, Vāda 55.

avikṛtasyaiva sahakāricakra sannipātena
kālaviśeṣa niyata kāryārambha upapatteḥ.

when the effect is produced. For in the production of an effect there is change only in the causal state and not in the causal substance. There is thus an agreement between the cause and the effect only so far as the substance is concerned but not with reference to their actual states or form for it is by the negation of the causal state that the effect state arises.[1]

It is argued that an effect is illusory because it is neither permanently existing nor permanently non-existing. But this argument is untenable. The fact that an entity may be destroyed at a later moment does not mean that it was non-existent at the moment when it was perceived. Destruction only means that an entity which was existent at a particular moment was non-existent at another time. This is to be distinguished from *bādha* or sublation. *Bādha* means that a thing does not exist even when it is perceived.[2] Hence, non-existence is not destruction, for the prior non-existence would also be called destruction since it is also non-existent. Non-existence at a later point of time also does not mean destruction, for even chimerical entities would also be called destruction. The case of shell-silver is not an instance of destruction, for it is obviously a case of sublation. Thus, the concept of effect can never be regarded as illusory. An effect, even if it be subject to origination and destruction, does exist in its own time (*svakāle*) and as such it cannot be treated as illusory. The conclusion which can be drawn from this is that the universe even though it be an effect does not become on that account illusory.

[1] *S.D.*, Vāda 55.

[2] Ibid.

svakāle sata evārthasya svottarakālā-sattvam nāśaḥ;
bādhyatvam tu svapratītikālepi asatvalakṣaṇam.

CHAPTER SEVEN

# THE DOCTRINE OF AVIDYĀ

We discussed in the previous chapter the theory of the illusoriness of the universe. If the universe, as the Advaitin contends, is only an appearance, the question arises as to why there is an appearance? In other words, why does the one Absolute appear as many? The solution to this problem is sought in the doctrine of *avidyā*, the pivot of Advaita Vedānta. It is because of *avidyā* that Brahman appears as the manifold Universe.

What is *avidyā*? According to Advaita Vedānta, it is the name given to the cosmic principle which gives rise to the world-illusion. The same when subjectively considered stands for *ajñāna* or ignorance which is the cause of all illusions, (*bhramopādāna*). It is not a mere absence of knowledge but a positive entity (*bhāva-rūpa*) and beginningless (*anādi*) but removed by right knowledge.[1] Just as the nature of the world of common experience is *anirvacanīya*, likewise its source too viz., *avidyā*, is *anirvacanīya* because its character cannot be defined either as *sat* or *asat*.[2]

Does this theory satisfactorily solve the problem? According to the critics of Advaita, it does not. It explains away the problem instead of giving any satisfactory account of the universe. The critics, therefore, have subjected the doctrine to a severe criticism. In fact, no other doctrine has been so vehemently attacked as that of *avidyā*. In the first place, its very nature (*svarūpa*) is shown to be riddled with contradictions. Secondly, its description as something inexplicable (*anirvacanīya*) is held to be untenable. Thirdly, it is argued that the theory is not supported by any of the pramāṇas. Fourthly, it is pointed out that neither Brahman nor the individual self can be its locus (*āśraya*). Fifthly, its function as obscuring the true nature of Brahman (*tirodhāna*) is proved

[1] See Citsukhi's *Tattva-pradīpika*, p. 57
"anādi bhāvarūpam yad-vijñānena vilīyate;
tad-ajñānam-iti prājñāḥ lakṣaṇam sampracakṣate".

[2] See *Iṣṭasiddhi*, p. 47.

to be unintelligible. Sixthly, it is contended that the removal of *avidyā* by right knowledge (*nivartaka*) is untenable. Finally, the very conception of the cessation of *avidyā* (*avidyā-nivṛtti*) is held to be a riddle. This is the seven-fold criticism (*saptavidhā-nupapattiḥ*) levelled against the Advaitin's doctrine of *avidyā* by Rāmānuja.[1] Vedānta Deśika adopts these criticisms and elaborates them further in his *Śatadūṣani*, devoting a separate *vāda* for each of these issues.[2] An exposition of the salient points of these criticisms is given in this chapter.

## I *Is Ajñāna a Positive Entity?*

The issue whether or not *ajñāna* is a positive entity is first taken up for consideration. The Advaitin maintains that it is a positive entity (*bhāva-rūpa*). The implication of it is that *ajñāna* is not a mere absence of knowledge, a negative concept, as the Viśiṣṭādvaitins hold, but it is a state preceding but terminated by right knowledge.[3] This theory is sought to be established by means of perception, inference and scripture.

That perception establishes the positive nature of *ajñāna* is shown by the fact that it is impossible to have perceptual knowledge of the mere absence of knowledge, as the two are contradictory. We have perceptual experience in the form, 'I do not know', 'I do not know either myself or others'. Apparently this is an experience of *ajñāna*. Now the question is whether the *ajñāna* referred to here is of a positive nature or of a negative character. In other words, is the *ajñāna* referred to here a positive idea or a mere absence of knowledge? The Advaitin's contention is that the perceptual cognition in question does not refer to the mere absence of knowledge but indicates a positive concept. The argument adduced in support of this contention is that knowledge itself cannot know its absence in so far as the two are

[1] *Śrī-bhāṣya*, I. 1. 1. pp. 73-107. (Ananda Press Edn.)

[2] These have been discussed in the following Vādas:

| | |
|---|---|
| brahmāśrayā-jñāna nirāsa vādaḥ | (Vāda 19) |
| tirodhānā-nupapatti vādaḥ | (Vāda 35) |
| bhāvarūpā-jñāna bhanga vādaḥ | (Vāda 39) |
| jivā-jñāna bhanga vādaḥ | (Vāda 40) |
| avidyā-svarūpā-nupapatti vādaḥ | (Vāda 41) |
| māyā-vidyā vibhāga bhanga vādaḥ | (Vāda 42) |
| nivartakānupapatti vādaḥ | (Vāda 43) |
| nivṛttyanupapatti vādaḥ | (Vāda 44) |

[3] Cp. Bergson's idea of nothing. See *Creative Evolution*, pp. 289-313.

incompatible. That is, to know its absence, the knowledge itself will have to be first known. If the knowledge of the object whose absence is to be preceived is brought within consciousness, how can at the same time its absence too be asserted?

It cannot be said that the cognition of the non-existence of knowledge is known through a pramāṇa other than perception. For in the judgment, 'I do not know myself as well as others', *ajñāna* is known to be present at the time of cognition. If the individual is questioned whether he knows, he would reply, 'I do not know'. Hence, the knowledge generated by other pramāṇas is opposed to the non-existence of knowledge. Even that very knowledge about the non-existence of knowledge militates against the non-existence of all knowledge.

This difficulty does not arise if *ajñāna* is considered as a positive entity. What is positive in character can be known by its own nature, that is, without the knowledge of the counter-correlate. It is only a negative entity that presupposes the knowledge of the counter-correlate but not that which is positive as it could be described by its very nature (*svarūpeṇa*). In fact, there is the cognition of *ajñāna* in its positive form in such judgments as 'I am ignorant', 'I am foolish'. Hence even in the judgment 'I do not know anything', what is referred to is *ajñāna* which is positive in character and not the mere absence of knowledge whose cognition is impossible.[1]

That nescience is a positive entity can also be proved by inference. The inference is thus stated, "All knowledge established by one of the *pramāṇās* (which is held in dispute) is preceded by something else which is different from the prior non-existence of knowledge, which obscures the object of knowledge and which exists in the same place as knowledge; because knowledge possesses the property of manifesting things not illuminated before, just as the light of a lamp lit in the dark place manifests things.[2]

[1] *S.D.*, Vāda 39.
See also *Śrī-bhāṣya*, p. 76.
Cp. *Pañca-pādika-vivarṇa*, pp. 12-3.
Both Rāmānuja and Deśika have drawn the arguments from this work.

[2] Ibid.
viprati pannam māna jñānam sva prāgabhāva vyatirikta svaviṣayāvaraṇa svanivṛttya svadeśagata vastvantara pūrvakam, aprakāśitārtha prakāśakatvāt, andhakāre prathamotpanna pradīpa prabhā-vad-iti.

Cp. *Vivarṇa*, p. 13.

The inference is intended to prove that all knowledge is preceded by a positive state of ignorance, which is removed as soon as knowledge arises. This state of ignorance is not the same as that of prior non-existence of knowledge. The analogy of the light of a lamp lit in the dark place explains the point clearly. The objects are hidden by darkness and the light of the lamp only makes them manifest by removing the *āvaraṇa*, viz., the darkness. Similarly ignorance like darkness is a positive entity in the sense that it hides the true nature of things. With the onset of valid knowledge the ignorance is removed when the true nature of the things becomes revealed.

The scriptural texts also point out that *ajñāna* is a positive entity. Thus, it is said, " Hidden by what is untrue ". " Of them which are true, the untrue is the covering ".[1] " Then there was neither non-being nor being; there was darkness, hidden in darkness ".[2] " Indra, through *māyās*, takes on many forms ".[3]

Vedānta Deśika examines the above theory in detail. In the first place, it is shown that perception does not prove that nescience is a positive entity. If *ajñāna* as a positive entity is known by perception, it is asked whether *ajñāna* manifests itself to perceptual cognition as opposed to it or as unopposed to it? If it be the former, the contradiction pointed out in respect of the view that *ajñāna* is a prior non-existence of knowledge would also arise in respect of the present view. If *ajñāna* is opposed to knowledge, then its cognition obviously presupposes the knowledge of its opposite viz., knowledge itself. If that knowledge be known, its *ajñāna* which is opposed to it would cease to exist. Thus, the perception of *ajñāna* would also be impossible.

It may be contended that the *ajñāna* that is known through perception is only opposed to the specific knowledge but not to the knowledge in general. But this explanation, Vedānta Deśika replies, does hold good in respect of the view that *ajñāna* is prior non-existence of knowledge. The prior non-existence of knowledge is also not opposed to the knowledge

[1] *Ch. Up.*, VIII-3-1 & 2.
anṛtena hi pratyūḍāḥ.
teṣām satyānām satām-anṛtam-apidhānam

[2] *Yajurveda*, II, 8-9 nā-sadāsin-no-sadāsīt-tadānīm tama āsīt-tamasā guḍham-agre praketam.

[3] *Ṛgveda*, VI, xvii, 18. indro māyābhiḥ puru-rūpa īyate.

in general but to that specific knowledge whose prior non-existence is in question.[1]

Nor is the second alternative viz., that *ajñāna* is unopposed to knowledge, tenable, since there is no such experience. Even in such judgments as, 'I am ignorant', 'I am a fool', the words *mugdha* and *mūḍha* imply the negative character of *ajñāna*. Though the negative particle viz., *non* (*na*) is absent in these terms, they do not bear any positive sense as in the case of the words *pradhvamsa*, *vināśa* etc. Because of the mere absence of the negative prefix these words should not be regarded as positive terms. Thus, it is difficult to prove by means of perception that nescience is a positive entity.

Nor can it be proved by means of inference. The syllogistic argument put forth by the Advaitin suffers from logical defects. Thus, in the probans, viz., *aprakāśitārtha prakāśakatvāt*, what is meant by the term, *prakāśakatva*? It may be resolved into six alternatives: (1) being knowledge, (2) being the distinctive cause of knowledge, (3) being an aid to the sense organs, (4) being merely the cause of knowledge, (5) being the cause of the manifestation (*prākaṭya hetutvam*) and (6) being in a general way the cause of the empirical usage about the object either directly or indirectly.

It cannot be the first, because the probans would be defective in respect of the illustration in so far as the light of the lamp is not knowledge. Nor is the second alternative valid since the probans would not be present in the subject of the syllogism (*pakṣa*). Besides, the light of a lamp (*dīpa*) cannot be a direct distinctive cause since it is only an aid to sense organs.

Nor is the third alternative tenable as the probans would not be present in the subject of the syllogism. What is an aid to the sense organs is not the means of valid knowledge. The fourth alternative is also inadmissible because of the inconclusiveness of the probans in respect of the sense organs. The sense organs which are not preceded by anything, unlike knowledge, are the causes of knowledge. The fifth alternative is also wrong since the probans would be defective in respect of the illustration. The rays of the light of a lamp cannot generate *prākaṭya* or manifestation in the objects. Not even the sixth alternative is correct because of the defect of inconclusiveness in respect of the sense organs.

[1] *S.D.*, Vāda 39.

The main point of criticism, as given in the *Śrī-bhāṣya*, is that the probans in the syllogism is inconclusive. The function of manifesting what is not already manifest belongs to knowledge only. Manifestation of an object does not merely consist in dispelling what is opposed to its relation. On the contrary, it consists in defining the objects. This function belongs only to the knowledge. The light of the lamp serves only as an auxiliary in as much as it reveals the object to the sense organs by dispelling darkness. If the power of manifestation of what was not already manifest were admitted to the auxiliary factors also, then it should be admitted in respect of sense organs as well. But sense organs are not preceded by anything different from that which is terminated by their activity and as such the probans would become inconclusive.[1]

The scriptural texts also do not support the theory of *ajñāna* as a positive entity. The texts quoted by the Advaitin in support of his view do not refer to *ajñāna* as conceived by the Advaitin viz., that it is inexplicable. An entity which cannot be regarded either as real or as unreal does not exist. In the scriptural texts such as " Hidden by the untrue ", the word *untrue* (*anṛta*) does not denote the inexplicable; it rather denotes *karma* or such actions as cause contraction of knowledge (*jñāna-sankocahetu-bhūta karma*). That karma is opposed to knowledge is established by numerous śruti and smṛti texts. *Anṛta* means that which is different from *ṛta*. The term *ṛta* denotes such actions which aim at the propitiation of the highest person (God) and thus enable the devotee to attain the supreme goal. This is evident from such texts as " Enjoying the *ṛta* " (*rtam pibantau*). The word *anṛta* therefore means actions of a different kind, that is, actions which aim at worldly results and thus stand in the way of the realization of Brahman. This interpretation is in consonance with the scriptural text, " They do not find that Brahman world, for they are carried away by *anṛta* ".[2] The term *anṛta* also means sin (*pāpa*) in as much as it is a hindrance to the attainment of release.

Likewise in the text, " There was darkness, hidden in darkness ",[3] the word *tamas* refers to the primal nature (*mūla*

[1] *Śrī-bhāṣya*, p. 80.

[2] na sukṛtam na duṣkṛtam sarve pāpmānaḥ ato nivartante.

[3] tama āsīt tamasā gūḍam-agre praketam.

*prakṛti*). This is established by such texts as " Tamas becomes one with the supreme Self ",[1] " Whose body is tamas " [2] and " This (universe) was darkness then, being unknown by any one ".[3]

Again, in the text " Then there was neither non-being nor being ", the denial of its being neither *sat* nor *asat* only indicates that the intelligent and non-intelligent beings, which at the time of origination are called *sat* and *tyat* are merged during the period of dissolution in the collective totality of non-intelligent matter which the texts denote by the term *tamas*. There is thus no reference whatsoever to something not definable either as being or non-being. The terms ' being ' and ' non-being ' are applied to the different modes of Reality at different times.[4]

The scriptural texts wherein the term *māyā* appears do not also support the Advaitin's view. As explained in an earlier chapter, the term *māyā* in such texts refers to *prakṛti* only. Moreover, the term *māyā* does not necessarily mean what is *anirvacanīya*. On the contrary, the term is applied to that which produces wonderful effects (*vicitra sṛṣtikaratva*). Vedānta Deśika, therefore, comes to the conclusion that nescience as a positive entity cannot be proved by any of the pramāṇas. (*Pramāṇā-nupapattiḥ*).

## II *Nature of Avidyā*

The theory of *avidyā* advocated by the Advaitins does not even stand logical examination. Nescience is held to be the cause of the illusion of the universe in Brahman whose nature is constituted of nothing but self-luminous consciousness. Vedānta Deśika asks whether this nescience is real or non-real? If it be real, is it different from Brahman or non-different from it? If it be different, it would amount to the admission of two reals. If it be non-different, then Brahman itself would become responsible for the illusion of the world-appearance and Brahman being eternal, the world-appearance too would be eternal. If it be said that illusion arises when Brahman is associated with some other accessory cause (*sahakāri*) and when that is absent illusion does not arise, then it would follow that the accessory cause is the defect

[1] tama ekī bhavati.

[2] yasya tamaḥ śarīram.

[3] āsīdidam tamo bhūtam.

[4] *S.D.*, Vāda 39.

that produces illusion. And about this also the old question may be raised as to whether the accessory cause or causes are different from Brahman or not and whether they are real or not. Thus all the old difficulties would crop up again.

As regards the second alternative also viz., that nescience is non-real, the same difficulties would follow. Is nescience which is illusory (*aparamārtha*) different or non-different from Brahman? Obviously it is different from Brahman. The appearance of what is illusory is always due to some defect (*doṣa*). Now, what is that defect on which the illusory nescience depends? If a defect be admitted as the source of the manifestation of nescience, then that defect would require another defect for its manifestation and so on *ad infinitum.* Just to overcome this difficulty if it be held that Brahman itself causes the manifestation of *avidyā*, then Brahman being eternal, the appearance of *avidyā* too would be eternal.[1]

It may be argued that *avidyā* is beginningless (*anādi*) and hence there is no need to postulate another defect to account for its manifestation. This will not do, contends Vedānta Deśika. If *avidyā* be beginningless it would only mean that it is not caused by anything and on that ground it cannot be said that it is not dependent on a defect. Nescience, in so far as it is illusory, must depend on a defect for its appearance even though it be beginningless. If on the contrary it could manifest itself without an object, it would become real like Brahman. If a defect be admitted to account for the manifestation of *avidyā*, then it would lead to an infinite regress.

Vedānta Deśika further proceeds to show that the postulation of *avidyā* in order to account for the world-appearance is superfluous. Does *avidyā* appear or not to Brahman which is defectless? If it appears to Brahman then it will do so eternally. If it is urged that there is the appearance of *avidyā* to Brahman only prior to the onset of the knowledge of Reality, while after the dawn of knowledge there is no appearance of it, then it amounts to saying that the prior non-existence of the knowledge of Reality is itself the cause of the Brahman's knowing *avidyā* (*avidyā darśana nibandhanam*) and the same may be admitted to be the cause of world-appearance. Why then the admission of *avidyā* as a third factor?

If it is argued that the prior non-existence of knowledge cannot be regarded as the cause of the varied production of

[1] *S.D.*, Vāda 41.

world-appearance, then in reply it is asked whether positive entities like a pot etc., have been found to be the cause of them? If it is held that a positive defect in the eye such as cataract often produces many illusory appearances, then it can be argued with equal force (on the view of non-existence) that the non-apprehension of difference (*bhedā-graha*) is also often capable of producing many illusory appearances.[1]

It may be argued that non-existence is limited by time and is, therefore, incapable of producing the diverse kinds of illusion under different conditions of time, and it is for this reason that nescience is admitted. This will not do, contends Deśika, for it may as well be asked how a beginningless nescience unconditioned by time can continue to produce the diverse world-appearance conditioned in time till the dawn of true knowledge. If in reply to this it is said that such is the nature of *avidyā*, then it may as well be asked why not that be admitted in respect of the prior non-existence of knowledge?

The Advaitin may argue that prior non-existence of knowledge is formless (*nirākāra*) and as such it cannot undergo a series of illusory transformations, while *avidyā* being a positive entity, can pass through a series of illusory manifestations (*vivarta-pāramparyāt*). This will not do, replies Vedānta Deśika. Is this *vivarta paramparā* the very nature of *avidyā*? Or is it its product? Or some other thing? It cannot be regarded as the very nature of *avidyā*; if it be so, then since it is the nature of *avidyā* to have a succession of diverse kinds of transformations, there would be illusory manifestations at all times. Nor can they be regarded as the products of nescience, for what is to be explained cannot itself be the explanatory principle.[2] Nor is the third alternative tenable. If the *vivarta-paramparā* be regarded as some entity other than nescience, then the old question would recur regarding the reality or unreality of it. If that be real it would result in the admission of dualism. If it were non-real, it would lead to an infinite regress. That is, if it be illusory, the succession of it as various appearances conditioned by diverse kinds of time and space would presuppose such other previous appearances and so on *ad infinitum*.

[1] *S.D.*, Vāda 41.

[2] Ibid.

nirvāhyasyaiva nirvāhakatvā-nupapatteśca.

If it is held that there is no logical defect in supposing that the earlier transformations determine the later transformations in an unending series, as in the case of the transformations of Brahman or of *prakṛti*, even then it is not necessary to postulate *avidyā* in order to account for such a view. For it may well be supposed that the different transformations arise in Brahman without depending upon any extraneous cause. It may be objected that such a supposition as Brahman is continually undergoing the diverse transformations would inevitably lead to the conclusion that there is no Brahman beyond such transformations. This is untenable because our perceptual experience shows that the transformatory change of a lump of clay does not destroy its *svarūpa*. This explanation does not hold good in respect of *avidyā* since the pramāṇas put forth in support of that view have been refuted separately.[1] Nor would there be the contingency of illusions arising being devoid of a substrate, for Brahman is admitted to be the ground of all illusory manifestations. The illusory *avidyā* itself cannot be regarded as the substrate; in that case Brahman itself would not be established and as such the position would land in nihilism.

It may be said that the existence of Brahman as the basis of everything is admitted not on the assumption that it is the ground of all illusory manifestations but on the strength of the scriptural texts declaring the reality of Brahman. In that case, *prakṛti* and its transformations too would have to be admitted as real because there are scriptural texts pointing out the reality of change and the material cause viz., *prakṛti*. If the texts pointing out the reality of *prakṛti* and its transformations be sublated, then it would be possible to sublate the texts that declare the reality of Brahman.[2]

Again, it may be asked whether *avidyā* manifests itself or not? If it does not, it becomes a non-existent. That which is not known by any pramāṇa is a non-existent. If it manifests, is this manifestation that of the nature of *avidyā* itself or is it of the very nature of Brahman? Or is it the characteristic of either nescience or of Brahman?

It cannot be of the nature of Brahman. As Brahman is eternal the manifestation of *avidyā* too would be eternal and as such there would be no release. Release according to an

[1] See Section I.

[2] *S.D.*, Vāda 41.

Advaitin is the removal of *avidyā* and if *avidyā* persists ever, there would be no release.

Nor can it be the characteristic of either *avidyā* or Brahman since neither of them has been admitted to be the knower. That which is the substrate of *prakāśa* or knowledge is a knower. Neither Brahman nor *avidyā* is admitted to be a knower and therefore *prakāśa* does not inhere in either of them as an attribute. The admission of the superimposed knowership will not solve the difficulty. For even such a superimposition is only caused by nescience and as such the position would involve reciprocal dependence.[1]

The theory of *avidyā* examined in respect of its locus, also stands untenable.[2] Vedānta Deśika, therefore, urges that from whatever point of view the theory is subjected to logical examination, it is found to be riddled with contradictions.

Against all these criticisms the Advaitin may contend that these are only applicable to what is real and an existent but not to nescience which is of the same status as the swallowing of a palace by a magician. In fact, unintelligibility itself is the very characteristic feature of *avidyā*. It is just an ornament to it but not a blemish.[3] Even though the conception of *avidyā* stands unintelligible, non-dualism is established.

This contention does not hold good, argues Vedānta Deśika. If the Advaitin holds the above position then his attempt to refute the nihilists would be futile. Supposing the nihilists argue that *Śūnya-vāda* in spite of being unintelligible becomes established, what is the Advaitin's reply to them? If he gives the following reply, viz., if everything being *Śūnya* is unintelligible (*durghaṭa*), then there is victory for the opponent, the same argument may be urged against the Advaitin too. In other words, it is wrong to argue that the criticisms do not apply to nescience as it is not a real entity, since such a doctrine would be almost like nihilism, for all criticism against nihilism are accepted by the nihilists as not invalidating their doctrine.[4]

[1] *S.D.*, Vāda 41.

[2] This issue is discussed in detail in the subsequent sections (III and V).

[3] *S.D.*, Vāda 41.
durghatatvam avidyāyā bhūṣaṇam, na tu dūṣaṇam.

Cp., *Brahmasiddhi*, p. 10.
na hi māyāyām kācid-anupa pattiḥ;
anupapadya mānārthaiva hi māya.

[4] See Dr. Dasgupta's *History of Indian Philosophy*, Vol. 3, p. 334.

### III *Brahman as the Locus of Avidyā*

*Avidyā*, like *jñāna*, implies some person to whom it belongs and some object to which it refers. That is, there must be some person whom it characterises and some object which is misapprehended through it. In the case of the shell-silver illusion, the person that mistakes the shell for silver is its seat or locus (*āśraya*) and the shell is its object (*viṣaya*). It is *ajñāna* thus determined that is regarded as the source of error.[1]

Now what is the locus and content of cosmic illusion viz., *māyā* or *avidyā*? According to one school of thought, Brahman itself is both the locus and content of *avidyā* as there is nothing else besides the Absolute.[2] But Brahman in the Advaita system is self-luminous intelligence. How can it be the seat of *ajñāna* which is opposed to its nature and which is avowedly sublated by knowledge? Just to overcome this difficulty some Advaitins hold that jīva or the individual self is the locus of *ajñāna*.[3] Vedānta Deśika examines both the theories in detail and shows that both are untenable.

The first view that Brahman is the locus of *avidyā* is taken up for consideration. If Brahman, as the Advaitin holds, is of the nature of knowledge alone or omniscient as the scriptural texts declare, in either case it can never be the locus of nescience for the following reasons: Brahman is not the knower, secondly, it is self-luminous, thirdly, Brahman is eternally free; and lastly, it is omniscient. Each one of these points is explained in detail.[4]

If *ajñāna* is something which is to be removed by knowledge, then it is in the fitness of things that it should reside in the knower or that which is the substrate of knowledge. For knowledge can remove only that ignorance which is located in its own locus. Thus, for instance, the knowledge of 'X' cannot remove the ignorance located in 'Y'. Brahman

[1] See Hiriyanna's Introduction to *Iṣṭasiddhi*, p. XXVI.

[2] See *Samkṣepa Śārīraka*, I, 319.
āśrayatva viṣayatva bhāginī nirvibhāga citireva kevalā.

See also *Panchapādikā-vivaraṇa*, pp. 45-6.

[3] Bhāmati is credited with this view.

See Introduction to *Bhāmatī Catussūttri* (T.P.H.), p. XXXIV.
Maṇḍana also holds the same view.

See *Brahmasiddhi*, p. 10.
yattu kasya-vidyeti; jīvānām iti brūmaḥ.

[4] *S.D.*, Vāda 19.

according to the Advaitin is not the knower and hence it cannot be the locus of *ajñāna*. Illusory knowership is, however, admitted in respect of Brahman, but this will not improve the situation. Brahman is regarded as a knower in the sense that it is qualified *per accidens* by *ahamkāra*. (*Ahamkaropahita-veṣeṇa*). But this will not overcome the difficulty. For during the state of deep sleep *ahamkāra* becomes extinguished and as such the self alone will have to be accepted as the locus of nescience. The Advatin is thus forced to admit either the individual self as the locus of *ajñāna* or to give up the theory of ignorance.

The second objection against the theory is that Brahman is self-luminous. According to the Advaitin nescience is removed by the knowledge of Brahman. Brahman which is of the nature of knowledge is eternally self-luminous. It is opposed to nescience like light and darkness.[1] How then can it be the locus of *avidyā*? Nevertheless if Brahman can allow the presence of nescience in it, what is it that can put an end to nescience? If *vṛttijñāna* having for its content Brahman removes nescience, then Brahman would become the object of that knowledge and as such the theory that Brahman is *avidyā* stands contradicted. Besides, what is there to distinguish between these two types of *jñāna, svarūpajñāna* and *vṛttijñāna*? This point will be discussed in a subsequent section.[2]

Brahman cannot be the locus of *ajñāna* because it is admitted to be eternally free from bondge. Bondage means being associated with ignorance (*ajñāna*) while release means to be devoid of it. Thus, the two are opposed to each other. Hence, it is a self-contradiction to say that Brahman who is eternally free is the locus of *ajñāna*. It may be argued that there is no opposition involved in the above theory since the presence of *avidyā* in Brahman and its removal take place at different times. In that case, the eternal freedom of Brahman would stand contradicted. If it be said that eternal freedom is not contradicted since the relation of nescience to Brahman is only illusory, then the temporal sequence of bondage and release would be hardly intelligible.

[1] The Advaitin does not admit that there is opposition between the two. He contends that the analogy of light and darkness does not hold good here.

See *Advaita-siddhi*.

[2] See pp. 144-6.

nitya muktatvā-bhyupagamācca.

The last argument against the theory of Brahman being the locus of *ajñāna* is that Brahman is omniscient (*sarvajña*). If Brahman is omniscient, it cannot have ignorance. For it cannot be said that Brahman knows all and that it does not know either something or anything at all. Nor can it be argued that Brahman is not omniscient as this position would conflict with numerous *śruti* and *smṛti* texts. Brahman, therefore, cannot be regarded as the locus of *ajñāna*.[1]

Further, Brahman which is eternally free, self-luminous and of the nature of pure consciousness, cannot even experience nescience which is located in it.[2] For bondage is the experience of nescience and its products (pleasure and pain), while release consists in its removal. If Brahman which is eternally free is bound, it is no more eternally free, since bondage is eternal. If there is no bondage, then release is also inconceivable.[3]

It may be argued that the experience of nescience by Brahman is only illusory and hence it would not affect the eternal freedom of Brahman. This will not do, argues Vedānta Deśika. For, that very illusory experience of ignorance is considered by the Advaitin as bondage. If Brahman is eternally free and self-luminous its association with nescience is unintelligible.

## IV *The Distinction between Māyā and Avidyā*

Before discussing the view whether the jīvā is the locus of nescience, there is another issue to be considered here which has a bearing on the foregoing topic. With a view to overcoming the defect involved in the view that Brahman is the locus of *ajñāna*, some Advaitins make a distinction between *avidyā* and *māyā* and call the *avidyā* or *ajñāna* located in

[1] ataḥ nitya sarvajñatvāt brahmaṇaḥ na kadācidapi tasya ajñānā-śraaytva sambhavaḥ.

[2] *S.D.*, Vāda 18.

nitya mukta sva-prakāśa caitanyaika svarūpasya
brahmaṇaḥ ajñānā-nubhavaśca na sambhavati.

See also *Śrī-bhāṣya*.

[3] Ibid.

nitya muktasya bandhaścet nitya muktiḥ na
sambhavet; bandhasyā-pi ca nityatvāt
bandhābhāvetu amuktatā.

Brahman by the name of *māyā*.[1] Vedānta Deśika dismisses the view by showing that such a distinction between *avidyā* and *māyā* will not in any way improve the situation.

What is the ground on which the distinction between *māyā* and *avidyā* is made? There are three views as pointed out by Vedānta Deśika in support of this theory?

According to the first view *māyā* is that which deludes others while *avidyā* is that which deludes one's self.[2] This view does not hold good, argues Vedānta Deśika. Delusion of others is possible only when others are seen. If others are seen, does Brahman look at them because the perception of others is natural to it or because of *ajñāna* or because of *māyā* itself? If looking at other individuals is natural to Brahman it would follow that other individuals are real in so far as they are the content of defectless cognition. Besides, it would follow that knowership is natural to Brahman. If Brahman looks at other individuals because of *ajñāna*, then it would lead to the conclusion that Brahman is associated with *ajñāna* (*Brahmā-jñāna*) and as such there is no need to postulate *māyā* as distinct from *avidyā*. Nor does Brahman see other individuals because of *māyā*. Since *māyā* serves only as a means of deluding others when they are seen, it cannot cause perception of others.

The distinction between *māyā* and *avidyā* may be maintained on a different basis. *Avidyā* is the cause of the false perception (*viparīta darśanahetuḥ*) as in the case of the perception of nacre-silver. *Māyā*, on the contrary, does not cause any such false perception to Brahman. All that is outside Brahman which is illusory is made known as illusory.[3]

The above argument is also untenable, contends Vedānta Deśika. Does Brahman know this world-appearance which is illusory, as illusory because it is the product of its own illusion (*svabhrama-siddha*)? Or because it is the product of

[1] See Vāda 42.
ye tu brahmaṇo doṣam pari-jihīrṣantaḥ
brahmā-jñānam māyā śabdena upacaranti.

The distinction between *Māyā* and *Avidyā* is not admitted by all the Advaitins.

See *Panchapādikā-vivaraṇa*, pp. 31-2.

Bhāmati also does not admit such a distinction.

[2] *S.D.*, Vāda 42.
paravyāmohanahetur-māyā, sva-vyamohana-hetur-avidyā.

[3] *S.D.*, Vāda 42.

the delusion of another individual (*parabhrama-siddha*)? Or does Brahman merely apprehend illusory character of it without being aware that it is the product of illusion? The first alternative will not do since it would amount to the acceptance of the view that Brahman is associated with *ajñāna*. Nor is the second alternative tenable. If Brahman does not know others, it cannot even know the world-appearance as the product of illusion of other individuals. If Brahman be admitted to know others, then it would mean, as has been shown, that Brahman is subject to *avidyā*. Not even the third alternative is sound. If the world-appearance is not known to be the product of illusion, then its illusoriness also cannot be cognised. That is, the cognition that a thing is illusory cannot take place unless it is known that the thing in question is the object of illusion. Illusoriness is not the mere non-existence of an entity but its appearance in a locus where it does not exist. If Brahman sees others as merely illusory then it is difficult to conceive how Brahman desires to delude them. A magician, for instance, does not show his magic to delude either a barren woman's son or the shadows of persons or even the persons depicted in a picture.

The Advaitin may put forth another argument to prove that *māyā* is not *avidyā*. It is true that when other individuals are deluded they should be seen and the perception of others who are illusory is not possible without being subjected to *avidyā*. Nevertheless the defect viz., the *māyā* of Brahman, which causes the perception of others, cannot be called *avidyā* since *avidyā* is defined as the cause of illusory experiences that produce undesirable effects in respect of the percipients.[1] But in the case of Brahman, *māyā*, though it manifests these illusory selves who are to be deluded, does so without giving rise to any undesirable effect in respect of Brahman. That is, it manifests them to Brahman as a *puruṣārtha*. Hence *māyā* is not *avidyā*. This is the third view put forth to account for the distinction between *māyā* and *avidyā*.

Even this contention is inadmissible, replies Vedānta Deśika. If *māyā* is the cause of a *puruṣārtha*, it cannot be considered as a defect. If it be a defect, it cannot be a *puruṣārtha*. Nothing that produces a desirable end is treated as a defect. It may be said that *māyā* is not

[1] *S.D.*, Vāda 42.
**apuruṣārthā-paramārtha-darśana-hetur-avidyā.**

a defect of Brahman but it is only a quality (*guṇa*) in the sense that it is beneficial to Brahman. If that be the case, then is it to be removed through the desire of Brahman or through anything else? If it is to be removed through Brahman's desire how could it be considered as a (*puruṣārtha*) to him? For nothing that is not connected with an undesirable effect needs to be removed. Nor can it be removed by means of anything else. The individual selves being deluded by *māyā* are endowed with limited knowledge and power and as such they are incapable of removing *māyā* that serves the purpose of the omniscient and omnipotent Brahman. Nor would it be destroyed by itself without any cause for that would land the Advaitin in the doctrine of momentariness. The only alternative which we are driven to is that *māyā* is undestroyed. This would lead to the conclusion that *māyā* is eternal and is associated with Brahman—a position which is not acceptable to the Advaitin. Vedānta Deśika, therefore, concludes that it is impossible to draw a distinction between *māyā* and *avidyā* on the view which maintains that *māyā* is illusory and Brahman is pure and indeterminate.[1]

### V *Individual Self is not the Locus of Avidyā*

Can the individual self be the locus of *avidyā*? The Advaitin who answers in the affirmative argues as follows. Necience and bondage are not directly associated with Brahman. For, Brahman which is reflected in the nescience or the internal organ is the jīva and that jīva is the locus of *avidyā* and bondage. It is true that the reflection should be of the same nature as the prototype. Nevertheless the defects found iṇ the reflection do not belong to the prototype. Thus, for instance, the defect of the mirror is found in the face reflected in it but it does not in any way belong to the face, even though the prototype (face) is not different from its reflection. In the same way, the defects found in the jīvas, which are the reflections of Brahman, do not belong to Brahman but are located in the jīvas only. Further, these defects are due to the adjuncts just as the defect found in the reflected face is due to the mirror. Hence even if the jīvas are ultimately identical with Brahman, the purity of Brahman is in no way affected.[2]

[1] *S.D.*, Vāda 42. [2] *S.D.*, Vāda 40. Cp. *Brahmasiddhi*, p. 11.

How can the jīvas be the locus of *avidyā*? When *avidyā* is first established, then the reflection in it viz., jīva is possible; when that is possible, *avidyā* as residing in it is established. In other words, there would be no jīva except as the product of nescience; how then can nescience itself reside in it?

This objection is untenable, replies the Advaitin. The interaction of nescience and jīvahood is regarded to be beginningless like the seed and the sprout. The Advaitin does not say that at any time *avidyā* was and the jīva was not or that the jīva was and *avidyā* was not. The two, on the contrary, are beginningless. Nevertheless if the above explanation is unintelligible, it is answered that it is absurd to expect intelligibility in the case of nescience since it is of the very essence of nescience to be unintelligible in the last resort.[1]

Vedānta Deśika refutes the above theory. At the very outset he points out that the reflection of consciousness in the inner organs or the nescience is an impossibility and the postulation of the plurality of jīvas on that ground is untenable. Reflection, in other words, is invariably of objects possessing colour in media possessing colour; when neither the prototype (pure consciousness) nor the reflecting medium (nescience) possesses colour, how can there be a reflection of one in the other? Even assuming that the reflection is somehow possible, the jīvas cannot be the locus of nescience. What is the nature of individual selves wherein the nescience is supposed to rest?

(1) Does nescience reside in the jīvas existing in their natural state (i.e., as Brahman), or (2) in the jīvas existing in a different state, i.e., not in their natural state but in their ordinary supposed nature as having rebirth etc., or (3) in the svarūpa of jīva qualified by the imagined form (*kalpitākāra viśiṣṭa svarūpeṇa*)?

The first alternative is untenable, as it would result in the admission of the theory that Brahman is the locus of nescience.

Nor is the second alternative valid since it would follow that nescience is associated with the material stuff and as such can never be removed; for the material limitations of an individual can never have a desire to remove *ajñāna* nor have they the power to remove it.

[1] See Introduction to *Bhāmatī Catussūtri*, p. XXXIV (T.P.H.).
tad-eva-avidyānām avidyātvam.

See also *Brahmasiddhi*, p. 10.
na hi māyāyām kācidanupapattiḥ; anupadyamānārthaiva hi māyā.

Not even the third alternative is tenable. Does nescience rest in the entity qualified by an imagined form (*kalpitākāra*) which has been caused by itself? Or does it reside in the entity qualified by a form that has been caused by another *avidyā*? In either case the argument would involve a vicious circle.

Further, is *avidyā* that constitutes the difference of individual jīvas one or many? In the former case, with the emancipation of one, *avidyā* being removed all the jīvas would be released. If one jīva is not released, *avidyā* too would exist and as such there would not be the release of even a single individual. In the latter case, it would be difficult to determine whether *avidyā* comes first or the difference between the individual jīvas, and it would thus lead to the fallacy of reciprocal dependence *anyoṇyā-śraya*. When the jīvas are established to be many, it then follows that *avidyās* are many; when *avidyās* are determined to be many, the plurality of jīvas stands established. The Advaitins do not admit that the difference between the jīvas is real. If that were admitted, then there would be no need to postulate the plurality of nescience in order to account for the difference of the jīvas.[1]

The Advaitin cannot say that the plurality of jīvas is known through perception and on that ground the plurality of *avidyā* too is admitted. If the difference of the jīvas as established by perception be real as has been admitted by the Viśiṣṭādvaitins, then the postulation of the plurality of *avidyā* is futile. If, on the other hand, the difference of the jīvas be false as has been held by those who hold that *ajñāna* is associated with Brahman, even then there is no necessity to admit the diversity of *avidyā* in so far as jīvas on that view are admitted to be identical. In any case *avidyā* whether it be real or fictitious, cannot account for the diversity of jīvas.[2]

Again, do the *avidyās* that are supposed to produce the plurality of jīvas, reside in Brahman or in the jīvas themselves? If the former, the position would amount to saying that Brahman is the locus of *avidyā* and not the jīvas. If it be the latter, the argument involves a vicious circle. When the *avidyās* as located in the different jīvas are known to be diverse, it follows that the jīvas are many; when the jīvas are

[1] *S.D.*, Vāda 40. [2] Ibid.

established to be many, then there is the plurality of *avidyās* as abiding in them.

It is not possible to overcome the difficulty by maintaining the view that the interaction of nescience and jīva is beginningless like the seed and the sprout. Does the Advaitin mean to say by the analogy of the seed and the sprout that the *avidyās* which condition the jīvas have the latter for their locus? Or does he mean to say that the earlier *avidyās* residing in the earlier jīvas condition the subsequent jīvas? If it be the former, the analogy of the seed and the sprout does not apply at all to the present issue. The sprout brought forth by a seed cannot itself be the cause of that seed.[1] Nor is the latter tenable.

If the *avidyās* of the previous jīvas produce the later jīvas, then the jīvas would be destructible. And such a position would conflict with the scriptural texts which declare that jīvas are eternal and indestructible. Thus, from whichever way we may try to understand the view that *avidyā* rests in the jīvas, we are faced with logical difficulties.

It is logically unsound to say that untenability itself constitutes the very nature of *avidyā*. If that be the case, then why not admit, asks Deśika, the presence of nescience in the released soul in as much as it is not a defect but a *bhūṣaṇa*? The argument that untenability is not a blemish is no solution to the problem. The implication of it is that any theory which is not logically sound is to be given up instead of being adhered to under the pretext that unintelligibility itself is the characteristic of the theory.

## VI *Brahman as the Content of Avidyā*

After having shown that *ajñāna* or *avidyā* cannot reside either in Brahman or in the individual self, Vedānta Deśika points out that Brahman cannot also be its content. Brahman is said to be the content of *avidyā* in the sense that the latter conceals the true nature of Brahman, which is pure consciousness devoid of all determinations. The concealment or obscuration (*tirodhāna*) of the true nature of Brahman is unintelligible, contends Vedānta Deśika. What is meant by

[1] Ibid. na hi yadankurotpādakam yad bīiam tadeva tasyārambhakam.
See *Caṇḍamāruta*, Vol. 3, p. 350.
tadankurameva tad-bījārambhakam.

*tirodhāna* or concealment? It may be resolved into eight alternatives: (1) the removal of the relation of the sense organs to the object; (2) the removal of the object being the content of the cognition generated by the sense organs; (3) the removal of the object being the content of all cognitions; (4) the absence of its being the object of itself (its own knowledge); (5) the cessation of its being self-luminous; (6) to render what is distinctly manifest indistinct; (7) the denial of one of the accessory factors that cause the manifestation of Brahman; (8) something that is indescribable.[1]

The first three alternatives are untenable as Brahman has to be admitted in some sense or other as the content of knowledge generated by the sense organs or of knowledge in general. This would not be acceptable to the Advaitin.

The fourth alternative is also not acceptable to the Advaitin. The fifth and the sixth alternatives are of some importance. Concealment of the nature of Brahman should either mean the destruction of self-luminosity (*sva-prakāśa-bhanga*), or making what is distinctly manifest indistinct (*viśada svarūpasyāpi aviśada svarūpatvāpādanam*). In neither sense, Deśika contends, is the concealment of Brahman intelligible. In the former case, does the term *svaprakāśa-bhanga* mean the destruction of the *prakāśa* that is already existing? Or the obstruction of the rise of *prakāśa*? If it be the former, Brahman would become perishable. If it be the latter, then Brahman would be subjected to origination.

As regards the other alternative, the distinction between distinct and indistinct manifestation in respect of Brahman whose nature is pure self-luminous consciousness is hardly intelligible. Brahman which is always of the nature of immediate consciousness cannot admit in itself any manifestation which is mediate. Nor is it possible to conceive any kind of manifestation other than Brahman itself in so far as it is immutable and indeterminate in character.

In conclusion, Vedānta Deśika points out that in respect of the indeterminate and eternally self-luminous entity, which is neither open to the knowledge of oneself nor of another, the conception of its concealment is unthinkable.[2]

[1] See Vāda 35.

[2] Ibid.

na kathanchidapi nirviśeṣa nitya svayamprakāśe svasya parasya vā jñānāntara agochare vastuni tirodhāna vācoyuktiḥ ghaṭate.

## VII *Removal of Avidyā*

It is contended that *avidyā* or *ajñāna* is removed by the knowledge of the non-dualism (*advaita-vijñāna*). This theory is unsound, argues Vedānta Deśika. What is the nature of this *advaita-jñāna* which is supposed to remove the nescience? (1) Is this knowledge different from the knowledge which constitutes the very *svarūpa* of Brahman? (2) Or is it non-different from it? (3) Or is it both different and non-different? (4) Or is it neither different nor non-different? (5) Or is it something whose nature is inconceivable? [1]

Taking the first alternative into consideration, Vedānta Deśika asks whether the knowledge in question has any content or not. If it is without a content, it ceases to be knowledge. For even according to the Advaitin the knowledge of the psychosis is related to an object. If it has a content, then what is it that figures as the content of that knowledge? Is Brahman itself its content? Or the same associated with *avidyā* or something different from it or illusoriness of everything other than Brahman or something else?

If Brahman itself be the content of the knowledge in question in no way would it be distinct from the knowledge which constitutes the very *svarūpa* of Brahman inasmuch as both refer to the true nature of Brahman. Hence, as in the case of the knowledge that constitutes the *svarūpa* of Brahman, even the knowledge in question cannot remove nescience. If the knowledge in the form of the psychosis can remove nescience, then Brahman-knowledge itself would have to put an end to it.[2]

It may be argued that there is a distinction between the two kinds of knowledge in question. Brahman-knowledge is of the nature of manifestation of the substrate (*adhiṣṭāna*) which is essential for the illusion to take place as in the case of the manifestation of *this* in the illusion, 'this is silver'. Hence, it cannot remove nescience so far as it is not opposed to illusion. What is actually opposed to illusion and which alone can remove it is the manifestation of the *viṣaya*, that is, the *svarūpa* of the object. In other words, the mere manifestation of the substrate cannot remove illusion while the

[1] *S.D.*, Vāda 43.

[2] Ibid.

ubhayorapi yathāvasthita brahma svarūpa
prakāśarūpatvā-viśeṣāt.

manifestation of the *svarūpa* of it can. The knowledge which is Brahman itself is of the former type while the knowledge of the psychosis about Brahman is of the latter type.

The above argument is untenable. There is no doubt a distinction between the knowledge of the *this* and that of the shell in so far as the contents of the two are of a different nature. The manifestation of *this* has for its content that feature which is common to both the silver and the shell, while in the manifestation of the shell, the reference is only to the object qualified by shell-ness which constitutes the difference of the shell from silver (*rajata-vyāvartaka*). There is thus a difference in respect of content (*viṣayabheda*) which renders one capable of removing the illusion of silver while the other not. As regards the content of Brahman-knowledge and the knowledge of the psychosis, no such distinction exists between them. The knowledge of the psychosis does not have for its content any new factor other than that which constitutes the nature of Brahman itself. If any such factor were admitted, either it should be real or illusory. If real, then it would be admitting Brahman as determinate. If illusory, then it would not remove the world-illusion, since that psychosis itself is of the nature of illusion.[1]

It may be said there is a distinction between the Brahman-knowledge and the knowledge of the psychosis in respect of their effects (*sādhyabheda*) as in the case of the knowledge by acquaintance (*abhijñā*) and knowledge by recognition (*pratyabhijñā*). The knowledge by acquaintance which is expressed in the form of the judgment, 'He is Devadatta', does not remove the illusion viz., that he is not Devadatta, while on the other hand, the knowledge by recognition which is expressed in the judgment, 'He is *that* Devadatta' which confirms the identity of the person with the one previously seen is capable of removing that illusion. In the same manner, as between the Brahman-knowledge and the knowledge of the psychosis, though the content of the two is the same, viz., Brahman, the latter is capable of removing nescience inasmuch as it is of the form, "I am that (Brahman)" (*So'ham*).

This distinction does not hold good, argues Vedānta Deśika. In the case of *abhijñā* and *pratyabhijñā*, the distinction is apparent in respect of the objects manifested by them. *Pratyabhijñā* or the knowledge by recognition refers to the distinctive feature

[1] *S.D.*, Vāda 43.

of the person in the form *so'ham*, while *abhijñā* or the knowledge by acquaintance refers only to the person in general as *asau*.[1] Hence the contents of these two types of knowledge are not the same. In the case of the *svarūpa-jñāna* and the *vṛtti-jñāna*, no such distinction can be found. The knowledge of the psychosis referring to Brahman is the same as that of the knowledge constituting the nature of Brahman. If any additional characteristic feature be admitted in the latter, other difficulties pointed out earlier would follow. That is, if the additional characteristic feature (*ākāra*) be real, it would result in the admission of the view that Brahman is qualified. If it be illusory, the knowledge itself would be illusory and as such it could hardly put an end to the world-illusion.

It may be said that the Brahman-knowledge manifests things other than itself, whereas the other one does not and as such there is the distinction between the two. But this does not improve the situation in any way since these factors are not the determinant of sublatership and non-sublatership.[2] The *vṛtti-jñāna* is the sublater because it is of the nature of the manifestation of the true nature of Brahman and not because it is a psychosis.

The second alternative viz., that Brahman associated with *avidyā* is the content[3] of the final psychosis, is also inadmissible. If the psychosis has for its content Brahman associated with nescience, then like witness-consciousness (*sākṣi-pratyakṣa*) it would not remove *avidyā*. The witness-consciousness does not remove illusion but on the contrary, it is favourable to illusion in so far as it manifests it (*bhramopakāraka*). Similarly, if the final psychosis too has for its content nescience, then it can hardly put an end to it.

As regards the third alternative that something other than Brahman is the content of the psychosis, it is pointed out that there is absolutely no chance of its being the sublater since that itself is of the nature of illusion. The cognition of shell-silver itself cannot sublate the cognition of silver.

Nor can it be maintained that the manifestation of things outside Brahman as illusory is the content of the final

[1] *S.D.*, Vāda 43.

[2] Ibid. bādhakatvā-bādhakatve prati aprayojakatvāt.

[3] The view that final intuition is of the conditioned is ascribed to *Bhāmatī*. See *Bhāmatī*, p. 78 (T.P.H.).
See also *S.L.S.*, Vol. I, p. 63 (Madras Univ. Edn.).

psychosis. For without knowing the substrate of illusion, it is not possible to know the illusory character of things.

Further, does this psychosis which is supposed to remove the world-illusion apprehend its content, viz., illusoriness of everything except Brahman, as something illusory or as real? If it apprehended it as real, then it would imply dualism. If it apprehended it as illusory, then it would follow that the world-illusion is real. That is, if what is illusory is regarded as illusory, it would mean that it is real. To cite an instance, if the illusoriness of the true silver is illusory it is obvious that the silver is real.

The Advaitin may argue thus: If we say that everything other than Brahman is illusory, it not only means that the world is illusory but also that the illusoriness of the universe is also illusory, just as in the statement ' the world is real ', the reality of the world as well as the reality of the reality are established. This will not do, contends Deśika, as there is a wide difference between the two views. The former view involves a self-contradiction, while the latter is free from it. If the illusoriness of true silver is illusory, it does not follow that silver too is illusory. If the shell-silver is illusory, the illusoriness of this cannot be non-real. Thus it is summed up: " If the illusoriness of a thing is illusory, the illusoriness itself stands sublated, while the reality of a thing if real, the reality of it stands established.[1]

May it not be said that as in the supposition of the death of a barren woman's son both the barren woman's son and his death are illusory, so also both the world and its illusoriness are equally illusory? This cannot be. In the above instance, the attributes viz., being the son of a barren woman and his death could be false since there is no basis for them.

Is this knowledge of the psychosis which is supposed to remove the world-illusion generated at the time of hearing the texts that teach the identity of the self and Brahman? Or does it arise at some other time? If it be the former, then the world-appearance should cease for those who teach non-dualism at that very moment. The persistence of the trace of nescience in the form of the body etc., even after the

[1] See Vāda 43.

mithyātvasya ca mithyātve mithyātvam bādhitam bhavet;
satyatvasya ea satyatve satyatvam sādhitam bhavet.

This objection is not admitted by the Advaitin.
See *Advaita-siddhi*, pp. 210-222 (Nirṇayasāgara Edn.).

sublation of nescience is hardly intelligible. This point has been discussed later.[1] As regards the latter, does that knowledge (which comes) later serve as the *nivartaka* either as being the same as the previous knowledge or as being different from it (i.e., having some new content)?

If it be the former, then the previous knowledge itself would remove the world-illusion. If that were not capable of putting an end to it, then the latter one too could not do it. The latter view is also untenable. It cannot manifest any new element which has not been already revealed by the previous knowledge. There is no other real form or element (*ākārāntara*) in Brahman that has yet to be manifested.

So far the view that the *nivartaka-jñāna* is something different from Brahman was examined and shown to be faulty. Vedānta Deśika proceeds to show that the other views about the nature of *nivartaka-jñāna* are also untenable. The *nivartaka-jñāna* cannot be even non-different from Brahman. If Brahma-svarūpa were to remove the world-illusion, then there would be no illusion at all since the Brahma-svarūpa is beginningless and eternal. It may be said that Brahman itself can be the cause of the world-appearance as well as its destruction just as the one and the same stick can produce as well as destroy a pot. Vedānta Deśika replies that this analogy does not hold good. The stick does not cause both origination and destruction simultaneously which would be a self-contradiction. It does in succession and with the help of other accessories. The stick, for instance, does not break the pot when it is serving as one of the accessories of the production of the pot. On the contrary, it affects its destruction only after the pot has come into existence.

The third, the fourth and the fifth alternatives regarding the nature of *nivartaka-jñāna* are also inadmissible as they are self-contradictory.

Thus, the theory that nescience is removed by knowledge of the psychosis referring to Brahman is untenable.

## VIII *Cessation of Avidyā*

Vedānta Deśika further proceeds to show that the very conception of the cessation of *avidyā* is also unintelligible

[1] See Chapter VIII, section V.

(*nivṛttyanupapattiḥ*). According to the Advaitin the complete cessation of nescience is effected by the onset of the knowledge of the meaning of the texts teaching non-dualism, a knowledge which is distinct and which is perfected by the process of hearing the Vedānta texts, reflection thereon and the repeated contemplation of the truth taught therein. Vedānta Deśika asks whether the cessation of nescience (*avidyā-nivṛtti*) is itself illusory in character or not. If it be illusory, how could there be a complete cessation of *avidyā*? While cessation which is itself of the nature of illusion exists, *avidyā* too which is its cause should exist, since there could be no effect without a cause. It cannot be said that the cessation of *avidyā* has as its ground the *ātman* (*ātmopādāna*), for then the *ātman* would be subjected to change. If it is without any further ground like Brahman and *avidyā*, then there is no meaning in associating *avidyā* with it. And there is also no reason why even after the cessation of *avidyā*, it may not appear again.[1]

It may be pointed out that the function of the cessation of nescience is to show that everything else except Brahman is illusory and as soon as this function is fulfilled the cessation of *avidyā* also ceases to exist. This will not do, argues Deśika. If the cessation of *avidyā* itself ceases to exist and if that be illusory, then that would mean that there is a cessation of cessation which means either that *avidyā* is again restored or that it is real.

It may be urged that when a pot is produced it means the destruction of its prior non-existence and when the pot is again destroyed, the prior non-existence of it does not again come into being. Again, to give another example, the light seen in the dream which is the cause of the cessation of darkness seen in the dream, ceases to exist in the waking state; yet the darkness seen in the dream does not become real. In the same way, the cessation of *avidyā* is not restored, nor does it become real.

Vedānta Deśika easily disposes of this argument. In the case of the prior non-existence of the pot and the dream-darkness, their being non-restored and being illusory respectively is intelligible because the destruction that removes the pot and its prior non-existence, and the waking state, that

[1] *S.D.*, Vāda 44.

Cp. the arguments in *Iṣṭasiddhi*, p. 83.

contradicts the dream darkness and dream light both exist, whereas in the present case there is no other entity as opposed to *avidyā* and its cessation. If it be said that there is the Brahman which negates the cessation of *avidyā*, then the difficulty would be that Brahman, the negation of both *avidyā* and its cessation being eternal, there should be no appearance of the universe at any time. As such there being an end to the appearance of difference etc., the study of *mokṣa-śāstra* need not be undertaken. If it were not contradictory to it previously, then it could not be opposed to it even afterwards.

The second alternative viz., that the cessation of nescience is not illusory is also untenable. If it be not illusory, then it is asked whether it constitutes the very nature of Brahman or not. If it be included in the nature of Brahman, then Brahman being beginningless, *avidyā* would stand always sublated. It may be possible to say that just as the very existence of the pot itself is the negation of its prior non-existence, likewise the existence of Brahman is itself the cessation of *ajñāna*. In that case, Brahman which is of the nature of cessation of its *ajñāna* should have to be admitted as arising subsequent to it (cessation) as in the case of the pot and the negation of its prior non-existence. This would mean that Brahman is non-eternal.

The Advaitin puts forth a different argument. The cessation of nescience is not real, being different from Brahman. It is not even of the nature of real and unreal, as this involves a contradiction. Nor is it something different from the real and the unreal since that would not lead to a real cessation. So ultimately it must be either unreal or something different from any of the above four alternatives (*pancama-prakāra*). *Ajñāna* is something different from the real and unreal; its cessation is also valid being amenable to proofs. Hence, in accordance with the principle viz., "Oblation conforming to the ghost" (*yakṣānurūpobaliḥ*), the cessation of *avidyā* has to be described as something unique and different from all existent and non-existent entities.[1]

[1] Ibid. This argument is given in *Iṣṭasiddhi*.

See *Iṣṭasiddhi*, p. 86. The same has been stated by the author of *Nyāya Makaranda*. See *Nyāya Makaranda*, p. 355.

na sannāsan-asadāsanna-nirvachyipi tatkṣayaḥ.
yakṣānurūpo hi balir-ityācārya vyāchicharan.

See also Introduction to *Iṣṭasiddhi*, p. XXXV.

The whole position is unsound, argues Vedānta Deśika. The first three alternatives have been set aside by the Advaitin himself. As regards the fourth that the cessation of nescience is like a non-existent entity (*asatva*), if by *asat* or non-existence is meant another existence (*bhāvāntara*), then the contingence of dualism is unavoidable. If on the contrary, *asat* means chimerical (*tuccha*), then it would be a non-existent like the horns of the hare. And such a chimerical entity being unopposed to bondage, there would be no emancipation at all. The fifth alternative also is unsound. If the cessation of nescience be regarded as different from existent, non-existent, existent-non-existent and different from both, then it is virtually the admission of the Mādhyamika doctrine of indescribability of all phenomena as being of this type. Thus, they say: "The reality (*tattva*) is neither real nor unreal, nor real-unreal, nor different from the four alternatives."

Again, the maxim, *yakṣānurūpobaliḥ* does not apply here. If there should be conformity without opposition, then the cessation of nescience which is regarded as indescribable would follow to be indescribable. If there is conformity by opposition, then the opposite of indescribability being describability, its being different from real-non-real would not stand.

Vedānta Deśika, therefore, concludes that such an absolutely unique and indefinable category is inconceivable.

CHAPTER EIGHT

# ŚĀDHANA AND MUKTI

THE present chapter is devoted to the discussion of some of the important issues arising out of the interpretation of the first aphorism of Vedānta[1] by Śamkara and Rāmānuja. Though both of them agree with regard to the general meaning of the *Sūtra*, they differ fundamentally in respect of the interpretation of the word *then* (*atha*) appearing in it. This word significantly points out that the enquiry into the nature of Brahman (*brahma-jijñāsā*) is to be preceded by some preliminaries. It implies that something must have gone before to which Brahman-enquiry is invariably related. What is that something? Śamkara's answer to this question, which every student of Vedānta must be familiar with, is that there are four factors which constitute the pre-requisites to Brahman-enquiry. These are discrimination of things eternal and non-eternal, possession in abundance of calmness, equanimity and other such means, non-attachment to the enjoyment of fruit here and hereafter and desire for release.[2] Rāmānuja, on the contrary, maintains that the study of the rituals (*karma-vicāra*) invariably precedes Brahman-enquiry.[3] The main reason for holding such a view is that *Pūrva-Mīmāmsā*, which is concerned with the ritualistic portion of the Vedas and *Uttara-Mīmāmsā* which deals with Brahman-knowledge constitute one integral whole and as such the study of the rituals is an indispensable prolegomena to the Brahman-enquiry.

This raises further questions: (1) What is the relation of the *Pūrva-Mīmāmsā* to the *Uttara-Mīmāmsā*? (2) What is the relation of karma to Brahman-knowledge? (3) If karma also serves as a means to Brahman-knowledge, what then is the

[1] *Vedānta-sūtra*, I. 1. 1. Athā'to brahma-jijñāsā.

[2] See *S.B.*, I. 1. 1. p. 36 (N. S. Edn.).
tasmāt kimapi vaktavyam, yadanantaram brahma-jijñāsopadiśyata iti. ucyate, nityānitya-vastu-vivekaḥ, ihāmutrārtha-bhoga-virāgaḥ, śmadamādi-sādhana-sampat, mumukṣutvamca iti.

[3] *Śrī-bhāṣya*, p. 2.
pūrva vṛttāt karma jñānādanantaram tata
eva hetoḥ brahma jñātavyam ityuktam bhavati.

nature of the means (*upāya*) to *mokṣa*? (4) Finally, what is the nature of *mokṣa* itself?

All these questions, important as they are, relate to the nature of *Sādhana* and *Mukti*. These have been discussed fully by Rāmānuja at the very outset of his monumental work, *Śrī-bhāṣya*, in the sections known as *Laghu-pūrva-pakṣa* and *Laghu-siddhānta*. The arguments given therein have been further developed by Deśika in his *Śatadūṣaṇī*.[1] An exposition of these arguments is given in the present chapter.

### I *Pre-requisites to the Study of Vedānta*

Whether *Sādhana-catuṣṭaya* constitute the pre-requisites to the study of Vedānta is first taken up for consideration. The *prima facie* view is that the word *atha* mentioned in the first aphorism can be accepted in the sense of immediate succession if it fulfils three conditions. First, it must precede invariably the desire to know Brahman; secondly, it must be a distinctive factor, and thirdly, it must serve some definite purpose (*saprayojana*). The twinkling of the eyelids though it precedes every act, does not serve any purpose as a preliminary to the study of Vedānta. Mental alertness may be necessary for the study of Vedānta, but it cannot constitute a distinctive factor for the study of Vedānta alone as it is required for the study of any other subject. Hence, that which is useful, distinctive and has invariably to be gone through before, is, according to the Advaitin, the possession of the four means—the discrimination of eternal and non-eternal, possession in abundance of calmness, equanimity and other such means, non-attachment to the enjoyment of fruit here and hereafter, and desire for release. These are invariably related to Brahman-enquiry because in their absence there would be no desire to know Brahman. They also serve the purpose of defining the eligibility of the person to the study of Vedānta.

Vedānta Deśika refutes the above theory on the ground that the four factors in question do not invariably precede Brahman-enquiry. The main point of the criticism is that

[1] See Vādas 3-6, 8 and 31.

aika-śāstrya-samarthana vādaḥ (3)
avidheya-jñāna-bhanga vādaḥ (4)
bādhitānuvṛtti-bhanga vādaḥ (5)
vividiṣā-sādhanatva-bhanga vādaḥ (6)
sādhana-catuṣṭaya-pūrva-vṛttatva-bhanga vādaḥ (8)
jīvan-mukti-bhanga vādaḥ (31)

the discrimination of things eternal and non-eternal becomes possible only after one has made a study of Vedānta and as such it cannot be a pre-requisite to the study of Vedānta.

Each one of the means suggested by Śamkara is examined in detail. What is meant by the discrimination of things eternal and non-eternal? Does it mean that 'this thing is eternal' and 'this thing is non-eternal'? Or does it mean, as Vācaspati-Miśra interprets, the discrimination of the substrates which are eternal and non-eternal, as also of their attributes—the discrimination between that which is to be rejected and that which is to be accepted (*heyatvo-pādeyatva*). In other words, to be eternal is to be true, that in which this is found is eternal and it is therefore to be accepted (*upādeya*); to be non-eternal is to be untrue, that in which this is found is non-eternal and is thus to be rejected (*heya*).[1]

The first alternative is taken up for examination. The discrimination in the form, 'this thing is eternal' and 'this is not', cannot take place without the study of Vedānta texts. It is only from the study of the Vedānta texts that one learns that the self is eternal and ether etc., are non-eternal. In other words, the discrimination between the eternal and the non-eternal is possible only after the study of Vedānta. But the study of Vedānta, according to the Advaitin, cannot take place without a knowledge of such discrimination. The argument thus involves a vicious circle.[2] It cannot be said that this knowledge of discrimination arises from the study of other systems which one would have completed before commencing the study of Vedānta. In that case, the study of Vedānta would become superfluous since the knowledge that is to be obtained from it would have already been derived from the study of other systems.

It may be argued that the study of Mīmāmsā is enjoined and hence it is undertaken. Even then the discrimination of things eternal and non-eternal is dependent upon the study of Mīmāmsā only and as such it cannot be prescribed as a

[1] See *Bhāmatī-Catussūtri* (T. P. H.), p. 95.

Vācaspati uses the terms *āsthāgocara* and *anāsthāgocara*, i.e., that which is in the sphere of desire and that which is not in the sphere of desire. Corresponding to these terms Vedānta Deśika uses the terms *upādeya* and *heya* respectively.

[2] Vāda 8.

vedānta śravaṇe siddhe nityā-nitya viveka dhīḥ;
nityā-nitya vivekena vedānta śravaṇam-tviti.

preliminary to the study of it. Further, if the study of Vedānta is undertaken because it is enjoined, then the study of the *karma-mīmāmsā* or that portion of the Mīmāmsā dealing with the ritualistic texts would have to be undertaken since it is also covered by the same injunction. In fact the study of *Uttara-Mīmāmsā* follows only after the study of *Pūrva-Mīmāmsā*. Accordingly the study of the ritualistic portion should precede the study of the Vedānta (*karmabhāga-śravaṇa-pūrvaka meva brahma-bhāga-śravaṇam*).[1]

On the same ground the second alternative is also refuted. If the discrimination between that which is to be rejected and that which is to be accepted follows after ascertaining through the pramāṇas what is eternal and what is not eternal, then the same difficulty pointed out in respect of the first alternative would arise. In other words, the ascertainment of what is eternal and what is not eternal would not be possible without the study of the Vedānta texts. If, on the other hand, it be maintained that the discrimination is of the form 'if it is eternal, that is to be accepted, and if non-eternal, that is to be rejected'—even then the position does not improve. For even a thing which is eternal is to be rejected if it does not constitute the human goal. Likewise a thing which is non-eternal, if it comes within the sphere of *puruṣārtha*, is to be accepted. The *mokṣa-sādhana*, for instance, is *anitya* and yet it is acceptable (*upādeya*).

Nor can the discrimination be in the following form viz., "If there is anything eternal among the human goals, that is to be accepted, otherwise it is to be abandoned". For such a discrimination which is more in the form of a doubt cannot be a distinctive factor for the study of Vedānta in so far as it can initiate one into the study of rituals as well as the study of other systems.

The second means viz., the possession in abundance of *śama*, *dama* etc., is examined. What does this mean exactly? Does it mean the possession of mental concentration at the time of hearing the Vedānta texts? Or does it mean the perfect control over the sense organs (*jitendriyatva*)?

If it be the former, the Viśiṣṭādvaitins also admit it. But it cannot be regarded as a distinctive factor to the hearing (*śravaṇa*) of the Vedānta texts alone, as it is required for the

[1] *S.D.*, Vāda 8.
This issue is discussed at length in the subsequent section.

study of any other subject. If it be the latter, that again cannot be a pre-requisite to the hearing (*śravaṇa*) of the Vedānta texts. On the contrary, the control over the sense organs etc., constitutes an important means to self-realization (*darśana*). This is evident from the following Upaniṣadic text: "Hence having become possessed of calmness, equanimity, turning away (from objects), the desire to abandon (them) and faith, one seeing the self in the self alone, sees everything in the self".[1]

Further, mental control, equanimity etc., have been enjoined as auxiliaries to the knowledge of Brahman. This point has been discussed in the third chapter of the *Vedānta-Sūtras*.[2] How can these be helpful to the hearing of the Vedānta texts? The knowledge of the Pūrva-Mīmāmsa is required to understand that *śānti*, *dānti* etc., are the means to Vedānta study. As pointed out by Rāmānuja, the fact that these conditions serve as a means must be determined on the basis of *viniyoga* or the principle of application which determines the relation of the principal to the subordinate units. This *viniyoga* which depends on direct scriptural statement, inferential signs and so on, is treated in the third section of the Pūrva-Mīmāmsā Sūtras.[3] Here again, the study of Vedānta presupposes the study of Pūrva-Mīmāmsā.

As regards the third and the fourth means viz., non-attachment to the fruits here or hereafter and the desire for release, though these may constitute the antecedent factors to the study of Vedānta, yet it is more appropriate to hold that the enquiry into the rituals alone is the pre-requisite to the enquiry into Brahman for the following reasons: it suggests the order in which a person proceeds to study Vedānta; it also makes evident that an individual who enters on the study of Vedānta has understood well the arguments that are required for the purpose of knowing the nature of Brahman as well as contemplation thereon; it also facilitates an unhindered enquiry into Brahman through the removal of the *prima facie* superficial

[1] *Brah. Up.*, IV. 4.23.
Śānto dānta uparatas-titikṣus-samāhito bhūtvā ātmanyevā-tmānam paśyet.

[2] *V.S.*, III. 4. 27.

[3] *Śrī-bhāṣya* I. 1. 1. p. 13.
The reference made by Śrī Rāmānuja to the third section of the *Pūrva-Mīmāmsā* is only illustrative (*pradarśanārtham*). Vedānta Deśika tries to point out that not merely the third section but each chapter of *Pūrva-Mīmāmsā* is helpful for the study of Vedānta. See Vādas 8 and 3.

knowledge that the rites lead to the infinite and permanent result; more than all, by stating that the enquiry into the rituals has gone before, the two preliminaries under question become consequential (*artha-labdhatvāt*).

The scriptural text also says: "Let a Brahmin after he has examined all these worlds acquired by deeds, obtain freedom from all desires".[1]

Vedānta Deśika, therefore, concludes that in the aphorism, "Then, therefore, the enquiry into Brahman", the intention of the *Sūtrakāra* is that in immediate succession to the enquiry into the rituals and not in immediate succession to the possession of the four means that the enquiry into Brahman should follow. The author of the *Vṛtti* also says: "After the comprehension of the rituals has taken place, there follows the enquiry into Brahman".[2]

## II *Pūrva-Mīmāmsā and Uttara-Mīmāmsā*

The refutation of the view that the *Sādhana-Catuṣṭaya* constitute the pre-requisites to the study of Vedānta has a positive implication. The implication, which is of great importance for the Viśiṣṭādvaitin, is that the study of rituals (*karma-vicāra*) or more appropriately, the study of the Pūrva-Mīmāmsā, is the essential prerequisite (*pūrva-vṛtta*) to the study of Vedānta. There are three strong arguments in support of the above view: (1) the enquiry into the meaning of the Vedic texts which comprise the ritualistic as well as Brahman portion should cover the study of both Pūrva-Mīmāmsā and Uttara-Mīmāmsā; (2) the knowledge of Pūrva-Mīmāmsā is very essential for the study of Vedānta; (3) the two Mīmāmsās—Pūrva and Uttara—form one integral whole.

These arguments are discussed in detail by Vedānta Deśika with a view to refuting the Advaitin's contentions that the study of the Pūrva-Mīmāmsā need not be undertaken as it is of little value to the study of Vedānta and that the two are divergent śāstras since there is difference in respect of their authorship, content, aim and the persons eligible for their study.

The scriptural injunctions demand that the entire scriptural text including its subordinate branches (*angas*) should be

[1] *Mund. Up.*, 1. 2. 12.

[2] *Śrī-bhāṣya*, I. 1. 1. p. 2.
vṛttāt karmādhigamānantaram brahma vividiṣā iti.

studied. Its import also should be grasped, for it is the grasping of the import that must always determine the subsequent conduct. The enquiry into their meaning (*artha vicāra*) may be initiated either through a specific injunction, as the Mīmāmsakas believe, or it may take place through one's own desire (*rāgataḥ*) as the Viśiṣṭādvaitins hold. In either case, Vedānta Deśika argues that it covers the entire portion of the Vedas, as it cannot be restricted to any one part. Though it may be possible to restrict the enquiry that springs up from a specific injunction, it is not possible to do so in the case of the enquiry that springs up from a pragmatic purpose. It cannot be restricted to Brahman since one may desire to know all the four human ends (*puruṣārtha*) and a desire to realize all the four ends naturally leads to the enquiry into the meaning of the entire scriptural texts.

Nor is it correct to restrict the enquiry to the ritualistic portions only, as the Mīmāmsakas do. The Mīmāmsakas consider the Brahman-texts as non-authoritative since they refer to an existent. Words for them are significant only when they refer to a thing the existence of which was not known before. The Upaniṣadic texts which refer to Brahman, an existent, therefore, do not carry any import. Hence, the enquiry is to be restricted to the ritualistic sphere only. Against this the Vedāntins contend that even in respect of an existent words do carry import. The Upaniṣadic texts referring to Brahman are, therefore, authoritative. Hence, the enquiry cannot be restricted to the ritualistic sphere alone but should be carried on into the Upaniṣadic portion as well. Nor can the enquiry be restricted to the topic of Brahman alone in view of the fact that it gives the knowledge of the supreme human goal. If it were so, then the entire range of ritualistic programme would be an empty prescription and there would be no one to follow it. It cannot be said that the ritualistic programme is meant for one who is not aware of the supreme human goal. For he who has entered into the study of the entire Vedas including the Upaniṣads at the instance of the Vedic injunction cannot pretend to be ignorant of the supreme end. As will be shown presently, the ritualistic programme cannot be dispensed with as it forms a purificatory programme and aids Brahman-enquiry (*Brahma-jijñāsa*). The Advaitins too have admitted that the performance of the rituals is helpful in acquiring either the desire to know Brahman (*vividiṣā*) or as held by some, the knowledge of

Brahman itself (*vedanā*).[1] The enquiry into the nature of the rituals cannot therefore be excluded.

Further, Pūrva-Mīmāmsā actually aids the Uttara-Mīmāmsā. The aid is in the form that Vedānta requires the arguments and the principles of Pūrva-Mīmāmsā (*nyāyopa-jīvanam*). The first chapter of the Pūrva-Mīmāmsā establishes that Vedas are authoritative. This in general is very essential for Vedānta. The second chapter, *Bhedādhyāya* discusses the nature of difference etc. This aids the third section in the third chapter of the Vedānta which is called *Guṇopasamhāra-pāda*. Again, the third chapter of the Pūrva-Mīmāmsā which deals with the laws or the principles of exegesis is useful throughout the study of Vedānta. *Prayuktiḥ* or that which discusses the purpose of each ritual which comes under the fourth chapter of Pūrva-Mīmāmsā, is helpful in ascertaining whether the religious duty connected with the caste etc., is meant for the purpose of Brahman-knowledge or bound to the *āśrama* itself. Again, in the fifth chapter of the Pūrva-Mīmāmsā there is a topic dealing with the succession of the rituals (*kramaḥ*). This is helpful in studying the third section of the last chapter of *Śārīraka-Mīmāmsā*. The discussion relating to the nature of the agent etc., which is taken up in the sixth chapter of Pūrva-Mīmāmsā is useful in the discussion about the eligibility of persons to the study of Vedānta. Likewise, the other chapters of the Pūrva-Mīmāmsā are also useful either directly or indirectly to the study of Vedānta. Thus, the meaning of Vedānta texts is ascertained with the help of the principles and arguments set forth in Pūrva-Mīmāmsā.[2]

There is absolutely no contradiction between Pūrva-Mīmāmsā and Uttara-Mīmāmsā either in respect of the content or end or aspirant. The aspirant is one and the same. He who has studied the Pūrva-Mīmāmsā and understood the finite and impermanent character of the fruits of Karma enters on the study of Vedānta which refers to the supreme human goal. As regards the subject matter though there are minor differences there is an inherent unity between the two subjects. Ritualism is preliminary and philosophic quest is subsequent or developmental. One is apprenticeship, the other is

[1] There are two views on this subject, one ascribed to the school of *Bhāmatī* and the other to that of *Vivaraṇa*.

[2] *S.D.*, Vāda 3.

adeptship. One clarifies and illuminates the other. Thus, there is an organic unity between the two treatises (*śāstras*).

But how could the two treatises, the Advaitins urge, be considered to be one while they have been composed by different authors? Vedānta Deśika easily exposes the hollowness of this contention. One and the same person can plan, project and successfully execute many endeavours, many schemes; or again countless persons by combined or co-operative effort may accomplish a single object as in the construction of a tower of a temple. Even in respect of a literary work, one scholar can very well compose a number of independent treatises. From the other side, as in the case of the commentary on *Pāṇini* and *Kādambari*, even though different authors are involved, the treatise continues to be one.

May it not be said that the two *śāstras* should be bifurcated in view of the difference in content viz., the one asserts difference whereas the other teaches identity. This cannot be, for identity and non-identity do not relate to the same content. The Mīmāmsakas consider the end, means and the accessories and it is not the identity of these that the Vedāntins speak of but the non-difference of Brahman and the world.

It may be argued that in many of the *Vedānta-Sūtras* the position taken up by Jaimini is indicated as *pūrva pakṣa*, that is, a position to be repudiated. Does this not indicate that the two are incompatible? How then can they coalesce into a single unity?

This objection is baseless, argues Deśika. The differences referred to between Jaimini and Bādarāyaṇa relate to minor matters, almost to trivial formalities (*atyalpatara apradhānārtha*). These minor differences far from destroying the main unity of Karma and Brahma-Mīmāmsas really contribute to an added emphasis on their unity. If in a portion of a building some unusual part is removed and reconstructed the main unity of the building is never destroyed. On the other hand, the removal of the unusual part and its reconstruction add to the beauty of it. Likewise it should be understood here that the Pūrva-Mīmāmsā has been corrected by the Uttara-Mīmāmsā. Or again, the differences referred to between Jaimini and Bādarāyaṇa may be understood in a different way. Jaimini has given expression to such views not with the intention of opposing the views of Bādarāyaṇa but to exhibit his capacity or ability to establish the truth on logical grounds conceding the opponents' assumptions (*vaibhavokti*). Bādarāyaṇa re-examines them with the idea that laymen may not mistake them for truths. The position of Jaimini, therefore, is quoted with approval for removing likely doubts, for clarification of the issues and also for a reasoned reinforcement of main doctrines. All this is amply evidenced by references like 'so said Jaimini'. More than that, in many contexts Bādarāyaṇa refers to Jaimini by name for supporting his own position.[1] Similarly, Jaimini to support his own conclusion refers to Bādarāyaṇa and his authority.[2] These reciprocal references must prove convincingly that the two branches of literature dealing with *Karma-kāṇda* and *Brahma-kāṇda* constitute a totality.[3] In view of this Bodhāyana says, "The *śārīraka* of four chapters forms a textual totality with the sixteen-chaptered Pūrva-Mīmāmsā of Jaimini".[4] Thus, Śrī Rāmānuja also points out: It is a single *śāstra* beginning with *athāto dharma jijñāsā* and ending with *anāvṛttiḥ-śabdāt*. It is a single *śāstra* divided into three sections: *Karma-kāṇda* of twelve chapters, *Devatā-kāṇda* of four chapters, and *Para-devatā-kāṇda* consisting of four chapters. This twenty-chaptered literature is throughout gripped and dominated by a central plan and execution.

### III *Karma and Knowledge*

The foregoing discussion raises an important issue regarding the place of karma in the scheme of philosophic discipline. For the Advaitin, *mokṣa* or self-realization which is the goal of all human endeavour is secured through *Jñāna* as taught in the Upaniṣads and not through karma as taught in the Pūrva-Mīmāmsā.[5] Thus the question arises as to whether karma serves any useful purpose in the realization of the goal.

There are two views on this question. According to one which is generally ascribed to the school of Vivaraṇa, karma is useful in generating the knowledge of Brahman (*Vedanā*

[1] See *V.S.*, I. 2. 29; I. 2. 32: I. 4-18; III, 4. 40.

[2] See Vāda 3.

[3] For a detailed discussion of the subject see Vedānta Deśika's *Seśvara-Mīmāmsā*.

[4] *Śrī-bhāṣya*, p. 2.
samhitam-etat śārīrakam jaiminīyena ṣodaṣa lakṣaṇena iti śāstraikatva siddhih.

[5] See *Nāiṣkarmya Siddhi*, I. 19.

*sādhana*). The other view which is ascribed to the school of *Bhāmatī*, maintains that karma only subserves the purpose of generating the desire to know Brahman (*vividiṣā sādhana*). The chief argument adduced in favour of the latter view is that there is a conflict between knowledge and karma and as such the latter cannot be a subsidiary to the former. The śruti also says, " Brahmins desire to know Him (Brahman) through the study of the Vedas, by sacrifice, by charity, by austerity and by fasting ".[1] In the above text sacrifice etc., are enjoined as subsidiaries to the desire to know and not as a means of the knowledge of Brahman as it is specifically stated that they *desire to know* (*vividiṣanti*) and not that they actually *do know* (*vidanti*).

Vedānta Deśika refutes the above view and establishes that karma subserves upāsanā which is the direct means to *mokṣa*.

The issue whether knowledge is opposed to karma is first considered. Why is knowledge regarded as opposed to karma? Is it because knowledge cannot be generated by sacrifice etc., or is it because sacrifice etc., conflict with *śama*, *dama* etc., which are subsidiaries to knowledge? Or is it due to the fact that the results of knowledge and rituals are different?

The first alternative does not hold good for without the performance of the purificatory acts either in the previous birth or in the present life, knowledge of Brahman does not rise. If rituals subserve *vividiṣā* through the purification of the mind, this is true in respect of knowledge as well (*vedanā*).

Nor is the second alternative valid. There is absolutely no conflict between *śama*, *dama*, etc., the subsidiaries to Brahman-knowledge and the observance of rituals. It is only the non-prescribed and prohibited acts that are prohibited under *śama* etc., and not the prescribed acts. As a matter of fact the prescribed acts are enjoined as subsidiaries to Brahman-knowledge.[2]

Nor is there any opposition between knowledge and rituals in respect of their results. What determines the end or the results of a particular action is the motive of the person (*abhisandhi*). With a change of the motive, the

[1] *Brah. Up.*, IV. 4. 22.
tam-etam vedānuvacanena brāhmaṇā vividiṣanti yayjñena dānena tapasā-nāśakena.

[2] See *Tait. Up.*, 6-50: dharmeṇa papam-apanudati.
See also *Vedānta-Sūtras*, III. 4-26 and 27; III. 4-32 and 33.

rituals which are meant for the purpose of attaining *dharma* etc., may also be directed towards the attainment of release.[1]

The second issue is also examined. It is contended that the term *vividiṣanti* is to be understood to mean that they desire to know, not that they actually do know. The reason underlying this argument is that in a word which is a combination of the suffix (*pratyaya*) and the root (*prakṛti*) the former is primary as compared to the latter which is subsidiary. The meaning implied by the suffix is therefore more important than that of the root. In the text under question, since desire forms the meaning of the suffix, the term *vividiṣanti* is interpreted to mean ' they desire to know '. If this is so, how is it, Vedānta Deśika asks, in such texts as *so anveṣṭavyaḥ, sa vijijñāsitavyaḥ, nididhyāsitavyaḥ*, the meaning of the suffix viz., " desire " is not admitted to be the content of an injunction? The Advaitin may answer that desire is not the content of an injunction because it springs up by the very fact that the means for which one desires is prescribed as useful to the achievement of the supreme human goal. It is, therefore, a re-statement only (*anuvāda*). Also there are such texts as *dhyāyīta*, where no suffix is found and in such cases the root meaning forms the content of an injunction. In order to establish harmony with such texts, the meaning of the suffix is not held to be the content of an injunction in the texts under dispute. In view of this though the meaning of the suffix is primary, the meaning of the root is accepted, since the object of desire is primary as compared to the desire therefor (*icchāyāḥ iṣyamāṇa pradhānatvāt*).[2] If this be the explanation, then on the same ground it must be admitted, contends Vedānta Deśika, that *vividiṣanti* means that they actually *do know* since harmony with many other texts[3] is secured by adopting such an interpretation. That is, in order to avoid conflict with other scriptural texts which explicitly point out that rituals subserve knowledge directly, the present text too will have to be interpreted on the same lines. Vedānta Deśika, therefore, concludes that sacrifice etc., are subsidiaries to knowledge of Brahman. The author of the aphorism

[1] *S.D.*, Vāda 6. [2] Ibid.

[3] *Mund. Up.*, III, 1-4.

kriyāvāneṣa brahmavidām variṣṭhaḥ
karmaṇaiva hi samsiddhim
kaṣāye karmabhiḥ pakve tato jñānam pravartate.

also says, "Because of the scriptural text about sacrifice etc., there is need of all, as in the case of a horse".[1]

## IV *Jñāna and Upāsana*

After having shown that the observance of karma directly subserves knowledge (*vedanā*), we now proceed to examine whether knowledge, as conceived by the Advaitin, is the sole means to *mokṣa* which is the goal of all human endeavour. According to the Advaitin bondage consists of the superimposition of the non-real on the real (Brahman). Accordingly, the removal of what is illusory in character can be brought about by means of the knowledge of the substrate alone as in the case of the illusory silver and not by any other means, either karma or contemplation or unseen potency, that are scripturally enjoined. The knowledge of Brahman, in other words, is the sole means to *mokṣa*. This knowledge is generated by the hearing of the sacred texts that teach the identity of the individual self and Brahman, by reflection and contemplation thereon. Thus it is pointed out in the Upaniṣadic text: "Lo, the self is to be seen, to be heard, to be reflected, and contemplated thereon".[2] *Darśana* here stands for the self-realization, the final goal and as such it is not enjoined. In other words, it is only a restatement (*anuvāda*), while *śravaṇa*, *manana* and *nididhyāsana* are enjoined as auxiliaries to *darśana*. These three subserve *darśana* by removing the cognition of difference which is a hindrance to the onset of the knowledge of the meaning of the scriptural text. With the onset of Brahman-knowledge, *avidyā* which is bondage is also removed.

In examining the above theory, Vedānta Deśika points out that knowledge as derived from the hearing of the sacred texts (*vākyārthajñāna*) will not by itself serve as a means to *mokṣa*. If the universe were illusory, then its removal by knowledge would be possible. But it is real according to the Viśiṣṭādvaitins; it would therefore be wrong to hold that knowledge alone is the means to *mokṣa*.[3]

Even granting that the universe is illusory, there would be no contradiction in admitting that it is removed by means

[1] *V.S.*, III, 4-26. sarvāpekṣāca yajñādi śruteḥ aśvavat.

[2] *Br. Up.*, 6. 5. 6.
ātmā vā are dṛṣṭavyaḥ śrotavyo mantayo nididhyāśitavyaḥ.

[3] *S.D.*, Vāda 4.

other than knowledge. Thus, for instance, defects like cataract and jaundice are also illusory in character but they are removed by means other than knowledge. Similarly, we have to admit, contends Deśika, something else besides the mere knowledge generated by the hearing of the Upaniṣadic texts as the means to *mokṣa*.[1]

The Upaniṣadic text referring to the method of self-realization needs careful examination. It has to be interpreted keeping in view many other scriptural texts referring to the nature of the means to *mokṣa*. Taking the text under question, *ātmā vā are draṣṭavyaḥ śrotavyo mantavyo nididhyāsitavyaḥ*, the Advaitin urges that *darśana* here is not enjoined, while *śravaṇa*, *manana* and *nididhyāsana* are enjoined. *Darśana* is not the content of an injunction because it refers to the ultimate goal; that which is the goal, cannot be a product of an act in which case it would not be eternal and ultimate. Secondly, knowledge *qua* knowledge cannot be enjoined.

Vedānta Deśika sets aside the above interpretation. Why is knowledge not enjoined? Is it because knowledge is not produced as a psychological phenomenon? Is it due to the fact that it cannot be the object of direct effort? Or is it because it does not constitute the direct activity of the self?

The first alternative will not do. Knowledge whether it be the modification of the internal organ, as the Advaitins hold, or an attribute of the self as the Vaiśeṣikas believe, or a particular state of the self as the Viśiṣṭādvaitins maintain, is in any case dependent upon the sense organs (*karaṇa*) and as such it is originated.

Nor is the second alternative tenable. If that which is not an object of direct effort cannot be the content of an injunction, then even effort would not be the content of it. But in our ordinary experience effort is enjoined.

Not even the third alternative is valid. If that which is not the direct activity of the self cannot be enjoined, then sacrifices which are enjoined would cease to be injunctions in so far as they are not the content of the direct activity of the self.

If knowledge is not to be enjoined, then texts referring to the performance of sacrifices would cease to be injunctions. For *yāga* or sacrifice is the dedication of the sacrificial material to a certain deity or deities, and as such it is a particular

[1] *S.D.*, Vāda, 4.

mental act, a particular mode of knowledge (*buddhi viśeṣa*). Again, hearing, reflection and contemplation are specific mental activities and these too could not be enjoined. If these modes of knowledge could be enjoined, why not it be admitted that *darśana* too is enjoined?

It cannot be contended that if *mokṣa* is held to be the fruit of a means that is enjoined (*niyoga sādhyatve*), it would cease to be eternal. If by *mokṣa* is meant the destruction of sorrow, it would remain eternal since destruction or *dhvamsa* is also eternal. If, on the other hand, *mokṣa* is understood to be the revelation of the true nature of the self (*svarūpā-virbhāva*), even then it remains eternal. For the revealed form of the self brought about by the removal of the hindrances that had veiled its nature by means of actions enjoined is the very nature of the eternal self; *mokṣa* is therefore eternal.

Vedānta Deśika proceeds to show that in the text under question, contemplation (*nididhyāsana*) alone is enjoined as the means to *mokṣa*. *Śravaṇa* and *manana* are not enjoined. *Śravaṇa* is not the content of an injunction because it springs up from one's own natural pragmatic desire. That is, when a person studies the Vedas including the Upaniṣadic portion and their branches, he acquires a surface knowledge and comes to know something about the ultimate goal. This arouses a desire in him to know more about it and also the method to attain it. As a result of this he is prompted to hear the sacred text (*śravaṇa*). Whatever is thus heard about is to be kept in mind without confusion of ideas; for this purpose he proceeds to reflect on it. This too, like *śravaṇa*, springs up from one's own desire and hence it need not be enjoined. Thus, both *śravaṇa* and *manana* are mere restatements (*anuvāda*) and they only subserve contemplation. As for *nididhyāsana*, it is to be enjoined as it is not already accomplished.

Contemplation (*dhyāna*) too cannot be considered as an *anuvāda*, like hearing and reflection, on the ground that it aids *darśana*. There is no evidence to show that *dhyāna* aids *darśana*. If *darśana* is taken to mean ordinary sense perception, *dhyāna* does not generate it, as it is not borne by our experience. If by *darśana* is understood the super-normal perception, since that is generated only through an unseen potency *adṛṣṭa*, it would presuppose an injunction; in that case the text, "to be contemplated" will have to be admitted as an injunction. If *darśana* is a state similar to perception, then *dhyāna* cannot be a restatement in view of *darśana*. For in the text " to be seen ", what is enjoined is only a specific form of *dhyāna* characterised by vividness. This itself is enjoined in a general way in the text " to be contemplated ". Thus since *darśana* is nothing other than *dhyāna* qualified by vividness, the latter cannot be a means to the former. Hence contemplation is the content of an injunction, but not a restatement. The text, " to be seen " is not a separate injunction. What is enjoined here is *dhyāna* itself as characterised by vividness. Of the two terms *darśana* and *nididhyāsana*, the former is a specific term while the latter is a general term. Except this difference, they are synonymous terms.[1]

Vedānta Deśika proceeds to show that the above view has to be adopted if the scriptural texts are to be interpreted without any conflict. Some texts point out that *dhruvānu-smṛti* or steadfast contemplation is the direct means to *mokṣa*, while others point out that *darśana* is the means to *mokṣa*. They cannot be considered as alternative means. Steadfast contemplation is a difficult course, whereas *darśana* is an easy path to perfection and option between them is therefore unintelligible. Nor can we say that both of them jointly serve as the means to *mokṣa* since it is impossible to adopt them simultaneously. Nor can they be followed in succession, for the principal unit (*angi*) which directly subserves the end cannot be combined with the subsidiary unit (*anga*) which subserves the end indirectly.

Nor can it be contended that *darśana* is the principal means and its fruit is merely restated in *dhruvānu-smṛti* which is a subsidiary means to *mokṣa*. For it has not yet been decided which is the principal and which is the subordinate one. This, however, is not known by perceptible means and the assumption that it is known through imperceptible means is a prolixity. The only alternative, therefore, is to treat *darśana* as synonymous with *nididhyāsana* except for the difference that the latter is a general term, while the former is a specific term signifying contemplation as characterised by vivid manifestation. This interpretation is adopted on the principle known as *chāga paśu nyāya* set forth in Mīmāmsā. *Paśu* is a general term which refers to any kind of animal. But it is ascertained by subsequent specification that it bears the meaning of *chāga* or goat, which is a specific term. Likewise,

[1] See Vāda 4.

here also the terms *vedanā*, *darśana* etc., which refer to the general form of knowledge (*jñānasāmānya viṣaya*) are to be interpreted as bearing the meaning of the specific terms viz., *dhyāna*, *upāsana* and other such terms which refer to the specific or particular states of knowledge (*jñāna viśeṣa viṣaya*), since neither an assumption of alternatives nor simultaneity nor relationship of the principal and the subordinate would be possible.[1] Keeping this in view the text " to be seen " is to be treated as an injunction referring to the specific nature of *dhruvānu-smṛti*, since in the text " to be contemplated " *dhruvānu-smṛti* nas been specifically enjoined. Vedānta Deśika thus arrives at the conclusion that knowledge in the form of contemplation (*upāsana*) is the means to *mokṣa*. In view of this the contention that the knowledge generated by the hearing of the Vedānta texts is a means to *mokṣa* is untenable.

Further, the mere knowledge produced from the hearing of the texts is not found to destroy *avidyā*. If it be contended that for him who has attained the knowledge of the meaning of the texts, nescience is removed while for one who has not attained it nescience still continues, then the teaching of Advaita would become impossible. If knowledge were not attained, then the imparting of that knowledge would not be possible. If knowledge were attained, then nescience would become removed and consequently the act of teaching itself which presupposes the persistence of the body and *avidyā* would be hardly intelligible.

### V *The Theory of Bādhitānuvṛtti*

The above difficulty is overcome by advocating the theory that even after the onset of Brahman-knowledge embodiment is possible and so the teaching of Advaita by a preceptor who has attained knowledge can take place. Even after the onset of knowledge embodiment is possible because of the persistence of the trace of *avidyā*.[2] The analogy given to explain this position is the continuance of the cognition of the double moon even after it is sublated by the apprehension that the

[1] *S.D.*, Vāda 4.
Jñāna-sāmānyaviṣaya vedanādi śabdānām tasmin viśeṣa śabdārtha eva paryavasānam yuktam.

[2] There are different views regarding the possibility of the trace of *avidyā* in a *jīvan-mukta*.
See *Siddhānta Leśa Samgraha*, Ch. iv.

moon is single. The persistence of the trace of *avidyā* does not cause any bondage to the self since its root has been completely destroyed. This is again explained on the analogy of the burnt cloth which though it retains its configuration is hardly useful for wearing purposes. Nor does the trace of nescience require to be removed by another knowledge since it ceases to exist of its own accord as in the case of the flame, the final wave of the sound, and the final *samskāra* (*carama samskāra*).

Vedānta Deśika refutes this theory by showing that the persistence of the trace of *avidyā* is logically unsound.[1] If *avidyā* is sublated by true knowledge, how can the trace of it continue? Is it because that *vāsanā* is real like Brahman so that it is not destroyed by knowledge? Or is it because that even if it be illusory it is not the object of the sublatory knowledge? The first alternative will not do as it would conflict with Monism. The Advaitin also does not accept that view. The second alternative also will not do since the knowledge that arises at the time of hearing the text that everything other than Brahman is illusory does not exclude the trace of *avidyā*.

The persistence of the trace of *avidyā* cannot be accounted for on the analogy of the cognition of the double moon. What is it that makes the single moon appear as double? Obviously, it is the defect in the eye viz., the pressing of the eye-lid or cataract. It is not the defect in the eye but the cognition of the double moon that is sublated by the knowledge of the single moon. Hence, there is the persistence of the cognition of the double moon even after the awareness that the moon is single. This is not the case with the Advaitin's theory in question. Just as the nescience and its effects such as bondage are removed by knowledge likewise the trace of *avidyā* too should be removed and there is absolutely no room for its continuance.

Even granting that it continues, how is its removal effected? That its removal is effected by itself does not very much stand to reason. What removes a thing cannot itself be the thing removed. In other words, the destroyer and the destroyed cannot be identical since the two are incompatible. The pot, for instance, is destroyed never by itself. The analogies of the flame, the final wave of the sound, the *carama samskāra*

[1] See Vāda 5.

do not hold good here. In these instances their destruction, Vedānta Deśika contends, is effected by the will of God in association with particular spatial and temporal factors. The theory of *bādhitānuvṛtti* or the persistence of that which is sublated is therefore untenable.[1]

## VI *The Doctrine of Jīvan-mukti*

On the basis of the theory of *bādhitānuvṛtti*, the Advaitin advocates the doctrine of *jīvan-mukti*. According to this doctrine the self is released even when it is embodied. This is possible because the body persists even after the onset of knowledge and the consequent removal of *avidyā* as a result of the persistence of a trace of *avidyā*. The body which persists has no power to cause bondage, just as the burnt cloth is not useful for wearing purposes. The trace of *avidyā* as well as the body come to an end of their own accord as in the cases of the flame, the final wave of the sound and the final impression (*carama samskāra*). The continuance of the body even after the release of the soul makes possible the teaching of Advaita by the preceptors.

Vedānta Deśika argues that the conception of *jīvan-mukti* is a self-contradiction. What is the meaning of this term? He resolves the term into six alternatives: (1) the cessation of the body etc., while embodied (*dehādi-bheda nivṛttih*), (2) the cessation of the appearance (*pratibhāsa*) of the body, (3) the cessation of the activities depending on the body, (4) the cessation of the merits and demerits accruing from the function of the body etc., (5) the cessation of the pleasure and pain caused by it, (6) the cessation of something else.[2]

The first alternative will not do as it involves a contradiction. Embodiment is the association with the body (*saśarīratvam*), while release is disassociation with it (*aśarīratvam*). The two are thus opposed to each other and cannot be found together. It may be argued that though there is the illusion of one's being embodied, embodiment too is removed since that illusion has been sublated by the knowledge of Brahman. This does not hold good, argues Vedānta Deśika. If one's being associated with the body (*saśarīratva*) is removed, he becomes disembodied and how then can he who is disembodied be called a *jīvan-mukta*? Again, the release of him who

[1] *S.D.*, Vāda 5. [2] *S.D.*, Vāda 31.

is not embodied is nothing but the removal of the illusory cognition viz., that the self is attached to the body. Except the removal of this illusion the Advaitin does not admit the destruction of the body and as such there is absolutely no distinction between *jīvan-mukti* and *ajīvan-mukti*. The distinction may be pointed out on the ground that the cognition of one's being embodied, though it is sublated, continues just as the cognition of the double moon persists even after its sublation by the cognition of the single moon. This argument is based upon the doctrine of *bādhitānuvṛtti* or the persistence of the trace of *avidyā* after its sublation. This theory has already been pointed out to be untenable. Moreover, such a view is in direct conflict with our perceptual experience.

Nor is the second alternative tenable, because it stands contradicted by experience. Besides, it is opposed to embodiment. When the illusion of the difference of body etc., has been totally removed, there is no room for the continuance of embodiment.

For the same reason the third alternative also is untenable. Neither do we see nor hear of any who are deeply absorbed in the knowledge of Advaita (*advaita-niṣṭam*) as being devoid of all activities. In fact, only those who are supposed to possess a good knowledge of Advaita have written the treatises on Advaita Vedānta.

Nor is the fourth alternative valid. For even the prescribed and prohibited acts which are contingent upon caste distinctions and distinctions of social order are binding on Brahman-knowers as well.[1]

If it be argued that the Brahman-knower is untouched by sins committed unconsciously, even then he cannot be considered a *mukta*, for sins committed consciously and the deeds that have already begun to fructify cause him bondage. If *jīvan-mukti* refers to this view, then the Viśiṣṭādvaitins have no dispute with the Advaitins in so far as they also admit such a view on the strength of the Śruti texts.

For the same reason the fifth alternative also is inadmissible. It has not been admitted that the deeds done unconsciously bear fruit in respect of the Brahman-knowers. The deeds done consciously, however, give their results. As this is borne by experience, it cannot be denied.

[1] Cp. *Katha Up.*, I. 2. 24. nā-virato duścaritāt. *Gita,* XVIII-7.

The sixth alternative is also untenable. Is the cessation of something else opposed to embodiment or not? If it be the former, *jīvan-mukti* itself would be absurd as it involves a self-contradiction. If it be the latter, release would be unintelligible since experience of pleasure and pain which is the natural outcome of embodiment could not be avoided. Without the persistence of the residue of nescience, embodiment (*jīvana*) is unintelligible. If the residue persists, then release is inconceivable.

Vedānta Deśika, therefore, concludes that if one is embodied one is no more released; if released, then no embodiment is possible. Thus, the conception of *jīvan-mukti* is absolutely unintelligible.

## VII *The State of Mokṣa*

Before closing this chapter we have to discuss the Advaitic theory of *mokṣa* or the final release. There is no separate Vāda in the *Śatadūṣaṇī* devoted mainly to the discussion of this topic. The Vāda devoted[1] to the discussion of the nature of the individual self in the state of release contains some arguments relating to the nature of *mokṣa* and these may be noted down here as the subject matter is of great importance.

The issue under dispute is whether the individual self in the state of release becomes identical with the Absolute or does it remain different from the Absolute without losing its individuality. The former is the view held by the Advaitin while the latter is the view of the Viśiṣṭādvaitin. The Advaitin takes his stand on the scriptural text viz., *Brahma veda brahmaiva bhavati*.[2] This text which is understood literally is interpreted to mean that the Brahman-knower becomes Brahman, which implies the identity of the individual self and the Absolute. Vedānta Deśika, on the contrary, urges that the text in question does not so much refer to *tādātmya* or identity as to *sādharmya* or equality. The chief argument in favour of this issue is that Brahman itself becoming Brahman cannot constitute the goal as it has already been accomplished. Nor is it possible for one different from Brahman to become Brahman itself as it would result in an *apasiddhānta*. Two different entities cannot be identical. It is therefore logical to hold that the individual

[1] Vāda 51. [2] *Mund. Up.*, 3. 2. 9.

self attains the status of Brahman (*sādharmya*). This interpretation is also in consonance with other texts openly declaring *sāmya* of the self with Brahman.[1]

The individual self not only retains its individuality in the state of release but it also enjoys the *vibhūtis* of Brahman as is evident from the scriptural text *so' śnute sarvān kāmān saha.*[2] The Upaniṣadic passage wherein the text appears is very significant. The passage begins with the text "*Brahmavid āpnoti param*" etc., referring to the nature of Brahman, the contemplation thereupon, the attainment of it and ends with the texts, *So' śnute* etc., referring to the fruit of contemplation. The word *saha* indicates that Brahman together with his *vibhutis* is experienced by the individual self.

That the self becomes omniscient in the state of release is evident from the scriptural text "*sarvam ha paśyaḥ paśyati*". This omniscience is not something that is newly produced in the self. The self by its very nature is omniscient, but its omniscience was not manifest in the state of bondage owing to karma with which it was overlaid. With the removal of karma the true nature of the self becomes manifested. This is compared to the lustre of the gem which is hidden by dirt and which is made manifest by merely removing the dirt. Similarly, the self becomes omniscient like the Lord after its impurities in the form of karma are removed. The self then becomes almost equal to Brahman in every respect except in the matter of the creation, sustenance and destruction of the world.[3]

[1] *Mund. Up.*, 3. 1. 3. [2] *Tait. Up.*, I. 1. 2.

[3] See *V.S.*, 4. 4. 17: jagadvyāpāra varjam prakaraṇād asannihitatvācca.
4. 4. 21: bhogamātra sāmyalingācca.

## CHAPTER NINE

# GENERAL EVALUATION AND CONCLUSION

In the course of the previous eight chapters an attempt has been made to give an exposition of Vedānta Deśika's criticisms against the doctrines of Advaita Vedānta with an eye on conformity with the letter and spirit of the original work. The arguments which are found in the different Vādas of the *Śatadūṣaṇī* are brought together and discussed in a systematic manner under the eight broad headings: 1. Validity of Pramāṇas; 2. Perception; 3. Consciousness; 4. Individual Self; 5. Brahman; 6. The Universe; 7. Avidyā; and lastly, 8. Sādhana and Mukti. In the present chapter we shall bring together the main issues which we have discussed in the preceding chapters and examine their philosophical soundness.

The aim of the *Śatadūṣaṇī,* as has been fully explained in the Introduction, is to criticise the doctrines of Advaita Vedānta with a view to establishing the soundness of the theories of Viśiṣṭādvaita Vedānta. It raises several issues bearing on the epistemological, ontological, cosmological, religious and ethical problems and discusses them in detail adopting the dialectical method. Though the issues are many, each discussing a specific problem, they are focussed on one central doctrine of Advaita, viz., that Brahman which is the sole Reality and everything else is illusory. The same is expressed in the famous and often quoted couplet: *brahma satyam jagan-mithyā, jīvo brahmaiva nā' paraḥ.* This is the main thesis of the Advaita system, and its other associated doctrines, particularly the doctrine of Māyā which is unique to the Advaita, emerge from this. Rāmānuja also has the same thesis in view when he states the position of Advaita as *mahā-pūrvapakṣa* in the opening section of his *Śri-bhāṣya,* the commentary on the *Vedānta-sūtra.* All the criticisms that he levels against Advaita, are mainly directed to disprove this central doctrine of Advaita. Vedānta Deśika, who follows the same line of argument as set forth in the *Śrī-bhāṣya,* concentrates his attention on the same. The several Vādas of the

*Śatadūṣaṇī* are ultimately directed to set aside this central doctrine of Advaita.

In examining the soundness of the above doctrine, the first question that a critic of Advaita would raise is whether this doctrine, has the support of the pramāṇas, and if there are pramāṇas to support it how far do they go to prove it? Secondly, is the nature of Reality advocated by the Advaitin correct? Thirdly, is the universe illusory? Lastly, what is the ultimate goal of a philosophical system which teaches that every thing other than Brahman is illusory? If there is a *summum bonum* which is the fruit of all human endeavour, what is the means of realizing it?

Regarding the first question Vedānta Deśika has pointed out that the Advaitin cannot claim *śruti* as a pramāṇa in so far as he does not admit the absolute reality of the pramāṇas. He also has shown that perception as the foundation of our experience is of greater force than scripture, whenever the two are in direct conflict. He has also pointed out that perception cognises difference and a world of plurality and as such scripture cannot be taken to teach anything that is opposed to perceptual experience.

Coming to the second question regarding the nature of Reality, it has been pointed out that consciousness (*anubhūti*) cannot be identical with the Reality in so far as the former is found to be related to a subject on the one hand and an object on the other. There is no proof in support of the existence of a transcendental consciousness, which is eternal, self-luminous and undifferentiated in character. All that we know is a consciousness that is related to a knowing subject and an object. Such a consciousness cannot obviously be identical with the self. Nor is the self identical with the metaphysical Absolute. Further, the Absolute is not devoid of the attributes since such a theory is inconceivable. Besides, such a concept of Reality does not have the sanction of either the scriptural texts, or the smṛti texts or even the Vedānta-sūtras.

The third question which the critic of Advaita raises is whether the universe is illusory. This theory of universe is the main edifice of the philosophy of absolute Monism. The doctrine of *Māyā* is its necessary corollary. Vedānta Deśika has examined in detail all the important arguments that are advanced to prove the illusoriness of the universe and shown that they do not establish the theory. He has also subjected the doctrine of *Māyā* to a searching logical analysis following the seven-fold criticism by Rāmānuja and has shown how it is riddled with contradictions.

As regards the last question namely, the Advaitic theory of *sādhana* and the allied doctrines, he has examined them closely and refuted the same as untenable. This, in brief, is the main theme of the work.

The criticism of the doctrines of Advaita Vedānta has been attempted on three different grounds. First, the criticism is levelled on the basis of the accepted pramāṇas. That is, it consists in showing that the position held by the Advaitin is not well grounded on the pramāṇas. Of the three pramāṇas, perception, inference and scripture, the last one is very important. Most of the criticisms levelled against the Advaitins consist in showing that the position held by the Advaitin is not sanctioned by the scriptural texts.

From a purely philosophical point of view an appeal to scripture as the final court is not of great value for a modern student of philosophy, though it is considered important by the orthodox Vedāntins. This is specially so when the rival schools of thought appeal to the same scriptural text as authority in support of their theories. Scriptural statements being often vague and equivocal in terminology could be interpreted to serve polemical purposes in the hands of disputants with their own predilection. There are, no doubt, rules of interpretation laid down by the Pūrva-Mīmāṁsā but these are again adopted to suit one's own doctrinal stand.

An appeal to perception as a pramāṇa has no doubt some value in so far as it is the foundation of our experience. What is within the scope of our perceptual experience is to be accepted as valid. But the scope of perception is limited as it cannot decide things which are supernormal.

Inference from the standpoint of logic is of considerable importance. There are accepted canons of logic or reasoning. If an argument fulfils these conditions it will be accepted as valid; otherwise, it is rejected as fallacious. Any criticism that is based on logic or reasoning is of greater philosophical value than that based either on scripture or perception.

Secondly, criticism of the Advaitin's theories is also attempted on the basis of one's own theory or *siddhānta*. That is, the critic levels a charge against his opponent, taking for granted that the theory accepted by his school of thought is correct. The validity of such a criticism depends on the soundness of the theory held by the critic himself.

Thirdly, the criticism has also been made by accepting for argument's sake the position of the opponent and by showing that the opponent's view is full of inconsistencies. It is a criticism levelled within the frame-work of the same system. It is directed to expose the hollowness of the theory advocated by the rival school of thought on the basis of his own arguments. Such a criticism that points out internal incoherence is the soundest from a purely philosophical point of view.

It would be an interesting study to take up each of the criticisms of Vedānta Deśika and assess its soundness in the light of the possible answers of the Advaitin which may be found in some of the polemical works of post-Deśika period, particularly the *Advaita-siddhi* of Madhusūdana Saravati (1540-1647 A.D.) and the *Śatabhūṣaṇī* of Anantakrishna Sastri brought out in 1956 A.D. as a rejoinder to the *Śatadūṣaṇī* of Vedānta Deśika. Though it is desirable to make such an evaluation, it would not be an easy task and also it would not serve a useful purpose for the reasons explained below. Anantakrishna Sastri in his voluminous book under the title of *Śátabhūṣaṇī* has no doubt covered the examination of all the Vādas of the *Śatadūṣaṇī* except two.[1] Some of his narrations are brief, while others are very elaborate. However, he has not taken up for examination the relevant points of Deśika's criticism and answered them in a straight-forward manner. On the contrary, he has chosen to restate the Avaita position bearing on the topics covered in the *Śatadūṣaṇī* by drawing material both from the ancient Advaita works such as *Śaṁkara-bhāṣya, Brahma-siddhi, Iṣṭasiddhi, Naiṣkarmyasiddhi, Pañcapādikā, Vivaraṇa, Bhāmatī, Saṅkṣepaśārīraka, Tattvapradīpikā* and also contemporary works of post-Désika period such as *Advaitasiddhi, Siddhāntaleśa-saṅgraha, Pañcadaśī.* After stating the Advaita position as found in these works and also in a general way, he quotes briefly Vedānta Deśika's views which in most of the cases are unconnected with the Advaita theory referred to in the preceding paragraphs and sums up in one line that by this (Deśika's argument) stands refuted or by this it stands commented (*etena pratyuktāḥ etena vyākhyātāḥ*. A dispassionate reader of the

[1] The two Vādas which have been left our are: *niṣprapañcīkaraṇaniyoga bhaṅga vāda* (Vāda 46) and *alepakamatabhaṅga vāda* (Vāda 65) as they are not supposed to have a direct bearing on Advaita Vedānta.

*Śatabhūṣaṇī* fails to understand what the criticisms of Sastriar against Vedānta Deśika are and in what manner they are answered. Anantakrishna Sastri assumes that Vedānta Deśika has levelled criticisms without a proper understanding of Advaita position. This is far from the truth. In fact Deśika was fully aware of the views of Advaita Vedānta as set out in their original works that were extant at his time. This is evident from the fact that he generally states either briefly or in details the *prima facie* view (*pūrvapakṣa*) faithfully as found in the original Advaita works before he commences his critical analysis. Nowhere does he exhibit his ignorance or imperfect understanding of the Advaita doctrines. Nor does Deśika present the views of the rival school in a prejudicial manner. He may not have been aware of the contents of the later Advaita works, particularly *Advaita-siddhi, Pañcadaśī* and *Siddhāntaleśa-saṅgraha,* but the dialectical method adopted by him in the *Śatadūṣaṇī* by subjecting a particular theory or concept to several alternatives indicates clearly that he has anticipated all possible views that an Advaitin could conceivably advance even at a leter period. Thus for instance, the concept of *mithyātva* or illusoriness of the universe is subjected to seven alternatives which cover all possible definitions of the term. The concept of *akhaṇḍārthaparatva* or that which denotes one unitary undifferentiated entity is subjected to eight alternatives to cover exhaustively all conceivable meanings. The critical analysis of a theory by Deśika is so exhaustive that it becomes difficult for any Advaitin to offer a direct reply to his criticism. If inspite of this one attempts to counter his criticism it would only end up in a restatement of the original Advaitic position and dogmatically, assert that Advaitin's view is correct and Vedānta Deśika is wrong without any convincing arguments. This is what Anantakrishna Sastri has generally done in the *Śatabhūṣaṇī.* This is not the correct method of answering a criticism. The view of the critic needs to be subjected to logical analysis and the defects involved are to be brought out before rejecting the criticism. Sastriar has not done this and he has also not attempted to give a direct reply to the points of the criticism with supporting arguments. In several places he has even misunderstood or misinterpreted the views of Vedānta Deśika.

The *Śatadūṣaṇī* as polemical work (*vāda-grantha*) was written in the 14th century. For centuries thereafter no Advaita scholar ever attempted to write a reply to the criticisms of Vedānta Deśika. Why was it so? Presumably a direct and satisfactory answer to the criticisms of Deśika was not easy. Recently, Anantakrishna Sastri has ventured to write a rejoinder to the *Śatadūṣaṇī* but his *Śatabhūṣaṇī* does not provide a convincing answer to the criticisms levelled by Deśika.

However, as eminent Viśiṣṭādvaita scholar, Uttamur Veeraraghavacharya has written a rejoinder to the *Śatabhūṣaṇī* under the title of *Paramārthabhūṣaṇam,* published in 1959. He has covered in this book all the 64 Vādas in the same order as in the *Śatabhūṣaṇī* with the purpose of refuting the arguments advanced by Sastriar. In his attempt to answer the objections of Sastriar, he devotes greater attention to defend Viśiṣṭādvaita theories with the support of textual authority than replying in a straight forward manner to the criticisms raised by Sastriar. Throughout we find in his book an elaboration of Viśiṣṭādvaita theories instead of offering an appropriate counter-reply to the points of criticism found in the *Śatabhūṣaṇī.* There is also no attempt to assess dispassionately the soundness of the criticisms of Vedānta Deśika in the light of the possible counter-arguments of the Advaitins. Hence it would be of little use to evaluate the criticisms of the Vedānta Deśika with special reference to the arguments contained in the *Śatabhūṣaṇī* and also *Paramārtha-bhūṣaṇam.*

We are now confronted with the basic questions: (1) Are the criticisms of Vedānta Deśika against Advaita unanswerable (2) Are the Advaita doctrines defective? An orthodox Viśiṣṭādvaitin would answer these questions affirmatively. Similarly an orthodox Advaitin would answer them negatively. Both the approaches would be doctrinaire and motivated unless we examined the theories dispassionately. It is nothing uncommon for a follower of a particular school of thought to claim validity for his own system and denounce the views of the rival school as fallacious. For instance, the Nyāya-Vaiśeṣika school upholds its theories as valid, while condemning the teachings of the Buddhists. In the realm of Vedānta, the followers of Madhva vehemently condemn the theories of Advaita, while they cherish their own as the soundest ones. This is the case to a large extent with Anantakrishna Sastri, as the champion of Advaita and Uttamur Veeraraghavacharya, as the staunch Viśiṣṭādvaitin. But for discerning student of philosophy who owes no allegiance to any one system, such claims do not carry much weight. The Advaita Vedānta of Śaṁkara has survived through centuries in spite of strong criticisms levelled against its doctrines by powerful critics both from the camps of Rāmānuja and Madhava. Similarly, Rāmānuja's Viśiṣṭādvaita Vedānta and Madhva's Dvāita Vedānta are alive in spite of the criticisms against their teachings by the opponents. What then is the value of the criticism? The Indian philosophical systems have employed polemics as a necessary and even indispensable part of their philosophy. The function of such a polemic is not to drive the opponent out of existence but only to define and distinguish one's position from that of others with a view to establishing the soundness of his position. The function of a criticism, in other words, is primarily to clarify one's position and not merely demolish the opponents. In such attempts there is great gains in clarity. It also brings out fully the philosophical implications of the basic theories or issues. Herein lies the philosophic value of a polemical work.

In the light of these observations, we shall now attempt an objective and critical evaluation of the major issues covered in the *Śatadūṣaṇī* with a view to finding out whether or not Vedānta Deśika's criticisms are justified. In making this assessment we shall take into consideration the relevant arguments advanced by Sastriar in the *Śatabhūṣaṇī* as criticism of Vedānta Deśika and also the counter-arguments made by Veeraraghavacharya in the *Paramārtha-bhūṣaṇam.* This exercise will help us to understand and appreciate better Vedānta Deśika's criticisms of the doctrines of Advaita. We shall take up the topics in the same order as followed in the preceding chapters.

In the first chapter some of the important issues relating to the validity of the pramāṇas have been discussed. The importance of the subject lies in the fact that pramāṇas are considered indispensable prolegomena to all metaphysical investigation. Two issues have been raised against the Advaitin. The first issue is whether the pramāṇas which have only empirical reality can be evidence to what is absolutely real. Secondly, whenever there is a conflict between perception and scripture which of them is to be regarded as of greater validity? Both these issues arise as a result of the metaphysical position held by the Advaitin. The first one involves and important epistemological problem viz., whether what is illusory can have any practical efficiency or cause real effect. The second one refers to the status and value of perception as a source of knowledge.

The Advaitin justifies the first issue on the ground that even what is illusory can cause an effect of higher grade of reality, as in the case of dream object causing joy. The Viśiṣṭādvaitin denies this contention on the ground that an illusory object cannot have any practical efficiency; it is its cognition that is the cause of the real effect and cognition by its nature is real.

The whole controversy rests on one epistemological question namely, whether knowledge can be real when its object is not real. We get two different answers to this question from the Advaitin and Vaśiṣṭadvaitin. According to the Advaitin it is the nature of the object that determines the nature of the knowledge. Accordingly, if the object be illusory its corresponding knowledge cannot but be illusory. According to the Vaśiṣṭādvaitin, knowledge can be real even though its corresponding object is non-real. All that is necessary for a knowledge to be real is that it should have a content and the mere appearance of an object serves this purpose.[1] There is thus a wide difference in the theory of knowledge upheld by the two systems. If we accept the Advaitin's theory of knowledge, then what is illusory can certainly have a practical efficiency and as such *Śruti* can be a pramāṇa, in respect of Brahman, which is absolutely real. If, on the other hand, we accept the Vaśiṣṭādvaitic theory of knowledge as correct, the Advaitin's theory stands refuted.

Coming to the other issue regarding the relative validity of perception and scripture, the Advaitin argues that all scriptural texts are not of greater force than perception. Only purportful texts are held to be superior in validity to perception. This particular argument which is developed in *Bhāmatī* does not come in for criticism in the *Śatadūṣaṇī*. The Advaitin decides on the basis of the six marks that determine the purport of the scriptural texts (*ṣaḍvidha-tātparyaliṅga)* that non-dualism alone is the main purport of the scriptural texts. On the strength of the teaching of the scriptural texts it is argued that perception is of lesser validity than scripture in so far as the former conflicts with the latter. Where scripture contradicts experience as in the statement that "stones float" it is not admitted to be authoritative. "When however,

[1] See p. 20

perception pretends to declare the nature of the ultimate reality, it is obviously doing something outside its scope; and its sublation of *Śruti* is legitimate."[1]

The above position is sound as far as it goes. But there is one difficulty involved in it, which the Viśiṣṭādvaitin stresses strongly. How can scripture override perception which is the foundation of our experience and which offers subsistence to inference and scripture (*upajīvya*)? Secondly, it is established by perception that difference is real and as such how can scripture teach something as opposed to perceptual knowledge?

Both these questions are answered by the Advaitin. As in the previous case, the answers given to these objections only bring out the difference in the standpoints of the two systems rather than offer any final solution to the questions. Regarding the first question, it is argued that perception no doubt is the *upajīvya* of scripture in so far as the latter is dependent on it for the perceptual knowledge of words and sentences etc., All that is needed for its dependence is the empirical validity of words etc., and not their absolute validity. This much is not contradicted by scripture.

Regarding the second question, it is argued that perception does not cognise difference. This is an important subject of controversy and it is examined separately in chapter II.

The discussion covered in chapter I relating to the validity of the Pramāṇas and the overriding authority of scripture over perception, does not help us to arrive at any final conclusion as to which of the views held by the two schools is correct. Both the Advaitin and Viśiṣṭādvaitin argue on the basis of two different standpoints of their respective systems. According to the Advaitin there is a difference between the concept of empirical reality and the concept of illusoriness, though in the last analysis from the metaphysical point of view everything other than Brahman is illusory. The rope-snake or the dream-elephant does not enjoy the same degree of reality as the scripture which is empirically real. The Viśiṣṭādvaitin, however, in his criticism treats both as belonging to the same order of reality. Whether or not the critic accepts the degrees of reality is a different matter. It he accedes to it, he cannot reject the views of the Advaitin on the mere ground of

[1] See Introduction, S.L.S., Vol. I, p. 27

empirical reality of the pramāṇas. All these polemical arguments against the validity of the pramāṇas are therefore of academic nature and not philosophically important.

Chapter II discusses the concept of difference. This is of cardinal importance to Advaita Vedānta. The importance of the subject is evident from the fact that it has occupied the attention of all the Advaita thinkers beginning from Maṇḍana down to Brahmānanda. Similarly, in the rival schools of Vedānta the problem of difference had exercised the minds of all the thinkers who unsparingly have attacked Monism on this ground. The issues involved in the problem are mainly two: Is difference known by perception or not? Secondly, is difference real or not? The first is an epistemological issue, while the second is an ontological issue and the two are complementary.

According to the Advaitin difference cannot be known by perception. Nor is its nature logically intelligible. It is therefore not real but illusory. According to the Viśiṣṭādvaitin difference is known by perception. Its nature is also logically intelligible. It is, therefore, real and not illusory. Thus, the two schools stand fundamentally opposed to each other on this subject. Both have attempted to justify their theories with elaborate arguments.

The concept of difference is held to be logically unintelligible because it cannot be conceived either as the nature of the thing or its attribute as in either case logical difficulties would arise.[1] The Viśiṣṭādvaitin refutes this contention on the ground that difference can either be the nature of the thing or its attribute. Difference is defined as that which gives rise to the judgement that things are different (*vyāvṛtta-vyavahāra-hetuḥ*). Generally it is the characteristic of the thing that gives rise to the judgement of difference, for it is on the basis of the characteristic which the one possesses and the other does not, that we differentiate the two objects. Sometimes the *svarūpa* of the object may also give rise to the judgement of difference and as such difference is the *svarūpa* of the object. On further analysis it is pointed out that the exclusive characteristic of the object (*asādhāraṇa dharma*) which is known as *jāti* constitutes the difference of one object from another.[2]

[1] See pp. 32-33.
[2] See p. 35.

The above explanation of difference by the Viśiṣṭādvaitin appears to be perfectly intelligible both from the standpoint of logic as well as that of our common experience. The difficulty only arises when we take the question whether difference is known by perception. If difference is considered a relation, which is the meaning of the term according to the Advaitin, its cognition would necessarily presuppose the knowledge of the relata; but in a single act of perception both the relation as well as the relata are not known simultaneously.

The Viśiṣṭādvaitin tries to get over this difficulty by pointing out that even in a single act of cognition it is possible to cognise both the object as well as its difference in as much as both are capable of being known by the same sense organ. This contention is based upon the fundamental supposition of the Viśiṣṭādvaitic theory of knowledge that all knowledge is of the characterised. Whenever we see an object we see it along with its particular structure (*saṁsthāna*) which is the exclusive characteristic of the object. This structure which is technically known as *jāti* in the Viśiṣṭādvaita system is itself the difference of the object from others in so far as that alone gives rise to the judgement of difference. Since that is apprehended along with the *svarūpa* of the object, difference is said to be as much the content of perception as the *svarūpa* of the object is.

There is nothing to say against the above theory in as much as it is supported by our common experience. Even if the mental act subsists for one moment only, it can grasp a vast area of the objective field. As Madhva points out, we see thousands of lamps at a glance. But the question may be asked: when we see an object do we see it as different from others? We may see the object as characterised but do we also at the same time see that the object is different from others. The Viśiṣṭādvaitin answers in the affirmative. As Rāmānuja points out, when an object is seen along with its special characteristic (*jāti*), it is as good as cognising it as different from others. If difference were not cognised at the moment an object as qualified by its generic character is seen, a person searching for a horse would not be satisfied with finding a buffalo.[1] However, when a judgement or empirical usage that a particular object is different from another is made, it needs the knowledge

[1] *Śrī-bhāṣya* I.1.1.

of its counter-correlate (*pratiyogi*).

All these arguments and counter-arguments relating to the concept of difference are more of dialectical nature than they being constructive criticism of a theory. Difference between two entities, whether they be ontological or empirical, as also between a substance and its attribute, is an accepted fact and needs no proof. The Avaitin is not unaware of this fact. Yet, he argues by using a dialectic to prove that difference is not ultimately real but an appearance. Similar dialectic is adopted by the western idealist, F.H. Fradley to disprove the reality of difference.[1] The main objective of denouncing difference is to uphold the Absolute Monism which does not allow for plurality. The acceptance of difference for practcal purpose as empirically real and not ultimately real, does not hold good unless the theory of two grades of reality is proved as valid. When difference between two objects or qualities is so obvious to perceptual experience, its denial purely on the ground of dialectic is not a satisfactory theory. Vedānta Deśika stresses this point and he is therefore justified in his criticism of the Advaitin's theory of difference.

The discussion on the nature of the consciousness (*anubhūti*) which is the subject matter of the third chapter of this book brings out in a greater measure the difference in the standpoints of the two systems. The Advaitin who approaches the problem from a transcendental point of view, if we may call it so, contends that consciousness is self-dependent (*svataḥ-siddha)*, eternal, one, undifferentiated pure knowledge which is the very Brahman. The Viśiṣṭādvaitin who approaches the problem from the empirical standpoint, that is, from the point of view of common experience, urges that consciousness is that which manifests itself as related to a subject on the one hand and an object on the other. A universal consciousness is held to be an abstraction, a fiction and not real existence.

There are seven contentions of the Advaitin regarding the nature of the universal consciousness as given in the *Śatadūṣaṇī*: 1. Consciousness is self-proved; 2. it is self-luminous in the sense that it is not an object of another knowledge; 3. it is eternal having neither a beginning nor an end; 4. it is not subject to transformation; 5. it is not many but one; 6. it is undifferentiated in character; 7. lastly it is the very self (*ātman*). Each one of these

[1] See p. 33 fn.2.

is an important issue emphasising the unity of consciousness and its transcendental character. In fact, they signify the nature of the Advaitic Reality as *cit* or consciousness.

Each one of these contentions has been criticised by the Viśiṣṭādvaitin on the ground that consciousness is that which is related to a knowing subject on the one hand and has a reference to an object. Obviously according to this theory, consciousness cannot be one eternal self-luminous light devoid of all determinations.

If consciousness is the very Reality, the Brahman itself as the Advaitin claims, the criticisms offered by Vedānta Deśika, which are primarily based on what Rāmānuja has stated in the *Śrī-bhāṣya*, appear on the face of it as unjustified because even for the Viśiṣṭādvaitin the ultimate Reality as conceived by him is one, eternal (*nitya*), without a beginning or end, and not subject to transformation, The Viśiṣṭādvaita Vedānta admits two types of *jñāna* - *jñāna* as the very *svarūpa* of both Brahman and *jīvātman* and *jñāna* as the attribute (*guṇa*) of Brahman and jīvātman. The latter is designated as *dharma-bhūta jñāna* or *jñāna* as a *dharma,* as distinct from the former which is known as *svarūpa jñāna* or *jñāna* as *svarūpa.* The *dharma-bhūta jñāna* and *svarūpa jñāna* are comparable to the Advaitin's concepts of *vṛtti-jñāna* and *anubhūti* respectively, though there is a wide difference between the theories advanced by the two schools. Most of the characteristic features of the *anubhūti* conceived by the Advaitin are applicable to the *svarūpa jñāna* admitted by the Viśiṣṭādvaitin. How then is he justified in criticising Advaitin's theory of *anubhūti* on the basis of the *dharma-bhūta jñāna* ? It may look unfair for the Viśiṣṭādvaitin, taking his stand on his own *siddhānta,* to criticise a theory of Advaita which is developed on different metaphysical position. Ananthakrishna Sastri, in his rejoinder to the criticism of Vedānta Deśika often emphasises this point.

Both Rāmānuja and Vedānta Deśika are not unaware of this point of criticism. If, however, they strongly criticise the theory of *anubhūti* of Advaita Vedānta, it is because of the fact that the transcendental consciousness as conceived by the Advaitin does not exist at all. It cannot be established by any of the pramāṇas, either perceptual experience and inference or scriptural texts. In the strongest terms Vedānta Deśika asserts that it is a non-existent like the sky-flower.[1] Even if it is admitted to be self-established (*svataḥ-siddha*) like Brahman, it cannot be altogether unknowable (*avedya*) or beyond any means of knowing by the pramāṇas. Scripture reveals the nature of Brahman and to that extent it becomes knowable. The assumption of the Advaitin that whatever in knowable (*dṛśya*) is material like a pot, is considered to be wrong logic and it is refuted by both Rāmānuja and Madhva.

Further, the *svarūpa jñāna* or *jñāna* as the very nature of Brahman and *jīvātman,* is not *jnāna* in the strict sense, since it is not functional like the empirical knowledge. The Viśiṣṭādvaitin is right in pointing out repeatedly that *jñāna* or *anubhūti* (the two terms are synonymous for him) is that which reveals an object and which is invariably related to the self on the one hand and to an object on the other. What constitutes the *svarūpa* of Brahman and *jīvātman* cannot have such a function and it is not therefore considered as *jñāna* in the ordinary sense as commonly understood.

Even it we admit that the *Svarūpa jñāna* conceived by the Viśiṣṭādvaita Vedānta is similar to the concept of *anubhūti* of Advaita Vedānta, it cannot be *absolutely nirviśeṣa* or devoid of all characteristics. In the case of Brahman, it may be one but not so in respect of *jīva,* because *jīvas* are infinite in number. Both admit differentiation or characteristics such as *nityatva, jñānatva, ānandatva* and *amalatva.* On the basis of the Upaniṣadic texts, the Viśiṣṭādvaitin admits that Brahman in addition to its being *jñāna-svarūpa* is also *jñāna-guṇaka.* If Rāmānuja and Vedānta Deśika strongly attack Advaitin's theory of *anubhūti,* it is for the reason of proving that Brahman is not *nirviśeṣa* but *saviśeṣa.* If *nirviśeṣa-Brahmavāda* is not tenable, the criticisms of Vedānta Deśika against the theory of *anubhūti* are justified.

The fourth chapter discusses the nature of the individual self. There are four important issues relating to this subject which come up for critical examination.

(a) whether or not the notion of ego (*aham-pratyaya*) is the Self.
(b) whether the *jīva* is a knower (*jñātā*) or mere *jñāna-svarūpa.*
(c) whether *jīva* is one only or many.
(d) whether *jīva* and *Īśvara* are identical.

On all these issues the Advaitin holds a view as totally different from that of the Viśiṣṭādvaitin and naturally the critic of Advaita

[1] See fn. on p. 60.

has to refute them to establish the soundness of his own theory.

Regarding the first issue, the criticisms of Vedānta Deśika are fully justified since these are based on sound and detailed arguments to disprove the wrong assumption of the Advaitin that the notion of 'I' or ego is associated with *ahamkāra tattva*, the product of illusion and does not persist in the states of deep sleep and release. The notion of 'I' persists at all times and even in the state of *mokṣa*. The *jīva* manifests itself always as aham.[1] This fact is conclusively established by Rāmānuja in the *Śrī-bhāṣya* and by Vedānta Deśika in the Śatadūṣaṇī.[2] The Advaitin can defend his position on the ground that *jīva* is not a distinct spiritual entity but it is the Brahman or consciousness conditioned by the internal organ (*antaḥ-karaṇa*). Whether or not such a theory is sound is a different issue. As we see presently, it is proved by Vedānta Deśika as untenable.

Similarly, the second issue relating to the nature of *jīva* as a knowing subject (*jñātā*) is based on the wrong assumption of the Advaitin that knowership involves change, whereas *jīva* is immutable. That this is not the case is conclusively established by Vedānta Deśika.[3] Further, if knowership is not admitted in respect of *jīva*, all the psychological and other functions of the individual self cannot be satisfactorily explained. The explanation offered on the basis of superimposition of knowership on the pure self-luminous consciousness is shown to be untenable.[4] More importantly, both the scriptural texts and *Vedānta-sūtra* strongly support *jñātṛtva* of the individual self.

The plurality of the individual self (*jīva*) and its identity with Brahman or *Īśvara* are major ontological issues for both Advaita and Viśiṣṭādvaita Vedānta. The Advaitin who is obliged to establish non-dualism as the ultimate truth of philosophy maintains that the plurality of individual souls is not ultimately real. Taking his stand on a few crucial Upaniṣadic statements such as "That thou art" (*tattvamasi*) he asserts the identity of the individual self with Brahman. To meet the empirical need of plurality of souls, which is warranted by experience, he resorts to the theory of the souls

[1] See *Tattva-muktā-kalāpa* II-6 *ātmā svenaiva siddhyati ahamiti...*

[2] See pp. 62-65.

[3] See pp. 67-68.

[4] See pp. 65-67.

as reflections of the one ultimate Reality in the several internal organs (*antaḥkaraṇas*) like the reflection of the single moon in the waves. Alternatively, he conceives that the one transcendental consciousness as conditioned by several internal organs constitute the individual souls. The Viśiṣṭādvaitin who takes his stand on the bedrock of experience and scriptural teachings refutes the Advaitin's contention and establishes that the individual selves are eternal spiritual entities distinct from Brahman.

The logical arguments adopted by the Advaitin in defence of *ātmādvaitavāda* or *eka-jīva-vāda*, which comes up for critical examination in the *Śatadūṣaṇī*, are proved to be defective by Vedānta Désika, as they do not stand the logical scrutiny.[1] The Advaitin cannot defend satisfactorily his thesis purely on the basis of logic as against the weighty scriptural authority and our common experience warranting the plurality of the souls. Even if the Advaitin depends solely on the scriptural texts to support his theory, he cannot prove his point convincingly as there are larger number of other *śruti* and *smṛti* texts pointing out the reality and plurality of the *jīvas*. Though this point is not taken up for discussion in the *Śatadūṣaṇī*, it is brought out in the *Śrī-bhāsya* and other Viśiṣṭādvaita treatises. Against these weighty arguments well supported with strong scriptural evidence, it is difficult for an Advaitin to prove this theory. In the last resort he may revert to the doctrine of *Māyā* on the basis of which the one Brahman is claimed to appear as many. But this theory, as will be seen presently, is not considered to be sound by the critic.

The fourth issue discussed in chapter IV relating to the identity of *jīva* and *Īśvara* (*jīveśvaraikya-vāda*) is also vital to Advaita Vedānta. All the arguments advanced by the Advaitin to prove his theory are critically examined in detail and set aside by Vedānta Désika. A large number of scriptural and smṛti texts including the *Vedānta-sūtras* and *Bhagavad-gītā* lend greater support to the Viśiṣṭādvaitin. The only way for an Advaitin to defend his theory against his critics is to resort to his fundamental metaphysical tenet viz., that Brahman alone is absolutely real and everything else other than Brahman is an appearance. But this theory can be sustained if the doctrine of *Māya*, the principle on the basis of which the illusory appearance of one Brahman as many can be explained. As will be shown presently, this theory is not tenable according to the critics. Hence the criticisms of

[1] See pp. 69-74.

Vedānta Désika against the Advaitin's theory of *jīva* stand justified.

The doctrine of *Nirguṇa* Brahman covered in the chapter V is unique to the Advaita Vedānta. It has attracted the criticisms of all the theistic schools of Vedānta who do not accept it. The major issue involved is whether Brahman is a pure Being devoid of all characteristics or whether it is a concrete Being endowed with infinite attributes. The primary source of authority on which both the schools of Vedānta rely to determine the nature of Brahman is the scriptural texts. The Advaitin takes his stand on the basis of a few Upaniṣadic statements, which in his opinion teach that Brahman is devoid of all differentiation. The Viśiṣṭādvaitin strongly questions the import of these statements as interpreted by the Advaitin and seeks the support of a larger number of Upaniṣadic statements which categorically point out that Brahman is endowed with attributes. Vedānta Désika does not take up in the *Śatadūṣaṇi* a detailed examination of the individual Upaniṣadic texts and the *smṛti* texts referring to the nature of Brahman as *saguna* or *nirguna* as this task has been covered extensively by Rāmānuja in his *Śrībhāṣya.* He, on the other hand, devotes his attention to the critical examination of the principles on the basis of which the Advaitin seeks to defend the *nirguṇa-Brahma-vada.*

The Principle of *apaccheda-nyāya* is adopted by the Advaitin to claim a greater validity to *nirguṇa-śrutis* as against *saguṇa-śrutis.* Vedānta Deśika has shown that *apaccheda-nyāya* as formulated in the Pūrva-Mīmāṁsā is not applicable to the present case.[1] He is correct in this respect.

The second principle to which the Advaitin gives greater importance is, that the *samānādhikaraṇa* or the sentence in which the terms are found in apposition, conveys an impartite and non-relational sense (*akhaṇḍārtha*). Applying this principle to the Upaniṣadic statement which defines Brahman as *satya, jñāna* and *ananta,* he interprets it in favour of *akhaṇḍārtha,* that is, as conveying the import that Brahman is the very *svarūpa* of *satya, jñāna* and *ananta* and not one endowed with these attributes. The criticism of this theory is very elaborate. The entire *Vāda,* which is one of the longest in the *Śatadūṣaṇī* and the most important one is devoted to prove, from all points of view that the *samānādhikaraṇavākya* cannot convey an impartite and non-relational

[1] See p. 79.

sense.[1] If the correct meaning of the *sāmānādhikaraṇya* as defined by the grammarian is taken, as Rāmānrya and Vedānta Deśika have done, his criticism of the theory is a unassaislable.

In the same way, a *lakṣaṇa-vākya* or a sentence defining the nature of an object (in this case Brahman) such as the '*satyam jñānam* and *anantam brahma*' cannot under any circumstances convey an impartite and non-relational sense because of the fact that a definition of an object is possible only in terms of its essential characteristics.[2]

Apart from the scriptural texts, it is conclusively established that neither perception nor the inference can prove the existence of a *nirviśeṣa* entity. Even the so called indeterminate perception (*nirvikalpaka pratyakṣa*) reveals an object as qualified with some qualities. Regarding the inference, in the logical proposition used as the major premise of the syllogism a relationship is to be established between the subject and the predicate. This would necessarily involve the predication of a quality to the subject.

The very term 'Brahman' taking its etymological meaning, implies a qualified Brahman possessing the attributes of *bṛhattva* (growing) and *bramhaṇatva* (causing to grow) since such characteristics connoted by the term are not applicable to a pure Being devoid of all attributes (nirviśeṣa)[3].

Leaving aside the scriptural texts and the other principles of interpretation, the Advaitin may finally resort to the *Vedānta-sūtras* to prove his theory of *nirviśeṣa-brahma-vāda.* Assuming that this is the case, Vedānta Désika examines in a general way to find out if the *sūtras* of Bādarāyaṇa support the thesis of the Advaitin. The concluding *Vāda* in the *Śatadūṣaṇī* is devoted to the critical examination of the different *adhikaraṇas* or topics in the *Vedānta-sūtras.* Though he does not go into the details of the interpretation of each *sūtra* offered by Śaṁkara in his *Brahma-sūtra Bhāṣya,* he advances adequate explanation to prove how the *adhikaraṇas* do not favour *nirviśeṣa-Brahman.* The trend of the *sūtras,* he contends, is definitely in favour of saviśeṣa-Brahman.[4]

Anantakrishna Sastri in his rejoinder to the *Śatadūṣaṇī* takes up this particular Vāda for a critical examination at the very com-

[1] See pp. 82-84.
[2] See pp. 85-86.
[3] See pp. 92-93.
[4] See pp. 96-99.

mencement of his *Śatabhūṣaṇī*. The greater importance given to this particular topic indicates the deep concern of the Advaitin to defend the *Vedānta-sūtras* in favour of *nirviśeṣa-brahma-vāda*. As is expected he comes to the conclusion that *sūtras* support the thesis of Advaita. In the same way, Uttamur Veeraraghavacharya, who writes a rejoinder to Sastriar arrives at the conclusion that the *Vedānta-sūtras* do not support the *nirviśeṣa-brahma-vāda*.[1]

The important point for our consideration is whether or not the views of Vedānta Désika on this matter are justifiable. Though *prima facie* Vedānta Désika is right in his criticism, we cannot make a categorical statement to this effect without making a thorough and dispassionate study of the *Vedānta-sūtras* without bringing in the views as expressed in the commentaries of Śaṁkara and Rāmānuja who have offered their own interpretations of the aphorisms of Bādarāyaṇa in accordance with the metaphysical positions of their system. This needs an independent study and is taken up in a separate book[2]. For the present it may be stated that according to Vedānta Désika the *Vedānta-sūtras* do not support *nirviśeṣa-Brahmavāda*, in spite of the claim of the Advaitin to that effect.

The theory of the universe as illusory (*mithyā*) and the doctrine of *Avidyā* which are dealt with in the chapters VI and VII constitute the edifice for the Advaita Vedānta. They are the logical corollaries of the absolute Monism. If Brahman alone is real how is the universe of plurality which we experience is to be accounted for? This is the vexed problem of the one and many which every monistic system has to face. The solution to this problem is offered by regarding the universe as an appearance. Again, if the universe is an appearance the question arises as to why there is an appearance? Why does the one Absolute appear as many? Here comes the doctrine of *Māya* or *Avidyā* which is admitted as a cosmic principle to account for the world-illusion.

The Advaitin does not, however, dogmatically assert that the universe is illusory. As we have seen in the chapter VI, he has several logical arguments, besides scriptural authority, to prove the illusory character of the universe. All these arguments have been refuted by Vedānta Deśika as untenable. Besides Rāmānuja and

1 See also *Tattva-sudhā* by E. S. Varadacharya.

2. See *The Philosophy of the Vedāntasūtra* by Dr. S.M.S. Chari.

Vedānta Désika, the followers of Madhva school of Vedānta have made this subject the main target of their attack on Advaita and as uncompromising critics they have strongly criticised the arguments of the Advaitin.[1] Madhusūdana Sarasvatī, in his famous *Advaita-siddhi* and Gauḍa Brahmānanda in his commentary on it have put up an equally strong defence of Advaita theory of *jaganmithyātva*.

How far are the critics justified in their criticism of this particular doctrine? We are concerned here with the evaluation of Vedānta Deśika's views as outlined in the *Śatadūṣanī*. If we look at this matter objectively, we cannot help feeling that there is a certain amount of misconception of the Advaita concept of *mithyātva* or illusoriness. The term *mithyā* bears a special meaning for the Advaitin. It does not mean false or non-existent (*asat*) as is commonly understood by the critics. Similarly, the term *sat* or *satya* does not merely mean what is real or what exists as is commonly understood. On the contrary, it is that which is not sublated at any time or that which exists for all the time (*traikālika abādhyatva*). Taking the special connotation of these two terms, *mithyā* means in a technical sense that which is neither real (*sat*) nor unreal (*asat*) (*sadasatvilakṣaṇa*). In other words, to use the Advaitin's terminology, it is *anirvacanīya* or indeterminable either as real or unreal. If we accept this exaplanation of the Advaitin, the categorisation of the universe as *mithyā* would imply that it is not absolutely unreal, like the sky-flower. Nor is it absolutely real as Brahman is. For all practical purposes, the universe is as real as it is for the critics. The Advaitins generally admit three grades of reality: a) *prātibhāsika satya* or apparent reality such as the dream object, b) *vyāvahārika satya* or empirical reality such as the objects of common experience and c) *pāramārthika satya* or absolute reality such as the Brahman. If we concede to this classification of reality and the definitions offered by the Advaitin for *mithyātva*, some of the criticisms against the doctrine of *mithyātva* of the universe appear to be unjustified.

Vedānta Deśika is not unaware of these facts. So also other critics. Though Śaṁkara himself has adopted a liberal view about the reality of the universe, the other Advaitic thinkers, both ancient and contemporary, have not been consistent in their

[1] See *Nyāyāmṛta* by Vyāsatīrtha and the two major commentaries on it by Vyāṣa Rāmāchārya and Ānandabhaṭṭāraka.

interpretation of the *mithyātva.* Thus Gauḍapāda even earlier than Śaṁkara, being influenced by the Buddhist teaching, takes the view that the world of experience is similar to the experience of dream objects. The post-Śaṁkara Advaitins offer definitions of *mithyātva* which go beyond Śaṁkara's liberal view. For instance the two definitions of the term: a) as being cognised in the same locus as its own absolute non-existence (*svātyantābhāva samānādhikaraṇatayā pratīyamānatvam*) and b) as being the counter-correlate of the negation of what is found in a particular locus (*pratipanna upadhau niṣedha-pratiyogitvam*), amount to saying that the universe does not exist. In the famous syllogistic argument, *dṛśyatvānumāna* adopted by the later Advaitins to prove the illusory character of the universe, the probans of the syllogism viz., that whatever is objective is illusory and the illustration (*dṛṣṭānta*) of shell-silver in support of it, amount to the denial of real existence to the universe. More important than these facts the concept of *bādhyatva* or negation by the dawn of knowledge of Brahman stands opposed to common experience. The dream objects may be negated by waking experience but the objects of experience are not. The critics place more emphasis on these points of inconsistencies or lacunae in the Advaitin's stand and also the extreme view of *mithyātva* of post-Śaṁkara Advaitins and repudiate the very theory of illusoriness of the universe. Inspite of these defects the Advaitin's theory of *jagan-mithyātva* can be defended on the basis of the *Māya,* which is the cosmic principle to account for the appearance of the universe in place of Brahman, on the analogy of the cognition of the snake in the rope. Is this theory of *Māyā* sustainable? This is the doctrine which comes up for much more detailed critical analysis in the *Śrī-bhāṣya* and Śatadūṣaṇī and it is covered in the chapter VII.

The criticism of the doctrine of Avidyā is very extensive and thorough. It is subjected to searching analysis from all points of view. Its very nature (*svarūpa*) is unintelligible. Either Brahman or *jīva* serving as its locus (*āśraya*) is untenable. Its functions as obscuring the self-luminous Brahman (*tirodhāna*) is inconceivable. Its removal by right knowledge (*nivartaka*) is not intelligible. The very conception of its cessation (*nivṛtti*) is a riddle. More than all, the very theory is not supported by any of the pramāṇas. All these criticisms are not easily defensible. The only defense that an Advaitin can put up is that it is not a real entity (*vastu*) and hence there is no point in subjecting it to a logical analysis. Unintelligibility itself is the characteristic feature of the theory. As the author of Pañcadaśī points out, "Wonder is its garment; inscrutable is its nature".[1] For the purpose of upholding the monistic system of philosophy which is claimed to be the main theme of the Upaniṣads, the admission of the cosmic principle of *Māyā* to account for the appearance of the world of plurality is inevitable. Whether or not a system of philosophy built on the basis of a questionable postulate is sound is a matter to be judged by an impartial student of philosophy.

In the chapter VIII we have discussed some of the issues arising out of the interpretation of the first aphorism of the Vedānta. They are more of academic interest than of philosophical significance. The question, for instance, what should precede the study of Vedanta—whether the four requisites laid down by Śaṁkara or the study of rituals as Rāmānuja emphasises—may not be of importance for modern students of Vedānta because Vedāntins belonging to either school do not strictly comply with these requirements before undertaking the study of Vedānta. Assuming that some exceptional individuals may fulfil the requisites, then we must concede in fairness to Śaṁkara, that certain amount of *vairāgya* or non-attachment to worldly pleasures and *mumukṣutva* or a desire for liberation from bondage are desirable requirements for the study of Vedānta. Both Rāmānuja and Vedānta Deśika concede to this but nevertheless in their opinion, the study of rituals is of greater importance as prolegomena to the study of Vedānta for more than one reason. According to the traditional scheme of scholastic study, a student is made to go through the study of other *śāstras*, particularly *Vyākaraṇa, Nyāya* and *Pūrva-Mīmāṁsā* before he takes up Vedānta study because the knowledge of other śāstras makes him better equipped for an intensive study of Vedānta. Both Śaṁkara and Rāmānuja possessed adequate knowledge of these *śāstras* as is made evident in their scholarly commentaries on the *Vedānta-sūtras.* The knowledge of *pūrva-mīmāṁsā* in general and in particular, the acquaintance with the rules of interpretation formulated in it would be useful to the study of *Vedānta-sūtras.*

It is also believed by some Vedāntins that *pūrva-mīmāṁsā* is an

[1] *Pañcadaśī* VI, 139.
See also Bhāmatī *Catussūtrī* p. XXXIV (TPH).
Also *Brahmasiddhi* p. 6.

integral part of Vedānta which is designated as *uttara-mīmāṁsā*. However, Śaṁkara does not consider the *pūrva* and *uttara Mīmāṁsā* represent two parts of the same one treatise known as *Mīmāṁsā-śāstra*, whereas Rāmānuja believes that it is one. There are sufficient arguments both in favour of and against this supposition. In the absence of sufficient historical evidence for the chronological order of the different *darśanas*, it is difficult to come to a conclusion. However, going by the authoritative statement of Bodhāyana, the oldest commentator on *Vedānta-sūtras*, the *Mīmāṁsā-śāstra* is one single treatise comprising two parts. The relevant statement of Bodhāyana which is quoted by Rāmānuja in the *Śrī bhāṣya* reads: "The *śarīraka* of four chapters forms a textual totality with the sixteen-chaptered *pūrva-mīmāṁsā* of Jaimini". (*saṁhitam etat śārīrarakaṁ jaiminīyena ṣoḍaṣa-lakṣaṇena iti śāstraikatvasiddhiḥ*). Based on this authority, Rāmānuja also points out: It is a single *śāstra* divided into three sections *karma-kāṇḍa* of twelve chapters (of Jaimini), *Devatā-kāṇḍa* of four chapters (compiled by Saṅkarṣaṇa) and *para-devatā-kāṇḍa* of four chapters (of Bādarāyaṇa). This twenty-chaptered work is throughout gripped and dominated by a central plan and execution. If we accept this ancient authority we cannot deny the fact that Bādarāyaṇa in the opening aphorism intended by the word *atha* that the enquiry into the Brahman (Brahma-*jijñāsā*) is to be preceded by the study of rituals. The Muṇḍaka Upaniṣadic statement[1] also supports this stand taken by Bodhāyana and Rāmānuja. Vedānta Deśika is therefore justified in his criticism of Advaita position on this subject.

It is yet for a different reason the Advaitin denies the need of the study of the rituals for the study of Vedānta. In his opinion, *karma* and *jñāna* are opposed to each other and the former does not directly serve the purpose of Brahman knowledge. These arguments of the Advaitin are refuted by the Viśiṣṭādvaitin. The justification for holding two different views on the subject can be offered on the basis of the different views held by the two schools regarding the nature of *sādhana* or means to *mokṣa* or Brahman-realization. The important issue involved here is whether *jñāna* or intuitive knowledge of Brahman alone is the direct means to *mokṣa*

[1] Mund. Up, I.2.12.
*Parīkṣya lokān karmacitān brāhmaṇo nirvedamāyāt nāstyakṛtaḥ kṛtena; tadvijñānārtham sa gurumeva abhigacchet samitpāṇiḥ śrotriyam brahmaniṣṭham.*

or the *upāsanā* (meditation) on Brahman undertaken after acquiring knowledge from the study of sacred texts would lead to *mokṣa.* These are the two different theories on *sādhana* to be pursued by an aspirant for *mokṣa.* The two schools of Vedānta justify their theories primarily on the authority of Upaniṣadic teachings. But the two schools adopt different interpretation of the same Upaniṣadic texts biassed by their respective metaphysical positions and it becomes difficult to judge as to which theory is sound purely on the basis of the scriptural texts.

Scriptural texts apart, the Advaitin justifies his theory on a different ground. According to Advaita Vedānta, bondage is caused by the ignorance (*ajñāna*) of the true nature of Brahman, just as the delusion of the snake in place of the rope is caused by the ignorance of the true nature of the rope. Unless *ajñāna* or *avidyā* as it is termed, is removed totally, it is not possible to attain *mokṣa.* The removal of such a bondage which is caused by *avidyā* is possible only by right knowledge, as in the case of the illusion of the rope-snake by knowledge of the rope and not by any other means. Against such a background, it is but appropriate that Advaita Vedānta accords greater importance to jñāna rather than *upāsanā* as the means of Brahman-realization.

The Advaitin's position looks sound if we concede to his conception of bondage and the doctrine of *avidyā.* The critic does not accept it. As we have already noted, the doctrine of *avidyā* and particularly the very concept of its removal by right knowledge is far from satisfactory. Vedānta Deśika is therefore quite justified in refuting this theory. Whatever defense the Advaitin may put up, as Sastriar has done in his *Śatabhūṣaṇī,* cannot stand the logical scrutiny. The Viśiṣṭādvaitin is right in claiming that *upāsanā* is the means to *mokṣa* as such a theory is well supported by a large number of the Upaniṣadic texts, the *Vedānta-sūtras* and the Bhagavad-gītā.

Incidentally, the theory of *jīvanmukti* comes up for criticism. Though it is an important feature of Advaita Vedānta, it is not acceptable to the critics because it involves a self-contradiction. The explanations offered by way of defense of the theory on the basis of the concept of *bādhitānuvṛtti* or the continuance of a trace of *avidyā* even after overcoming bondage by a *Brahma-jñāni,* does not stand to reason.[1] If an individual is alive with the association

[1] See pp. 168-69.

of physical body, he cannot be regarded as *mukta*; if he becomes a *mukta*, he cannot have the association of the physical body.

The theory of *mokṣa*, which is an important theory of Vedānta, does not come up for any detailed discussion in the Śatadūṣaṇī. The only issue which is discussed in connection with the consideration of the nature of knowledge of the released soul (*muktasaṁvit-nirviṣayatva*), is whether the individual soul in the state of *mokṣa* becomes identical with Brahman (*tādātmya*) or it attains a status equal to that of Brahman (*sāmya* or *sādharmya*). The view taken by the Advaitin is that the individual self becomes one with Brahman, on the strength of the Upaniṣadic text which states that *Brahmavit* becomes Brahman (*brahmaveda brahmaiva bhavati*)[1]. The words *brahmaiva* are understood in the literal sense and on that basis such a view is adopted. Vedānta Désika questions this interpretation. In conformity with many other Upaniṣadic statements relating to the status of the individual self in the state of *mokṣa*, he takes the view that the soul becomes like Brahman, that is, it attains a status equal to that of Brahman. It also becomes omniscient (*sarvajña*) and experiences Brahman in its full glory and as such it is not contentless knowledge.[2] This view carries with it greater relevance because the individual self is not totally obliterated in the state of *mokṣa* by becoming one with Brahman but exists with its own individuality by enjoying the glory of Brahman. The Advaitin's view on this subject can find a justification if the souls which are infinite in number are not distinct spiritual entities but reflections of one Brahman. But such a theory, as we have seen elsewhere is not plausible because the theory of *avidyā* on the basis of which one Brahman appearing as many souls is rejected.

We have so far made a general overall evaluation of the Vedānta Deśika's criticisms against the doctrines of Advaita Vedānta as given in the *Śatadūṣaṇī*. This comparatve analysis is not intended to denounce Advaita as a defective philosophical system and uphold Viśiṣṭādvaita as a sounder system. On the other hand, our objective is to bring to light the inherent inconsistencies in some of the theories of Advaita system as pointed out by Rāmānuja and Vedānta Deśika. An Advaitin may not accept these criticisms of

[1] Mund. Up. III.2.9.
[2] See pp. 172-73.

Vedānta Deśika, as is evident in the Sastriar's *Śatabhūṣaṇī.* Each school of thought tries to defend its own theories against such criticisms. Replies and counter-replies are true of all Indian derśanas. As we have observed earlier, the function of a polemic is not to refute an opponent out of existence but only to define and distinguish one's position from that of others with a view to establishing the soundness of one's theory. It is in this spirit that Bādarāyaṇa in the *Vedānta-sūtras* (part II sections 1 and 2) criticises some of the theories of Sānkhya, Nyāya-vaiśeṣika, Buddhists, Jains and Pāśupata as are opposed to the Vedanta.[1] Presumably Rāmānuja and Vedānta Deśika refute the doctrines of Advaita Vedanta with the same objective.

The defects pointed out in the *Śatadūṣanī* would not affect the Advaita as a system of Vedānta. Nor do the criticisms levelled against Viśiṣṭādvaita by its critics affect the value of this system. Ever since they were founded they have survived through several centuries and are alive even today with a large number of followers. The reason for their survival is that they have their own intrinsic vitality and are of appeal to different types of individuals. Every system of Vedānta claims to be based on the authority of sacred texts and tradition, logical stability and spiritual verifiability and proceeds on the principle of the establishment of truth by the repudiation of false theories. As observed by Prof. P.N. Srinivasachari, every Vedāntic system has a synthetic purpose as it claims to be a criticism of and fulfillment of previous systems.[2] Each satisfies a specific historic need and is pragmatically justified. The conflicts between two schools of thought do not in any way affect their value as a system of philosophy. On the other hand, they enrich them in so far as they serve as an impetus to further developmeht of philosophic thought.

[1] See RB II.2.1 *svapakṣa-raksaṇāya parapakṣāḥ pratikṣiphante* cp SB II.2.1.

[2] See The Philosophy of Viśiṣṭādvaita, p. 598.

# APPENDIX

## List of Topics Dealt with in the *Śatadūṣaṇī*[1]

1. According to the position held by the Advaitin the term Brahman cannot have any import either primary or secondary.
2. The enquiry into Brahman which is held to be pure and devoid of all determinations is unintelligible.
3. Mīmāṃsā which is scriptural exegesis is a single continuous śāstra but not a body of discontinuous and divergent śāstras.
4. Knowledge which is enjoined is not the means to release but Upāsanā.
5. After the removal of nescience, the continuance of the body is unintelligible.
6. Sacrifice etc., are not the means of *Vividiṣā* but of *Vedanā*.
7. Verbal testimony is not by itself the means of immediate knowledge.
8. The possession in abundance of the four means viz., Nityānitya-vastuviveka, etc., is not a necessary pre-requisite of Brahman-enquiry.
9. The Advaitin who does not acknowledge the Absolute Reality of the pramāṇas is not eligible for a debate.
10. There is no entity that is devoid of all determinations.
11. Even indeterminate perception has for its content a qualified entity.
12. Perception does not apprehend a mere ' Being '.
13. Difference is not illusory but real.
14. That scripture is the final authority in matters of spirit does not hold good in respect of the Advaitins.
15. The universe is not illusory; the inference on the probans *Dṛśyatva* urged in support of it is fallacious.
16. Even the Vyāvartānumāna does not prove the illusoriness of universe.

[1] These are given in the order in which they appear in the original text.

17. The relation of the consciousness to the object is quite intelligible and is also possible.
18. In respect of him who holds Brahman to be nothing but consciousness the external manifestation itself is not possible.
19. Brahman cannot be the locus of nescience.
20. That consciousness is self-luminous in the sense of not being an object of knowledge is untenable.
21. Knowledge is originated and as such it is not eternal.
22. Consciousness is also subject to change because it is produced.
23. Consciousness is many.
24. Consciousness is not indeterminate.
25. Consciousness cannot be identical with the self.
26. The entity denoted by 'I' (Ahamartha) is the self.
27. The notion of the self as the cogniser is not illusory; the self is the knower.
28. The pure consciousness cannot be held to be the witness.
29. When there is a conflict between perception and scripture, that scripture is superior in validity to perception cannot be established.
30. That real can be derived from what is not real is untenable.
31. Release while there is embodiment is impossible.
32. The supposition that in the appositional statements what is unreal stands stultified by what is real is wrong.
33. That consciousness is one but appears to be many in the form of knower, known and knowledge as qualified by them is inadmissible.
34. In the Advaita system the teaching (Upadeśa) cannot take place.
35. That nescience obscures Brahman is untenable.
36. The supposition that the self is one but appears to be many owing to the difference of the adjuncts does not stand.
37. The finite self cannot be identical with Īśvara.
38. That some scriptural texts denote an impartite sense cannot be proved.
39. That nescience is a positive entity though opposed to knowledge is neither established by perception nor by inference nor even by scriptural texts.
40. Nescience cannot rest even in the finite selves.

41. The view that nescience is a defect which is the cause of the illusion of Brahman is riddled with contradictions.
42. The distinction between *māyā* and *avidyā* does not hold good.
43. That a knowledge of non-duality puts an end to nescience is untenable.
44. The complete cessation of nescience is also unintelligible.
45. That Brahman is not denoted by any verbal testimony does not hold good.
46. It is wrong to suppose that Brahman is the content of an injunction that refers to the dissociating of Brahman from the world.
47. The view that all determinate knowledge is false because it is determinate in its nature is untenable.
48. The Advaitin cannot claim that Upabṛmhaṇas support *Nirviśeṣa Vāda.*
49. The teaching referring to the oneness of Brahman and the self is intelligible even without postulating nescience in Brahman.
50. The conditions laid down for eligibility to study the sacred texts are unintelligible in the Advaita system.
51. That consciousness is indeterminate in the state of release cannot be held as it contradicts a number of Śruti and Smṛti texts.
52. The contention that Nirguṇa Śruti is stronger than Saguṇa Śruti is inadmissible.
53. The material causality of Brahman does not consist in illusory manifestation but in the transformation of Brahman as qualified by the subtle *cit* and *acit* into the gross world.
54. *Māyā* cannot be held to be the material cause of the world.
55. The concept of effect is logically intelligible and it can never be regarded as illusory.
56. The concept of infinitude in Advaita is unintelligible.
57. If Brahman is *nirviśeṣā* it cannot be of the nature of pure bliss.
58. The concept of eternity too is inconceivable in respect of Brahman devoid of characteristics.
59. The term *advitīya* signifies a qualified entity.
60. That a thing is neither real nor unreal is self-contradictory.

61. The unity of the self is inconceivable.
62. The section viz., *Apaśudrādhikaraṇa* does not find full justification in the Advaita system.
63. A distinction between the persons eligible and non-eligible to study the Vedānta is difficult to draw in Advaita.
64. Asceticism as conceived by the Advaitin is opposed to the principle set forth in scripture and traditional codes.
65. The view that a sanyāsin is untouched by afflictions and worldly acts is inadmissible.
66. The Vedānta Sūtras are not in consonance with the teaching of Advaita.

# BIBLIOGRAPHY

## Sanskrit Works

*Advaita Siddhi*, edited by Ananthakrishna Sastry; Nirnayasagar Press, Bombay.

*Bhāmatī Catussūtri*, edited with an English translation by S. S. Suryanarayana Sastry and C. Kunhan Raja (T.P.H.).

*Bṛhadāraṇyakopaniṣadbhāṣyavārtikā*, Anandasrama Sanskrit Series.

*Brahmasiddhi*, edited by Kuppuswamy Sastry.

*Brahmasūtra Sankara Bhasyam*, edited by Mahadeva Sastri Bakre; Nirnayasagar Press, Bombay.

*Darśanodaya*, by Lakshmipuram Srinivasachariar.

*Iṣṭasiddhi*, Gaekwad's Oriental Series.

*Khaṇḍanakhaṇḍakhādya*, Chowkamba Sanskrit Series.

*Naiṣkarmya Siddhi*, Bombay Sanskrit and Prakrit Series.

*Nyāya Dīpāvalī*, Chowkamba Sanskrit Series.

*Nyāyamakaranda*, Chowkamba Sanskrit Series.

*Nyāyāmṛta*, by Vyasaraja.

*Nyāya Pariśuddhi*, Chowkamba Sanskrit Series.

*Pañcapādika*, Vizianagaram Sanskrit Series.

*Pañcapādikāvivaraṇa*, Vizianagaram Sanskrit Series.

*Paramārthabhūṣanam*, by Ullamur Viraraghavacharya.

*Śatadūṣaṇī with Candamāruta*, Sastramuktavali Series (4 Vols.).

*Śatadūṣaṇī*, edited with Tamil translation by Setlur Narasimhachariar; Nigamaparimala Press (2 Vols.).

*Śathbhūṣaṇī*, by N. S. Ananthakrishna Sastri.

*Siddhāntaleśasaṅgraha*, edited with a translation by S. S. Suryanarayana Sastry; University of Madras (2 Vols.).

*Samkṣepa Śārīraka*, Anandasrama Series (2 Vols.).

*Siddhitraya*, edited with translation by R. Rāmānujachari and K. Srinivasacharya; Annamalai University Philosophy Series.

*Śrī-Bhāṣya*, Ananda Press Edition.

*Śrī-Bhāṣya*, with Śrutaprakāśikā and other commentaries, edited by V. Ananthacharya and V. Krishnamacharya (2 Vols.), Published by Madras Sanskrit Book Depot, Madras.

*Tattvamuktā kalāpa with Sarvartha Siddhi*, Pandit Reprints.

*Tattvapradīpika* (2nd Edn.), Nirnayasagar Press, Bombay.

*Tattvaśuddhi*, edited by S. S. Suryanarayana Sastry and E. P. Radhakrishnan.

*Vādāvalī*, edited with an English translation by P. Nagaraja Rao (T.P.H.).

*Vedānta Paribhāṣā*, edited with a translation by S. S. Suryanarayana Sastry (T.P.H.).

*Vedānta Rakṣmaṇi-vimarśa*, by A. V. Gopalacharya.

*Vedārtha Sangraha.*

*Vivaraṇa Prameya Sangraha*, Vizianagaram Sanskrit Series.

## English Works

Bradley, F. H., *Appearance and Reality.*

Dasgupta, S. N., *A History of Indian Philosophy* (3 Vols.).

Dasgupta, S. N., *Indian Idealism.*

Datta, D. M., *The Six Ways of Knowing.*

Deussen, P., *The System of the Vedānta.*

Hiriyanna, M., *Outlines of Indian Philosophy.*

Jadunath Sinha, *Indian Psychology of Perception.*

Mahadevan, T. M. P., *The Philosophy of Advaita.*

Malkani, G. R., *The Philosophy of the Self.*

Max Müller, *Six Systems of Indian Philosophy.*

Mukerjee, A. C., *The Nature of Self.*

Nagarajasarma, R. N., *Reign of Realism.*

Radhakrishnan, S., *Indian Philosophy*, 2 Vols.

Radhakrishnan, S., *An Idealist View of Life.*

Radhakrishnan, S., *The Brahma Sūtra.*

Saksena, S. K., *The Nature of Consciousness in Hindu Philosophy.*

Srinivasachari, P. N., *The Philosophy of Viśiṣṭādvaita.*

Srinivasachari, P. N , *Ramanuja's Idea of the Finite Self.*

Srinivasachari, P. N., *The Philosophy of Bhedābheda.*

Thibaut, *Vedānta Sūtras with Rāmānuja's Commentary*, S. B. E. Series, Vol. XLVIII.

Varadachari, K. C., *Rāmānuja's Theory of Knowledge.*

# GLOSSARY

*abheda*: non-difference
*abhijñā*: knowledge by acquaintance
*acit*: primal matter
*adhiṣṭhāna*: basis, substratum
*adhyāsa*: superimposition
*adravya*: non-substance
*adṛṣṭa*: unseen potency
*advitītiya*: without a second, absence of a second similar to *Brahman*
*āgama*: revealed scripture
*ahamartha*: the entity denoted by the notion of 'I', the individual self
*ahamkāra*: egotism
*ajaḍa*: sentient, manifestation for itself
*ajñāna*: ignorance, absence of knowledge
*akhaṇḍārtha*: impartite and non-relational sense
*ānanda*: bliss
*anirvacanīya*: indeterminable
*anantam*: infinite
*anavasthā*: infinite regress
*antaḥkaraṇa*: internal organ
*anṛta*: untrue, *Karma* that causes contraction of knowledge, sin
*antaryāmin*: indwelling Self
*anubhūti*: consciousness, knowledge
*anupalabdhi*: non-cognition, non-recognition
*anupapattiḥ*: logical untenability
*anuvāda*: restatement
*anyathā-khyāti*: the theory of error according to which illusion is apprehension otherwise
*apaccheda-nyāya*: the principle of the later sublating the earlier
*āśrama*: stages of life
*āstika*: orthodox, one who accepts the authority of the vedas
*astitva*: existence
*avaccheda-vāda*: the theory that the *jīva* is the appearance of *Brahman* as defined by *avidyā*
*āvaraṇa*: concealment
*anyonyāśraya*: a logical fallacy, an argument involving a vicious circle
*avedya*: unknowable, not being an object of knowledge
*avidyā*: nescience, the cosmic principle which is the cause of world-illusion
*avyākṛtam*: unmanifest, devoid of manifestation with name and form

*bādha*: sublation

*bādhitānuvṛtti*: persistence of the trace of *avidyā* even after it is sublated

*bheda*: difference

*bimba-pratibimba-vāda*: the theory that the *jīva* is a reflection of *Brahman* in the internal organ

*Brahma-jijñāsā*: the metaphysical enquiry into the nature of *Brahman*

*bhrama*: illusion

*buddhi*: intellect

*carama-saṃskāra*: the final residual impression of experience

*cit*: individual self, consciousness

*dama*: self-restraint

*dānti*: equanimity

*darśana*: realization of the self, specific type of contemplation characterised by vividness

*dehātma-bhrama*: the illusion of the self in the body

*dhruvānusmṛti*: steadfast contemplation

*dhyāna*: contemplation, meditation

*dṛg*: seer, subject, self

*dṛśyatva*: cognisability, objectivity

*dravya*: substance

*ekajīva-vāda*: the theory that there is only one *jīva*

*Īśvara*: God, the supreme Self

*jaḍa*: inert

*jāti*: generic character, the distinguishing characteristic of an object

*jijñāsā*: desire to know, to enquire into the nature of *Brahman*

*jīva*: individual self, empirical self

*jīvanmukti*: release of a person while he is still embodied

*jñāna*: knowledge, cognition

*jñātā*: knower, cogniser, subject

*jvālābhedā-numāna*: the inferenee which proves that the flames of a lamp are distinct succeeding one another

*kalpita*: imaginary, having no real existence, false

*karma*: action, rituals, past deeds and their traces or results

*karma-kāṇḍa*: parts of the vedas dealing with rituals

*karma-vicāra*: study of the rituals

*Karma-Mīmāṃsā*: *Pūrva-Mīmāṃsā*, one of the six systems

*kārya*: effect

*mahat*: intellect, evolute of *prakṛti*

*manana*: logical reflection

*Māyā*: cosmic principle which gives rise to world-illusion, the phenomenal character of the universe, that which is an instrument of wonderful creation; primal matter

*māyin*: the wielder of *māyā*, the creator
*mithyā*: illusory
*mokṣa*: release from bondage, union with the Absolute, attainment of the status of *Brahman*
*mukhya-vṛtti*: primary import

*nāma-rūpa*: name and form
*nididhyāsanā*: contemplation
*nirguṇa*: devoid of qualities
*nirvikāra*: immutable, not subject to transformation
*nirviśeṣā*: undifferentiated, devoid of all characteristics
*nirvikalpaka*: indeterminate
*nivartaka*: that which removes
*nivṛtti*: cessation, removal

*pariṇāma-vāda*: the theory that the Absolute transforms itself into the universe
*pāramārthika*: transcendental, absolutely real
*pradhvamsa*: destruction
*pramāṇa*: evidence, means of valid knowledge
*prāgabhāva*: prior non-existence
*prakāśa*: illumination, manifestation, knowledge
*prākaṭya*: manifestation
*prakṛti*: primal matter
*prāṇa*: life breath
*pratyabhijñā*: knowledge by recognition
*pravṛtti-nimitta*: primary import, connotation
*puruṣārtha*: human goal
*pūrva-pakṣa*: the prima facie view, statement of an objection.

*ṛta*: righteousness, moral order

*sadasad-vilakṣaṇa*: different from the real and the unreal
*sādhana*: discipline, means for spiritual realization
*sādhana-catuṣṭaya*: the four pre-requisites for the study of Vedānta
*sādharmya*: equality
*sadvidyā*: meditation on Brahman as the *sat* without a second as described in the *Chāndogya Upaniṣad*
*saguṇa*: possessed of qualities
*śākha-candra-nyāya*: the analogy of the moon appearing through the branches of a tree
*sākṣin*: witness, one who knows in person
*śama*: tranquillity, calmness
*samanvaya*: harmony of the different texts, reconciliation
*sāmānādhikaraṇya*: syntactic equation of terms denoting the same thing but connoting different attributes
*samavāya*: inherence, internal relation
*sambandha*: relationship
*samskāra*: residual impression of experience

*samsthāna*: structure, exclusive characteristic of an object, the generic character
*samyoga*: external relation
*samvit*: knowledge, cognition, consciousness
*sarvajña*: omniscient
*satyam*: truth, reality
*savikalpaka*: determinate, differentiated
*siddhānta*: final view, final truth of an argument, established conclusion
*śravaṇa*: act of hearing
*śūnya-vāda*: nihilism, the doctrine advocated by the Mādhyamikas that nullity is ultimate nature of the Absolute
*suṣupti*: deep, dreamless sleep
*svarūpa*: essential nature, being
*svataḥ-siddha*: self-proved
*svayam-prakāśā*: self-luminous, that which does not require to be manifested by anything else

*tamas*: primordial matter, darkness, one of the three qualities of prakṛti
*tirodhāna*: concealment, obscuration

*uñcavṛtti*: receiving alms
*upabṛmhaṇa*: that which elucidates the meaning of the scriptural texts, *smṛtis* and *purāṇas*
*upādāna kāraṇa*: material cause
*upādhi*: adjunct
*upajīvaka*: that which depends on another
*upajīvya*: that which offers subsistence
*upahita Brahman*: qualified *Brahman*
*upalakṣaṇa*: a qualification *per accidens*
*upalakṣya*: that which is denoted by a qualification *per accidens*
*upāsanā*: contemplation, meditation
*upāya*: means

*vāda*: philosophical discussion aimed at the ascertainment of truth
*vāda-grantha*: a treatise containing philosophical discussion, polemic work
*vairāgya*: non-attachment to wordly objects, absence of desire for anything except the Lord
*veda*: revealed scripture
*vedanā*: knowledge of *Brahman*
*vibhūtis*: glorious manifestation of the Lord
*vikāra*: change
*vināśa*: destruction
*viśeṣaṇa*: qualification *per proprium*
*viśeṣya*: substance

*vivarta-vāda*: the theory that the world is an illusory appearance of *Brahman*
*vividiṣā*: desire to know *Brahman*
*vṛtti jñāna*: Knowledge of the psychosis
*vyavahāra*: empirical usage
*vyāvarta*: changing

*yāga*: religious sacrifice
*yogyānupalabdhi*: competent non-cognition, the *pramāṇa* by means of which non-existence or negation is apprehended

# INDEX